The Wholeness Map

The Wholeness Map

A REAL-WORLD WHOLESOME GUIDE TO HEAL LIFE'S
HOLES AND TRANSFORM FROM DIVORCE

By Sharon Owens

Author's note: Out of respect, some identifying characteristics in this work have been changed.

Editor: Daniel McIntire
Content Editor: Daniel McIntire
Copy Editor: Kathy Kelley
Author Photograph: Kanda Photography

SharonMOwens.com
@sharonmowens **f** ⓘ

MEDIA + SPEAKING: please contact sharon@sharonmowens.com
ALL INQUIRIES: sharon@sharonmowens.com

This book is dedicated to YOU, lovely reader.

*May you know how special you are and how much
I believe you deserve to be whole.*

*May The Wholeness Map guide you to your
inner peace and wholeness and open you up to the beautiful
gifts life, and the Universe, have for you.*

Love, Sharon

xo

IMPORTANT INFORMATION:

While this book is intended as a general information resource and all care has been taken in compiling the contents, this book does not take into account individual circumstances, and this book is not in any way a substitute for the medical or mental health advice of physicians. It is essential that you always seek qualified medical or mental health advice if you suspect you have a physical or mental health problem. The author and publisher cannot be held responsible for any claim or action that may arise from reliance on the information contained in this book.

Contents

"Finding Yourself"

Is not really how it works. You aren't a ten-dollar bill in last winter's coat pocket. You are also not lost. Your true self is right there, buried under cultural conditioning, other people's opinions and inaccurate conclusions you drew as a kid that became your beliefs about who you are. "Finding Yourself" is actually returning to yourself. An unlearning, an excavation, a remembering who you were before the world got its hands on you.

–Emily McDowell

INTRODUCTION

Why a Book About Divorce, Healing, and Transformation to Wholeness?

Any great chef will tell you, they're striving to take complex flavors and ingredients and create a simple, elegant dish out of them. The true essence of a master chef comes from highlighting key, and universal, flavors while blending in background flavors to play an important supporting role.

When you sit down at some of the world's highest-rated restaurants, you expect that the chef has done such a masterful job that you'll be able to find simplicity in the flavor, yet be awestruck at how much work went into creating that simplicity.

That is the essence of what I am trying to do here in the book, for you, right now.

How can I take something as complex and personal as divorce and make it simple and elegant? That really sounds like an impossible task. Yet I've never felt more at peace with my mission to do so. As this is my mission statement, it's important that I lay out the key elements that we will work on in this book.

The first key element is accepting the internal healing process. Internal healing is a building block that cannot be skipped over or hurried through. I know from my own personal experience with divorce how much fear and loss overcome you in the beginning stages. There is so much fear, and it comes on many levels. The fear of failure, lack of money, not having a support system, solo parenting, and never finding love are just a few that come to mind. Fear of the unknown is a battle that is best won head-on. From this point onward, throughout this book and after you've finished it, you will attack your new life with a fierce positivity! This is the only way to move past your fears, and you already have everything inside of you in order to overcome your fear. If you succumb to your fears, you are only delaying the true healing process that you must go through. Some people will spend the rest of their lives not attacking their fears head-on. They will hold onto anger, resentment, ego; blame others, complain, and much more. I am here to guide you past these low energy states and bring you into the strongest version of yourself–a version that you may not even know exists!

The second key element that will be important to acknowledge is time. I see this in nature everywhere. Time plays a fundamental role in not just healing from a significant life-changing event like divorce, but becoming even stronger than you were before. In the culinary world, time plays an absolutely crucial role in the development of complex flavors.

In Mexico City, world-renowned Chef Enrique Olvera offers patrons the experience of tasting mole that has aged over 1,000 days.

In Nagano, Japan the Hayashi family has created some of the world's most complex miso that is typically aged at least three years.

Scottish whiskey distilleries have long known that the longer you age fermented grains in a wooden barrel, the more complex and richer the final whiskey will be.

Healing yourself starts from the inside out, and time allows the process to, beautifully, bring you out stronger and happier than ever before. Think of yourself as a complex flavor, unlike anything anyone has ever tasted. We need time in order to unlock all that you have to offer. There is not a get rich quick scheme, and there is no healing process that happens overnight. I urge you to get excited about the time that lies ahead and about all the amazing experiences you've yet to have in your new life.

In this book, I'm going to talk about my own divorce journey, and how the stresses of divorce can lead to severe health problems and lack of mental clarity. It's important that I state, I am not a medical professional or a mental health professional. I am a certified life and health coach with years of experience working with clients going through their post-divorce life. I want to share my journey and my struggles with you in this book so that you can use my experience as a catalyst to overcome your divorce in a way that many think is not possible. This book is my experience, and the experiences of people I've worked with.

My desire is that your divorce will be a launchpad for you, like it has been for me, to learn about who you really are and what you can achieve in your new life. This book is titled *The Wholeness Map* because it's much more than a "how to" on getting past a divorce. I'm genuinely excited to help you develop wholeness internally that you can use to create abundance externally. My dream is, at the end of this book, you'll understand that massive abundance, in all areas of your life, is right at your fingertips. The only thing you need to do to harness this abundance is to accept that the internal healing process comes first, and it must take time.

All of the things laid out for you in this book are things that I am still working on within my own life today. This is a book that is evolving and will continue to evolve long after it has been published. I've written the book in stages, and no matter where you are at in your life after divorce, there is something for you in each section.

It all starts with honoring the story of divorce and decoding your own, self-made, story. It took me two years to understand that I was telling myself my own story each and every day. I will talk a lot about the Law of Attraction in this book because I believe it is a powerful way to harness your desires and create massive abundance. But before I ever started using the Law of Attraction to bring abundance to every area of my life, I had to understand what story I was telling myself.

In order to create a brand new, better-than-ever personal story, you must detach from the current narrative you are telling yourself. You will learn how to do this in the coming chapters.

We all tell ourselves a story each and every day. It's a story that we create, we direct, we narrate, and then we live it. Our own story is based purely on our outlook on ourselves. When I began healing internally from my divorce ten years ago, I spent the first two years telling myself a story of pain and stress. My health was in the gutter, and I was feeling my life slip away as disease seeped into my body. Stress is one of the biggest causes of death in the world, right next to heart disease. I was living the daily story of a newly divorced mother of five, struggling with financial loss in my divorce, and suffering from numerous stress-related illnesses. That was the story I was telling myself each and every day, by choice.

In this book, I will guide you along the path of identifying what story you are currently telling yourself and replacing it with a powerful story of abundance, self-acceptance, and joy in all aspects of your life.

You will learn all about what to expect from a divorce. Is divorce the right path for you? That is a question that isn't black and white. It's deep and complex. I will highlight the realities of divorce that set in as you begin your divorce. This is the place where you'll understand the emotions that come with a divorce, the chaos of lawyers, child support, and financial changes. In Part One, we will also learn one of the most important aspects of this book, the Law of Attraction.

The Law of Attraction—which has a basis in quantum physics—is the language of the Universe and I use it every day in my post-divorce life. I've learned to harness the Law of Attraction, and I'm going to teach you how to do the same thing. I want to share the world of intentional thinking and projecting your desires out into the world in order to tell the Universe what it is you really want.

You cannot use the Law of Attraction with a negative mindset. In your divorce, you will be surrounded by negative mindsets. Your ex-partner may be suffering from trying to turn your kids against you or hurt you in any way they can. Your friends may judge you in a negative or non-supportive way. Your family may be pushing you to "stick it out." You must charge forward with positivity in your heart because that is how you will attract the most beautiful and happy life in the shortest amount of time. The Law of Attraction responds only to positive thought patterns, and in *The Wholeness Map*, I'm going to help you build a foundation of positive energy and thought patterns.

For the sake of clarity and simplicity in this book, I will be speaking from my own personal experiences with my personal and spiritual development, as well as my own personal experiences with my health journey. Know that if I speak of the Universe or God, Goddess, Angels, Archangels, etc. throughout the book, they all mean the same thing. These are words and beliefs that are personal to me, and if they resonate with you, then they do; however, I speak to everyone in this book. Please know I do not believe that you have to "subscribe" to one way of personal development, spirituality, or way of healthy living. It's about knowing what is best for you and being open to the rest. As to the tools, beliefs, and health practices that I speak of, please take the information that you read and apply it to how it resonates to you. For example, if I talk about the Universe or God, interchange the word "Universe" or "God" for your personal belief; if I use, refer, or guide you to use meditation but yoga, praying, sound healing, or meditative nature walks are what calls you; please honor your practice and use the tools where you see fit. Please be open to using the methods to invite more peace into your soul.

I will use the Law of Attraction throughout the book because I am passionate about the benefits it can bring to you as you move through your post-divorce life. The Law of Attraction, to me, means accepting that the Universe will take care of you if you allow it to. If you can accept that your thoughts create your actions, then you can use the Law of Attraction to build a new life of happiness and abundance through positivity and clear intentions. I want to simplify this idea for you by saying this is just one way of explaining our thoughts. The phrase "Law of Attraction" can mean as much or as little to you as you want it to, but the theory behind it is universal. Your thoughts and intentions will create your reality. You can choose positivity and abundance or, like many people who struggle with post-divorce life, you can get stuck in a cycle of negative thought patterns and never truly heal.

I believe entirely that your life is in your hands, and only you can build it up or tear it down. You will hear me talk about key moments when I harnessed the Law of Attraction even when things were completely dark around me. It wasn't always like that for me though. I spent the better part of two years holding myself down with fear, anger, and stress. Part One of this book is so important in laying the foundation for the rest of the book.

In Part Two, we begin the healing process by diving deep into self-love, your body, and finances. The biggest stressors of your divorce are addressed in the healing section so you can experience even more significant transformations in Part Three.

Then in Part Three, we'll go within to begin the transformation process–connecting to your inner Goddess/God and deepening your relationships, including how you can be of service to others. This book is a fully encompassed mind, body, spirit journey, filled with intention and interaction every step of the way.

It doesn't matter what part of the divorce process you are in, each section in this book plays a role in creating *The Wholeness Map*. You need to understand what is happening in Part One to learn the lessons of Part Two and so on. It's important to check any ego at the door and go through the book from start to finish instead of skipping ahead. Again, this isn't a "how to" on getting a divorce but rather a map to finding wholeness in the midst of divorce. That is a significant distinction.

My Story

I am a survivor of divorce, and today I live a life of abundance, freedom, and free-flowing creative and spiritual energy. I am a single mother of five children and making the decision to become that person is one I would never change. I am thriving financially as a business owner and as a health-conscious human who knows the pitfalls of stress. My life is truly in my hands, and my story is one that I am telling myself every day. Life wasn't always like this when I was going through my divorce, especially post-divorce.

People have often asked me "how did you overcome so much to get to where you are today?" and "how were you able to overcome all the emotions?" The answers to those questions are in this book. In order to get to those answers, it's important to go back to before my divorce even came to be.

This sounds obvious, and it is, but no one goes into a marriage knowing they are going to get a divorce at some point. After years of marriage, there came a time when I knew things weren't working. I knew deep down in my gut that it wasn't working long before I ever made any changes to my (and our) lifestyle.

And then it happened. A series of events in our marriage that led to the first brick being laid in our inevitable fate.

We separated.

For two years my husband and I lived under the guise of separation with the intention of "working things out." Again, any competent person hopes that this will actually work out when the reality is it very likely will not. Hope is a powerful force, and I hoped for my sake, my children's sake, and my lifestyle's sake that everything would work out in the end.

At the beginning of our separation I started seeing a therapist. I felt this burning desire, this primal need to tell someone about what I was experiencing behind the closed doors of my home. There is no worse feeling to me then living in fear, anger, and even uncertainty inside the sacred walls of the place you call home. If you cannot relate to that feeling, good! It's generally not a feeling that I would wish upon anyone. However, more likely than not, if you have this book in your hands right now you know the exact feeling I am talking about.

The work I began doing with my therapist was a mix of one-on-one sessions as well as couples work. The couples sessions didn't yield the results I was hoping for and soon after they began, they fizzled out. While, again, I would have loved to have those sessions work, they didn't. On a personal level, however, they were bringing me closer and closer to myself. After years of mistreatment, misunderstanding each other, and constant emotional turmoil, I came to the conclusion that my marriage was not going to be saved.

During the second year of our separation, while still living in the same house with our children, I had my big moment. The moment that, deep down in my gut I knew was coming, yet hadn't yet actualized itself in reality was finally here.

I remember driving in my car on my way home and finally accepting that I was going to move forward with my divorce. There was nothing more I could do, give, take, or feel to change this one simple fact about the future of my life.

It felt amazing.

It was the most massive weight immediately lifting from my shoulders–my mental clarity was spiking as I could finally move forward with a resolution to the future of my life. It was a resolution to what wasn't bringing me joy. It was the answer to all the grief I had been put through, that my kids were being put through, and, I assume, that my soon-to-be ex-husband was being put through.

Divorce was, ultimately and unequivocally, the only road I had left to take in order to move forward with the rest of my life.

I suppose you could relate this release of fear and acceptance of fate to leaving a job that is sucking the life out of your soul, facing a multi-year addiction habit, or removing a toxic parent, sibling, or friend from your life. Of course it will not be easy in the days, weeks, months, and years to come but it must begin today.

For me, it was monumental. I called my therapist late that night and said "This is happening. This must happen and it's happening now!!"

I finally made my decision and my therapist was the first person to validate what my home life had become. I needed that validation because I knew it was from a pure, unbiased source. That validation gave me the first taste of self-belief that I needed to accept where my life was headed. I started to believe that I was a strong enough person to make the big decision, the best decision for myself and my kids.

Throughout the entirety of the two years in our separation period I was still putting out the image that I had the perfect, wholesome, American family. It was a facade, of course, but something in me needed to keep that image up for myself and my children. Once I decided it was time to end my marriage, that also brought down this perfect home facade with it.

Just like when you start dating a special new person, making a massive life decision has a short honeymoon period. All the weight that was just lifted off my shoulders started to get piled back onto my back in the coming months. The moment I knew I was going to get divorced I hired a divorce lawyer. In that same moment, two powerful emotions began to bubble to the surface inside me.

There was the fear of the unknowns that lie ahead and the reality that divorce is just plain hard. No one has a perfect marriage, and when there are children involved, no one usually has the perfect divorce. As we move deeper throughout this book together, you will learn why divorce isn't easy and how you can make it as manageable as possible for your children and yourself.

We have children together, between the ages of five months and five years old.

We have a house together.

We have friends and family.

We have all this stuff together.

We have money together.

I learned fairly quickly that what I wanted and what my husband wanted were quite different. I was more interested in how I was going to get the kids, how the custody would work out, and where they would live. My husband has his own intentions and focus that were different than mine.

This was a blessing actually, although hard to handle at the time, because we would both get more of what we want than what we didn't want. I didn't care much about money or the stuff. My fears stemmed from not being able to see my children all the time and not being able to provide the best upbringing possible. As a parent, my only concern was with the future of my children and I know many parents can relate to that.

My divorce was actually fairly quick compared to most divorces involving children and "stuff." It lasted nine months from decision to finalization. I contribute this to the differences in what my husband and I wanted from the marriage. If we had been fighting over the same things, I know that both our egos and our fears would have caused things to drag out much longer. For that I am thankful.

That feeling of finality after your divorce is over is another one of those massive reliefs you only feel a few times in your life. It was like I had been fighting an unwinnable war, stuck in cold, muddy trenches for what seemed like forever and then one day your commander tells you the war is over.

Sigh. Relief. Exhale.

It was over and it was time to move forward as a single mother, responsible for five young children. I knew deep down that I could create a beautiful life for my kids, I had energy, life felt light and airy. I wanted my kids to feel like this as well. The hardest part of life after the divorce was that I could now only control one half of the "home life" that my children would experience. I had to accept that I wasn't the only driving force in raising my kids. That brought stress, and massive amounts of worry into my daily life. I didn't know how and what my ex was going to do to provide my kids with the same bright future.

I wanted nothing but the best for my ex-husband because that would mean that my children would have an even better future.

A lot of things changed in the first two years after the divorce. I was making big decisions, such as selling the old house and moving to a smaller house at half the price in order to put money away. I also purchased an established business in the fitness industry that I was able to immerse myself in.

During my divorce I committed myself to a barre exercise class which helped with managing my stress. I had been passionate about fitness and exercise my entire life. My barre practice forced me to escape from reality for one hour each day and focus on a mind/body connection, tapping into specific muscles. When I had a chance to purchase that very same studio a couple years later, I jumped at the opportunity. I had this new outlet to focus on and give me more purpose in addition to my real estate business and being a single mom.

It was an established studio that offered barre classes but I wanted to add my story to this space. I wanted it to be a place that people could come and get strength in other ways beyond the physical sense. The studio itself became a place for people, mostly women considering the nature of the classes, to share their stories, and connect with someone on a real level.

I knew my customers' stories and they knew mine. The business became more successful because of the supportive energy that was created as we shared our stories freely.

I owned this business for five years and when I was ready to move on, I moved on. This was the same gut instinct I followed when I chose to move forward with divorce. My health was starting to be affected by the stress of putting everything I had into this business. After being a rock for the community I had built, and having them as my rock, I wanted to explore that side of myself more.

I decided that it was time to sell the business because it was thriving and I had given it what I needed to give it. In return, it gave me a clear path to my next move in life. I let it go and decided to get a degree as a Certified Life and Health Coach.

At first, I wanted to do it all. I thought to myself "I can help anyone with diet, exercise, love, raising kids, construction code violations, proper Thai cooking methods, healthcare reform" and so on.

Those last few are clearly not true, and my point is that I wanted to be a one-stop shop for living a great life. Luckily, over time, I started to shine as a coach for people going through a divorce, people in a negative or abusive relationship, and people who had gone through divorce and needed to heal.

These experiences have led me to this point, and to writing this book that you hold in your hands now. It's a culmination of my life experience of catapulting my life's trajectory after my divorce instead of letting my life slip away. It's a collection of years of experience of working through other peoples' divorces with them. These days I am not afraid to say I live in abundance, full of life and love for myself. I travel with my family, I take on new projects, I think positively and attract positivity back. I have problems or challenges that occur in life, just like you do. In some ways I'm still healing myself. I will always look at life from the eyes of a student, and learning and healing are a continual process. I am not perfect, nor would I ever pretend to be.

Divorce now affects 51 percent of marriages in America, and that number is likely to continue to increase. I am not lucky or special because I am living and thriving in my post-divorce life. Everyone can come out of a divorce to live the life of their dreams. The thing to remember is that it took me over a decade to get here, and that is a long time. I got through my divorce, and now I'm living as the best, yet still growing, version of myself, but it took a long time. I'm going to help you rediscover your true nature in your post-divorce life in a much shorter period of time through *The Wholeness Map*. You still need to go through the healing process, but with my help, you will identify the key aspects of your behavior and your understanding of these emotions in order to address them much faster than I did ten years ago.

There is no step-by-step guide to divorce, and there is no handbook on getting through it. I know that the complexity of emotions that come out of a divorce can either tear you down or, with the right mindset and direction, build you up even stronger than you were before. Nothing about surviving divorce is simple. It's a dark place for many people, myself included, but on the other side of that darkness is the brightest light I have ever seen. *The Wholeness Map* is my way of guiding you to that light.

I was the person who tried to keep everything positive while the house around me burned to the ground. I wanted to shield my children from the reality of the situation, and at the same time, I hoped that I could somehow convince myself that everything was going to be okay, for them and for me. I wanted to shield my kids from having to choose one parent over the other, but I was only able to control one half of the divorce: me. Accepting that you are only one half of the equation and that there are going to be things far beyond your control will make the healing journey much easier.

When you accept this to be the way things are, the internal healing process has begun. You will heal from the inside out, and as your inner light grows brighter, you will attract more and more external energy towards you. If you try and change the way others do things, whether that be your ex-partner, your friends, or your family, you will see little change in your life.

If you say, right now in your head, I am committed to rebuilding myself internally and allowing time for myself to heal then you're in the driver's seat. I see a lot of people who think that a divorce is the key to solving their problems, which is not the case. Finding abundance and happiness is not as simple as getting a divorce and assuming everything will be better. Happiness comes from the internal healing that you are beginning right now.

Why The Wholeness Map

Together, we are going to find out who you really are and use the catalyst of a divorce as the common ground to get started. The thing with divorce, a traumatic break-up (or any traumatic experience in life really) is that fear can stifle your journey. We need to allow ourselves time to heal. When you run and numb yourself from the pain, you aren't actually allowing yourself the feelings of self-love and acceptance that we so deeply desired in the first place.

The reason I chose the title *The Wholeness Map* was because we are watching our world evolve at a faster rate than ever before, and it's more critical than ever to be a healthy example for the next generation. The next generation, whether it be your children, nieces, nephews, or children around you, are watching as you go through a divorce. You, we, and all of us are examples for how we heal from stress, balance healthy boundaries, and love ourselves first.

The *Oxford Dictionary* defines wholeness as, "forming a complete and harmonious whole unity." Wholeness is a word that I embraced in my healing because I desired peace, and in order to have peace, I had to learn to love each of the "holes" and levels of emotion in my body. Do I believe that one person is ever completely, 100 percent whole and does not have to continue to work at it? No. I believe wholeness is a journey–it's wrapping your arms around your imperfections and finding acceptance for them; loving every state of your being, mind, body, spirit; restoring yourself back to whole without strings of pain. Wholeness is a journey for a lifetime, so that's why I encourage you to always visualize a simple circle and watch that circle get bigger and filled with more love, over the course of your lifetime. You will find that your own personal definition of wholeness will evolve and grow with you, especially after experiencing trauma.

The two most fundamental qualities that I want you to be aware of are the power of positive thinking and the power of attracting what you want through your intentions. Setting intentions in your life that come from a place of self-acceptance of your current situation and a positive outlook on life will be the fastest way to abundance.

We all have the capacity to manifest what we want. In order to do so, you must step into the light and stay connected to God, The Divine, Angels, Universe, etc. Important to note here: you will then attract what you are, and NOT what you want. Your character must emulate that of The Divine and God–your intentions must be pure gentleness, kindness, and service towards others. When you get to this place of not feeling judgment, condemnation, and criticism of others, you are living aligned with The Divine.

Just as the process of moving through your post-divorce life requires time and internal healing, the process of creating your new self requires an unobstructed positive outlook on life. If you are feeling angry and depressed, you can choose to change your thought. You place into your imagination what you want to feel and then feel the emotion it creates. This reprogramming of your mind and thoughts will allow you to change your state. If you tell the Universe and God that you are depressed and angry, the Law of Attraction is designed to send you more situations and reasons to be depressed and angry. You see, you have control over your own destiny.

Things will happen that make you angry. Your ex-partner may not have the same mindset as you and may be stuck in a place of negativity. You cannot control what happens to you. But you can control how you feel about it. It is your job to hold the space for only positive thoughts, and thus, positive actions. It would be wrong of me to say "after reading my book *The Wholeness Map*, everything will be smiles and roses!" Things will be tough, you will still face hardships and external negative forces outside your control for years after your divorce. That is the essence of the healing process! What I can say, without a shadow of a doubt, is that *The Wholeness Map* will be a guiding light, a rock, and a tool that will always be there for you to keep you on the right track.

My wish for you is that you embrace and love the wholeness journey for a lifetime and you are able to use this map and journey just as I have. These three simple words are packed with a powerful message: may you harness these words just as I have in order to thrive and continue to stay balanced in this beautiful journey called life.

Throughout the book, I'm going to refer to wholeness a lot, as a reminder and invitation to you to surrender to what emotions come up during this process. Remember, this is a journey. I'll be referring to it in coaching tips, visualizations, meditations, and it's my invitation for you to experience the best wholeness journey possible.

It does not matter what you got from your divorce or what you did not receive in the divorce, or how traumatic your experience was–what matters is what you do after the experience to grow, evolve, shift, and change. I believe that our greatest teachers are sometimes the ones that put us through the most pain. If you can, as I did, learn to honor and appreciate the experience as a magical gift from the Universe to redefine yourself and come back to self-love and wholeness, then you are engaging in the collective wholeness legacy, for self and generations to come.

This is my invitation for you to join me. It's not going to be easy to get to the other side of trauma and stress. What I do know is that vulnerability is the new sexy, having gratitude for everything is the biggest mindset and energetic shift, living a life of abundance on all levels brings a whole new meaning to life, and opening up to the lightmaster, God/Goddess, Spirit that you are is the greatest gift that God and the Universe can give.

I am here with you every step of the way to see and embrace your beauty. Are you ready to join me, to let wholeness be your legacy in this lifetime?

Let's begin *The Wholeness Map* journey!

Honoring the Story of Divorce

PART ONE - GET GROUNDED

Divorce is the second most stressful life event according to the Holmes and Rahe Stress Scale, a list of 43 stressful events that can cause illness. Therefore, you must get grounded and listen to what your emotions are telling you. Divorce brings up many natural thoughts and emotions, so it is essential to listen to them. Your thoughts and emotions can spiral your being out of control and wreak havoc, taking you towards a chaotic life from which these thoughts stemmed from in the first place.

It is important to honor the feelings that are coming up and deal with them responsibly and compassionately. As you make your way through Part One, we will be talking about some of the points I make below. Here are some ways to prepare for your journey of "getting grounded."

1. Educate yourself on how the divorce process works.
2. Learn the difference between an attorney and a mediator. A mediator is a much more peaceful option if you can both communicate fairly.
3. Get organized financially.
4. Remove emotion from your divorce negotiations with your spouse and treat it like a business transaction.
5. Practice mindfulness by becoming aware of your thoughts and emotions. Observe if these thoughts are stemming from fear. Learn how to observe and NOT react to your spouse.
6. Make children your number one priority and never bad-mouth your spouse in front of your kids.
7. Maintain integrity.
8. Build your support team. You need emotional, mental, physical, and spiritual support.
9. Paint your canvas. See the big picture of how life can be. Really begin to understand that your life can take on so many new colors and shapes. You must focus on creating a positive and nurturing existence with your spouse and the new life you are both going to create.

CHAPTER ONE

Is Divorce for Me?

As you read this book, regardless of whether you've gone through a divorce recently, two years ago, or if you are currently in an unhappy marriage contemplating divorce, you are going to open yourself to feelings and beliefs that will be different from the thoughts, ideas, and feelings of people around you. I promise you will, and I want you to soak into every one and feel them.

In the beginning process of your divorce, you're going to feel a mountain of emotions. You're going to have this feeling that I like to describe as internal shakiness. This shakiness stems from the strongest feeling of all: fear of the unknown. People will stay in an unsalvageable marriage, on average, five years longer because of the fear and anxiety of the unforeseeable future. I want you to take a pause for a second and think about this statistic: people are choosing to put fear and uncertainty first before their own happiness and well-being. And this is why I am happy that we're meeting here on this page because I don't want you to be part of a statistic to the detriment of your love, happiness, and health.

Think about the quote "Feel the fear and do it anyway" from here on out. The shakiness I am talking about stems from fear and the only way through that fear is to ride those shakes out. I am not talking about physical shakiness. Oh no.

I am talking internal shakiness. It comes up when you are alone, sitting with your own thoughts like an awkward ride on an empty subway and yet a stranger sits right next to you. Listen to me carefully here because this is a very important sentence. You need to ride that shakiness, often referred to as anxiety, out like a storm. Nerves will bubble up to the top of your mind when you are alone. You will need to fight the urge to run and hide from them.

During your divorce, your fears will be running high and when you have nothing to occupy your mind, you'll get that shakiness. Instead of calling a friend to have dinner, or watching Netflix with wine, or getting on social media, just sit alone, with yourself, in silence. Feel the fear of the unknown, and reason with it. Wrestle all the possible outcomes of all your fears in peace and quiet so that you remove that unknown aspect.

I made a point to avoid running from my shakiness. I ran at first too, but I quickly realized it wasn't getting me anywhere. I told myself that I would get rid of distractions and allow myself to feel my feelings. But that was easier said than done. The truth is your urge to run, and your ego will try to get you to not do the uncomfortable thing, which is dealing with the unknown.

Resist your urge to always make plans when you know you have free time. Remove the daily distractions, like your cell phone, during your alone time. Sit in silence, in a comfortable spot and ride out those shakes!

Even if you have already experienced a divorce some amount of years ago, you could still be feeling this way. How are you going to get through those shaky feelings? Well, friend, that's why you're reading this book. It's going to be like walking through or into a storm, and you don't know how long the storm is going to be. But I can promise you, if you read the entirety of this book, it will be your new best friend and tool to help you through every stage, step, and process of healing from your divorce and get you to a place of wholeness, self-love and even healthy dating.

This is the time in your life when all your biggest fears are going to come up. Divorce is a massive step for you. It was a massive step for me. I knew that if I ignored the "shakiness" it would eventually consume me. I see people who still haven't dealt with the silence yet, even years after their divorce. When my kids spent time with their father, that was my time to get away from everything and everyone. Another way to put things is that I decided not to run, and instead go over all possible outcomes of my fear. It's that simple.

Face the reality of your life, in the current moment, or run. Which do you think will bring you the most benefit?

These moments are your most significant opportunities to grow, so even though I say to honor the shakiness, honor the feelings of being scared, understand that there is a rainbow at the end of the storm. You can survive this storm, and you can survive beautifully. Also, know that you are not alone, I'm here as your friend, support, coach, a listening ear, whatever you need–I am here holding your hand through your storm. We are in this together.

Should I Stay or Should I Go?

I know all marriages have their ups and downs, right? Anyone who claims to have a perfect marriage is quite simply lying. Do you remember when you first met your partner, you were happy, things were in sync, they felt comfortable, and everything in life seemed to be moving smoothly? Even your bodies were in sync, releasing the feel-good hormones, serotonin, and oxytocin–all you wanted was to feel more of that. Am I right?

In marriage–especially the longer a marriage is–couples begin to fantasize and romanticize about what the feeling of no longer being accountable to their partner anymore might look and feel like. You can start to think about how it feels to be independent, what it would be like to go out and date again, to love deeply again, and not be in a loveless marriage. You begin to romanticize what mutual respect might feel like.

The day in and day out of marriage takes work balancing all the responsibilities of finances, kids, careers, schools, perhaps sick parents… it's a constant balance, and calls for a steady give and take from each partner. Sharing responsibilities can create significant areas of stress for couples, and the only person to blame when you feel pressured and overwhelmed is, of course, your partner.

Your thoughts will begin to fixate on the negative–focusing only on the negative parts of your marriage and all the stress. I think this is inevitable. If we cannot negotiate or manage these areas of pressure in our relationship, we begin to lose trust in each other and blame the other person for our stress. This can give birth to a lack of intimacy and trust in the relationship and marriage.

DIVORCE IS SEXY

The "Divorce is Sexy" syndrome is a daydreaming effect and tailspin that begins when you dramatize the negative parts of your marriage, instead of watering what's working. I see people fall into the pitfalls and traps of an ideological marriage. It quickly becomes easier to envision and focus on what is not working, rather than trying to participate in ways to make things better in the relationship. I know it's easier to complain about your spouse and point out all the things that he or she is doing wrong, so it becomes natural to want to daydream about an easier life.

My divorce was, at no point, sexy. In my two years of awkward separation (while still living under the same roof) did I think "Hey, this is pretty darn sexy!"? That happened a total of zero times. Instead I lived in fear and pain while trying to salvage what I knew in my gut wasn't salvageable.

A famous comedian once joked "No couple in a happy marriage has ever gotten divorced. It would be very sad if a happy couple ended up getting divorced, but that never happens. That would be sad, though, if a happy, loving couple had to get a divorce. That would be really sad. But that's never, ever happened".

During the nine months of dealing with divorce lawyers and going through the official process, I never stopped to enjoy it. There wasn't a whole lot to enjoy.

Divorce is not sexy. Divorce can be smooth, albeit rarely, but it can go smoothly. You can even be friends after the divorce. However, when you start adding in children, money, homes and property, things can get ugly, fast.

Of course, in this "divorce is sexy" syndrome, I want to highlight if you are in an abusive marriage (mental, physical and emotional abuse), then it's 100 percent necessary to get out of your marriage. I am not a mental health therapist, but if there is no hope of improving the abusive marriage, then it's time to leave.

Typically, when one partner begins to see divorce as something sexy, it's where affairs start to happen. Affairs can happen for all kinds of reasons, but typically affairs strike when one partner is unhappy and unwilling to simply face reality. They've given up but refuse to be honest with themselves and their partner so they hide it. This is a symptom, not a solution, to a failing marriage.

Perhaps you are watching your divorced friends make their new life look so easy, carefree, fun, and sexy! Sure, you are watching your girlfriends go out and date again, and guy friends have half their weekends free—these are observations of the benefits, not the emotional pain that comes with divorce. There is, with no doubt in my mind, a lot of pain being masked by people portraying that divorce is sexy. How often do you see someone on social media living the best possible life? Do you also believe that everything is perfect for them and they have no issues to deal with, ever?

Of course you know they have problems. Don't let appearances influence what you and I both know to be the reality. In time, you will look back and see that you made the right decision for your children and yourself. I know this is true because I've seen it hundreds of times. I also know that each of us who has gone through a divorce has had to fight for our happiness. There is very little to be admired except for the one simple fact—we are stronger for having gone through it.

There is going to be a healing process that you must go through before you begin to truly learn to love yourself and have a healthy new relationship. All the stresses that you share with your spouse currently, are now going to need to be dealt with alone. My divorce didn't allow me a secret passageway around my unhappiness to a place of bliss and abundance. Certainly not. My divorce forced me to step up and take control of my happiness and my children's future. I was forced to choose what I wanted for myself. I knew I didn't want to be married any longer. When I finally accepted the answer to that question, I equally accepted that I was in the driver's seat of my life. Did I want to be a single mom providing for five children? Not really. But the alternative would have left me far worse off.

In many cases, divorce is the necessary avenue to go down to preserve your own spirit. Being alone is better than being in an abusive (mental, physical, emotional) or loveless marriage. I get it, I genuinely do. I had five young children when I made the decision that I was much better alone than continuing in my relationship. Get divorced for the right reasons, and don't fall for the illusion that "my life will be better once I am not married and I have a new partner." Divorce is far from sexy, so let's not fantasize what is not reality!

FEAR OF THE UNKNOWN

Let's talk about a big obstacle concerning divorce–fear of the unknown. When you finally settle into the reality of divorce and begin to undergo your post-divorce life, it is now not looking so sexy. This fear seeps in and overtakes every cell of your body. This is no longer a romance story. For me, I had to get really comfortable and see my potential future experiences as something exciting. It was exciting because I knew deep down this was the right choice for me and my children. It allowed a tremendous wave of relief to wash over me when I really needed it. It felt good to finally admit what I wanted for myself! I was able to open my eyes up to the future I could create instead of continuing to live in a life that didn't bring me joy. That letting go feeling still feels good to me to this day, as I reflect back on it.

Fear is one of those things that can eat us alive if we let it. It needs to be looked at head-on, straight in the eyes, so to speak. Anyone who is going through a divorce or has already experienced divorce is going to feel these fears on every level: fear of being alone, fear of abandonment, fear of your partner not being able to survive the storm of divorce. There will be guilt, and there will be self-sabotage in this beginning stage of divorce. There will be a fear of how kids are going to survive the divorce.

One of the biggest fears of all will be finances. If you haven't worked in a long time, because maybe you were a stay-at-home mom or dad, you're going to have to survive off of a much smaller income. It takes a strong person to acknowledge this fear of being a sole provider. Later in the book, you will find the steps to healing, tools, resources, and spiritual growth tools to help you feel more empowered to step into the light of this new role.

In society, we get caught up in the "house of cards," which is the fear of living real. We feel we need to project a certain status to the outside world. The priority is "how my life looks to others," rather than "how it feels to me on the inside." Later in the book, I will introduce the "house of bricks," metaphorically speaking. This is the real, true, sturdy, stable, predictable, and vulnerable life, rather than a false "keeping up with the Joneses" persona.

Another big fear is family. What is going to happen to the family as a result of divorce? There is a common, and realistic, fear that breaking up a family will destroy the lives of your children. I'm here to tell you that fear doesn't have to exist. If anything, you and your children can be stronger as a result. Finances keep couples together, and children keep couples together, but research shows this is not the healthiest option for you or your children. You're reading this book because you genuinely hope there is a better life, and a better version of you.

You'll want to show your kids that you have strength and grace in this time of fear and the unknown. Your children are watching you. When they observe you living in a loveless relationship, fighting with your partner, not showing happiness, and always depressed, then staying together for the sake of the children is not showing a healthy example of love. This is a lesson and opportunity for your children to see that a loving relationship needs to be selfless and respectful but also prioritizes self-love. We are raising our future generation to carry forward the lessons, teachings, and observations of their present. If your children observe that there is no love in your marriage, then this is the only frame of reference for "normal marriage" they will have. That can result in a higher chance they are going to repeat and mirror that in their future relationships.

Another huge factor to show children what a healthy, loving marriage looks like is to show mutual respect for your partner. If you are in a stage of fear because you're thinking about divorce, that's normal! You can, and must, still show mutual respect to your partner by leading the positive communication. Show your children that you're choosing to communicate amicably, rather than yelling or screaming, lashing out or manipulating the other person. It is also showing love and respect for your children. Ideally, you want to manifest and work towards having genuine communication with your partner after divorce because it continues to show the children that you can trust each other.

You want to show your children what love really looks like. We will dive deeper into this topic of how children are affected by divorce in later chapters, but for now, I want you to simply honor where you are at. Know your biggest priority, for your children and immediate family, is to keep things as harmonious as possible. This is a massive goal if you are in the pre-divorce stage or if you're experiencing a divorce because you know there are a lot of emotions on the table. The reality is that it's doubtful that both parties have come to each other at the same time, expressing they want to dissolve the marriage. Therefore, we have two parties at very different stages of emotional acceptance. So having empathic communication with your partner is laying the practical groundwork for both the divorce process and post-divorce journey. To begin your journey of this new life, you must commit to loving yourself first, and being a healthy example for your children during this time.

HOW TO KNOW IF YOU'VE EXHAUSTED ALL RESOURCES

You're probably by this point, asking yourself many questions, processing many emotions and deep down, you and your inner warrior know that you can conquer this fear and be a better version of yourself. However, there might be one last question you're asking yourself: "How do I know if I have exhausted all my resources and divorce is my final option?"

I'm a huge proponent of marriage counseling, but there have to be two people that are both willing to really work through things together. I still remember my marriage counselor saying to me, "you'll just know." It's one of those things that I remember so clearly, and she was so right with those three simple words. I made the decision I was going to go through with my divorce because I received an "indescribable feeling in my gut," telling me "it was time to go."

The reality of divorce, especially in this time of going through a lot of emotions and sifting through the noise of knowing whether a divorce is for you or not, all begins to become clearer and present with the deep-down feeling in your gut. It's the gut-brain connection (which we will dive deeper into in future chapters) that will allow you to feel something in your gut and communicate the message to your brain. The message is clear: you're ready to go. This indescribable feeling that you get is no longer a love story being written together. It's you knowing when you're ready to grow more as an individual, without your husband or wife by your side as a partner anymore. Listening to your gut is an integral part of the divorce process, as it's where you're going to get the most consistent messages and answers.

Mastering Your Ego

Mastering your ego is paramount during and after your divorce. I want you to accept that if you have a relationship that involves big things (kids, homes, savings) you will feel fear, anger, wins, and losses. I have not always had great control over my ego but I've always believed that

I can get better at it. My ego had a strong hold over me during the beginning of my divorce process. It wasn't until I was stripped down to my bare emotions, forced to make a life-changing decision, and face all my fears around divorce that I was able to check my ego at the door.

What is your ego? You already know your ego, I'm not going to explain that to you now. So I ask you again, what is your ego? Think in your head about what your ego is right now...

Did you find an answer? Say it back to yourself again now.

It's important that you can acknowledge the ever-so-simple fact that you have an ego, in your own words.

My ego is always looking out for my comfort. My ego wants me to win. In most divorces, ego is usually what drags them out, adds even more fuel to the fire, causes emotional pain to all involved and sets the tone for the post-divorce relationship.

If your ego is telling you to "squash your competition" and you hire an expensive lawyer to destroy your spouse in court, it will take years to come back from that.

If your ego is not in alignment with your truth and your intentions, you will act in ways you normally wouldn't act.

If your ego is in alignment with your intentions but left unbalanced with power, you will need extended time to recover from that.

As you learn to manage your ego throughout this book, you'll learn that there are simple ways to identify when your ego is acting out of alignment with your true intentions. If you're biggest fear is not spending as much time with your kids after divorce as is possible, it would be wrong to focus on making sure that your spouse doesn't get the house or the car in the settlement. Even though your ego may be screaming at you to get everything that you can in the divorce, you need to stay focused. Your ability to focus on what truly matters to you in your divorce is the best weapon you have to quiet your ego down.

You might also know ego as shame, guilt, fear, self-sabotage, judgment, your inner critic, or bully, or maybe another creative name that's special to you. This is what I like to call the "ego umbrella."

I personally relate to my ego as an inner bully that criticizes me saying, *I'm not good enough, I'm not smart enough, I'm not pretty enough, etc.*

You are going to develop a regular mindfulness practice to help you quiet your loud inner ego because, to trust your gut and intuition, which we will talk more about later, you need to listen to the quiet, soft and gentle inner voice. That voice is love.

At the beginning of the divorce process, you're going to find a lot of your ego present. It's intense when there is a lot at stake, and egos don't normally go down without a fight. In many ways your ego is a natural defense for you, but when combined with high levels of emotion, the ego can become unhinged.

For months I was becoming full of anger and anxiety when I finally told my spouse that we needed a divorce. My ego couldn't fathom that he didn't or wouldn't accept the divorce. It wasn't until long after that I realized my mistakes in managing my ego. My ego was adding stress to an already stressful situation. That will never end well.

I'm going to help you keep your ego in check no matter what point you're at in your relationship. Beyond a relationship or a divorce, being in control of identifying your ego and moving past the voice it leaves in your ear is going to have a positive, lasting effect on your life–and certainly on your future relationships.

The opposite of ego and fear is love. I want you to control your fear and your ego from a place of love. And I want you to learn to do this quickly. I'm not saying that any tip or trick is going to eliminate your ego or fears all together. We are humans and it's a natural state to feel fearful. Instead, I want you to be excited to learn how to identify what your ego is adding to your life and how to avoid leaving it unchecked.

In the process of divorce, the ego is going to be consistently present; your ego is going to feel entitled to show up. It might be encouraging you into an unhealthy addiction to alcohol, prescriptions, or other poor coping mechanisms. It might be getting you to focus on what you're not getting instead of what you already have. More often than not, it will trick you into focusing your attention on the things you aren't really that attached to, like money over spending time with your kids.

The feelings of the ego are all based out of fear, and they flourish and grow when you give them power and validation.

Based on my own personal experience with my divorce, I learned that the person with the stronger ego is going to engage and encourage the other ego to react. And then all of a sudden, you're going back and forth in an argument because two egos feel entitled to win.

When two egos engage, you will set out to win because you feel right and justified. The thing is though, nobody has to win anything in an ego argument. The point of learning about your ego now is to help you not engage and react because it makes things more destructive, hurtful, and emotional than they need to be.

Operating from a place of empathy, being true to your feelings and gut will help the other person eventually shift their energy and tone. Think of this as a positive ripple effect…if you want to try and have a positive conversation with your partner about your feelings and divorce, then start with a soft, non-engaging, non-reactive quiet voice, with your ego checked and tucked away. Honor the fact that your partner has strong feelings as well. And if you can honor their feelings, then you will find your happiness much quicker, and with grace and ease.

Master your Ego Exercise:

In this exercise I'm going to guide you through a simple three-step process to identify and deal with your ego during high-emotion situations. This simple process helped shape my understanding of and ability to control my ego during– and after–my divorce.

Before we dive into practicing the master your ego exercise, I suggest you to take out your favorite journal or a piece of paper and a pencil. It is more beneficial to you to jot down a quick note or sentence during these exercises to drive home your intention of doing them.

Step 1: Reflect to Become Aware

Think about a time that you had an imaginary argument in your head with someone in your life. Typically, we all experience these situations during showers, while driving, or shortly after an "incident" with another person. It could be a co-worker, your boss, a friend who continues to ignore your texts and calls, or your significant other. You don't need to remember the actual argument that went on inside your head. Instead, think about the feelings and emotions that were coursing through your body during the imaginary argument. You'll probably notice that you have the best comebacks, points and counterpoints, examples, and so on during your imaginary arguments. This is your ego acting out its burning desire for you to win. This is a part of you, me, and everyone who has ever lived on this earth. Step one is done. You have acknowledged and understood the voice in your head that we call ego.

Step 2: Gracefully Put the Ego to Sleep

Step two of this exercise is equally accepting that you have an ego and that, at times, your ego will be a massive distraction inside your head. When you accept both of these things without reservation you can move forward with setting your ego to the side. Any time that you identify the voice in your head, acknowledge it as your ego straightaway. Sometimes, I found myself even laughing at it. It can be like a barking dog that goes bonkers every single day the mail truck pulls up to your house.

Your ego isn't there to distract you; it's there to protect you by guarding against what is perceived as a threat. Many times those threats are actually your own choices. Even though a dog has every intention of protecting its territory from the mail truck each day, we always invite the mailman to our porch to do his job. It's our choice. In that same example, there are times when a dog will alert you of something more serious, like a potential home invader. The dog is simply acting out of instinct and it's up to you as the voice of reason and love to decide when you listen to that dog (or your ego) and when you smile, laugh, and move on.

Step 3: Step into Love

The last step is one that gives this exercise a lasting effect as you move through big life decisions and everyday life situations. Stepping into love is the act of setting an intention to act in a certain way AFTER you've identified the voice of your ego in any given situation. A great example of this in everyday life is while driving. It's no mystery to anyone who has been driving for a year or more that road rage or simply yelling at other drivers is part of commuting. If you can acknowledge that as true (and trust me I know it is for me!) then you can step into love right now. The next time you get into your car, set your intention before you move an inch. Tell yourself, out loud, that you are going to drive and laugh at things that would normally make your ego react. Can you do that? I bet you can, and I bet in the past you already have.

What I'm asking you to do by stepping into love is to let the ego have its moment inside your head, and then set an intention that is independent of what your ego wants. If your ego is telling you to write a nasty text message back to your spouse who said something rude, simply ignore it. Or, write back a completely cordial response and see what they do.

In many instances you will diffuse a potentially volatile situation in a matter of seconds. Now, had you followed through on the emotions laid out by your ego, you'd most likely pour gas on a raging fire. Which do you think will bring you the most peace and happiness?

Taking Inventory

The reason I believe it's so important to take inventory of where you're at today is because it's essential to be honest with yourself. We all like to have some sense of what to expect, right? We acknowledged earlier that a primary fear of divorce is fear of the unknown. By taking inventory and really asking yourself the hard question of "is divorce the answer for me?" you're able to use your quiet voice of intuition and gut feeling to help guide you down the right path.

Taking inventory is also understanding and allowing yourself to feel that your love story is going to be much better written alone at this time. For me, I am beyond grateful to my ex-husband that we came into each other's lives and share our five children. I honestly, deep down to my core know, I wouldn't have expanded and become who I am today without disconnecting our energies in the divorce and moving apart from him.

The only thing harder than divorce itself is making the decision that your divorce is imminent. Maybe you're unsure whether or not this is the path for you. I remember my therapist at the time saying to me, "staying or going is like walking through a dark forest without a hatchet." You need to find your way to the light because it is within you. I stayed in a marriage that was not healthy for me. It was unsupportive, lacked genuine love, and didn't allow me to be the emotionally vulnerable person that I am. My ex-husband may have felt the same. I spent two years in counseling hoping the marriage could be saved, and once I realized it could not, I think I spent more energy on what my marriage and family looked like to the outside, rather than taking inventory and honoring my feelings on the inside.

I worked hard to present the "image" I wanted people to see–maybe if we looked like the perfect family from the outside, then I might actually feel like a happy and perfect family from the inside. In time, I realized that this wasn't ever going to work. I knew the only option of saving my soul was to fly solo in the next flight of life and

hope for the best. And over time I felt no bitterness towards my ex–
I hoped his personal love story would live on as well.

Taking inventory for me was understanding that I was ready to
step forward and move on–I was accepting the energy that I needed to
change, and that I was going to create a better life for myself and my
children. The person who takes inventory in this way is usually the one
who is initiating the divorce.

Research states that between 75-80 percent of divorces are
initiated by the woman. Whether it is a man or woman isn't all that
important, in my eyes. We are all complex people with unique life
experiences that shape who we are. As you take inventory, try asking
yourself the tough questions as well. What role did you play in your
marriage ending in divorce? How do you feel about your soon-to-be
ex-spouse as a person? Be honest and say it out loud. Give yourself a
long look in the mirror so that you can develop empathy towards the
situation and everyone involved.

The "taking inventory" stage is necessary for both parties. If you're
the one who initiates the divorce, gently encourage your partner to
take inventory as well. If you're just receiving news of the divorce,
do your own inventory-taking. Either way, you don't want to be in
a loveless marriage or be in a marriage with someone that doesn't
want to be married to you anymore. This is the time for being really
honest and realistic of what was working and what was not working in
your marriage.

It's a time of reflection. It's a time that is going to open your eyes,
no matter what (giving or receiving) end you are on. Your eyes are
going to have to be open to have the opportunity to make and create
a more satisfying life.

UNDERSTANDING RELATIONSHIPS

When going through inventory-taking, it's important to understand
the types of relationships that exist. Recognizing of course, that I
am not a therapist, but through my coaching, and watching friends
go through divorces, there are more common reasons and types of

marriages and relationships that lead to divorce: toxic relationships being the most prevalent.

Getting out is not giving up on someone if staying means giving up on yourself. There are plenty of resources and options for couples who are in an unhealthy relationship. However, sometimes we don't see the signs of trouble even though we are heartbroken, lonely, and frightened. It can be hard to admit to ourselves that our relationship is one that causes more emotional turmoil than satisfaction. People often don't recognize the marriage is toxic because too often they have been confused and manipulated to accept the abuser's actions.

TYPES OF RELATIONSHIPS:

Criticism and Ridicule: One or both constantly ridiculing and "making fun" of their partner in front of others, purposely trying to embarrass them.

Poor Communication: You have lost the ability to share in an open, honest, and loving way without conflict; which often turns into blaming and anger. One person or the other doesn't feel safe expressing feelings or self-doubt.

Passive-Aggressive Behavior: Passive-aggressive behavior can manifest as non-verbal negativity, resistance, and confusion. It can appear in behavior such as resentment, jealousy, procrastination, avoiding responsibilities, helplessness, or childish behavior in an attempt to manipulate and control the other person.

Codependent Behavior: Codependent behaviors describe anyone who focuses on another person to gain some kind of control over them. Codependency behaviors to look for are people who: have moods that are dictated by yours, seek to control your attitudes and actions, and have little or no life of their own outside of your relationship.

Addiction: Alcohol and/or drug addiction only serve as tools to mask much greater internal problems. People with drug or alcohol problems are running from themselves or from a more extensive internal struggle. It is challenging to have healthy intimacy on all levels with somebody who is struggling to face themselves in a sober way.

Disengagement: Disengagement happens when one or both people lose their desire to invest energy or emotion into the relationship. Communication or arguments are often entirely passive, and it is a sign that the person is ready to end the relationship.

Loss of Intimacy: Emotional intimacy is built on trust and open communication with each other. It allows us to be vulnerable in a safe, loving and accepting way. It also translates into our physical intimacy, making that connection even more profound. Physical touch is essential for each partner to grow as well. Without emotional intimacy and physical intimacy, marriage becomes very lonely and empty.

Mutual Respect: Respect shows us that we understand each other and honor each other's boundaries, values, and needs. Without respect, you cannot have a healthy marriage.

Irresponsibility with Money: When one partner is irresponsible with money regarding overspending, a gambling addiction, or a shopping addiction; it causes a great deal of resentment and stress. Money is a significant source of problems within a marriage, even in marriages that have healthy spending habits. Money spending can become strife that in the long-term, impacts trust and respect between couples.

Narcissistic or Controlling Behavior: A person with a narcissistic personality is self-centered and seeks constant attention, considers themselves better than others, and believes they're entitled to special treatment. Controlling people desire to be in charge, prove themselves, and get their own way by controlling their environment and the people around them. Neither personality is conducive to authentic connection and intimacy.

Inability to Forgive: Forgiveness is essential for the health and longevity of a loving marriage. If one partner holds a grudge and can't let go of the past hurt or anger, neither partner will feel safe and intimate together. Forgiveness must be a sincere apology and a consistent change from the person.

Physical Abuse: Physical abuse is the use of force that injures or endangers someone. It is impossible to have a healthy relationship when one partner is a victim of abuse. The abuse can include hitting, biting, scratching, slapping, kicking, punching, shoving, use of a weapon, or forced sex. Physical abuse often builds gradually, beginning with emotional abuse. A one-time incident could be a warning sign of a future abuse waiting to happen. The only solution is to let go and leave as soon as possible.

Infidelity: It is devastating and shocking to discover your spouse has been unfaithful. Emotional pain, mistrust and resentment, and never-ending arguments about betrayal are present in the relationship. Everything goes back to the deception. If you decide to stay, it will be hard to rebuild trust and mend the marriage following the crisis of discovering the affair. You can hardly breathe once you find out, and it becomes too painful to bear. You're flooded with emotions and can't believe this is happening to you. Shock, denial, despair, chronic depression, all hit you at once. The relationship as you know it is over and you must mourn the loss. The opportunity to rebuild is only present if two people are committed to rebuilding together and there must be full disclosure and no secrets to do so.

Verbal Abuse: Verbal abuse can be threats, blaming, demeaning, and using sarcasm. The abuse damages self-esteem and makes intimacy impossible in the relationship.

Gaslighting: As the National Domestic Violence Hotline describes, gaslighting is a form of manipulation that seems to sow seeds of doubt in a targeted individual hoping to make them question their own memory, perception, and sanity. *I never said that. You're making things up again. Are you sure? You tend to have a bad memory. It's all in your head.* Does your partner repeatedly say things like this to you? Do you often start questioning your own perception of reality, or your own sanity within your relationship? If so, your partner may be using this form of abuse. Gaslighting is an extremely effective form of emotional abuse that causes the victim to question their own feelings, instincts, and sanity, giving the abusive partner a lot of power and control. The abuser will project his or her behavior and twist it around, making you believe that you are actually responsible for their behavior. Once an abusive partner has broken down the victim's ability to trust their own perceptions, the victim is more likely to stay in the abusive relationship. Some signs of being a victim of gaslighting can include: constantly second-guessing yourself, feeling confused and even crazy, always apologizing to your partner, and knowing something terrible is wrong but you can't ever quite express what it is. You may start lying to avoid put-downs and reality twists, you feel hopeless, and you frequently make excuses for your partner's behavior to friends and family members. I know. It's a terrible place to be.

As you can see, there are many types of relationships and reasons why marriages end up dissolving. Some marriages can dissolve with less difficulty and push-back than others. If you are in an abusive relationship of any sort, I applaud you for reading this book. You are giving yourself the ability to save yourself, and you are choosing to find your way back to a place where your inner light remains vibrant.

Taking inventory is a time for you to sit quietly with yourself and reflect. You'll really look at what is working and what is not working, what can be saved or improved upon, and what is already too far along and can't be undone.

Sometimes we just need to have someone say to us that it's okay for you to want a better life and that the marriage and relationship are not working any more or making you happy. At the end of the day, when you marry someone, you're hoping that you're going to continue to grow together for a lifetime. That's what love is. It's having your partner by your side. They are your best cheerleader, encouraging you to grow, expand, and evolve into even more vibrancy and love than you were before. And if you are not becoming "more" and growing as a human being, not receiving the same level of encouragement and love from your partner, then sometimes you just need that validation from somebody else; for someone to say "it's okay that you want more, it's okay to set your spirit free." I'm here to be that validation for you, hear me when I say "it's okay to choose you–go embark on your personal love story!"

DOES DIVORCE CONFLICT WITH RELIGIOUS BELIEFS?

One thing that you might be thinking about when it comes to dissolving your marriage is that it conflicts with the vows you took when you were married. Many religions are built on the foundation of structured rules that go against divorce. It can bring intense feelings of guilt and shame to you, and, in most situations, to your family as well. I was raised Catholic, but when it came time to evaluate the state of my marriage one of the first people in my life to help me move forward was a priest. When I shared my dark story with him, his words were concise and supportive: "It is time to get out."

My marriage, which was causing emotional pain and a tremendous amount of turmoil for myself and my children who witnessed the behavior, is not in alignment with what I view as God or the Universe. I cannot tell you how to process deep-rooted religious beliefs other than to ask you, "Who is God?"

Is your God one that punishes those who are considering leaving an abusive relationship? I think God is not that way. I view God and the Universe as a source of love, as a deep-rooted power we all have inside of us and can access anytime. I see God as someone who is putting challenges in front of us so we can make decisions and move forth with any and all consequences. I see God as a beautiful means to evolving as a person by living your life the best way you see fit. I see God as pure love.

One thing that I am still surprised by is how big of a factor religion is when someone has a choice of being happy or continuing to be abused. I regularly see, with my friends and clients, that religion is one of the factors that holds people back from a divorce that they desperately want and need! People tell me that they made a vow that they will live out no matter what.

I believe that God and the Universe write a love story in all of us from the time we are born. And when you stand in front of your family, friends, and God, taking those vows to heart, your intention is pure and whole. However, my love story and partner's love story were no longer growing "whole" together. It was clear to me that my personal love story was going to be more enriched and purer continuing my journey alone. This is a self-love story, and if self-love isn't thriving in a marriage, it might be better off thriving alone.

If you feel that God is going to punish you for dissolving a marriage and not following through on the vows that you made in His presence, talk to someone who can give you a unique perspective. Take it from me because I confided in a priest who had been a family friend for years and still is. He offered me the greatest support and validation as I was paralyzed with fear. He encouraged me that I was on the right path by choosing "me" and my own "self-love" story.

I want to pause and make a note here, that I honor and respect your personal religious beliefs. God can look different for everybody, and there is no judgment here. Your spiritual beliefs are your own. Whoever your God is and whatever your beliefs, God will be there to support you every step of the way. I feel certain God wants us to expand our love story and surround ourselves with other beautiful souls that ignite and grow our stories further–creating a brightness and vitality that lights us up and the world around us. God wants us to create heaven here on Earth.

Our love stories only thrive when we create them from inner peace, wholeness, and love; and avoid toxic relationships. Marriage is no different. It helps to understand with marriage that sometimes people change and unfortunately harbor toxicities for themselves and others, have sabotaging behavior, and personally damage their ability to grow. Therefore, that person may no longer be a healthy partner with which to expand your unified love story together. At times, you must choose your own love story to take a path on its own. In making that hard decision, you will keep your light vibrantly shining and your pathways clear. A road alone, making your own love story is better than a loveless and toxic story, that not only has no vitamins to grow but is slowly blowing out your inner flame.

CHILDREN AND PARENTAL PARALYSIS

Not only do I see people have a fear of divorce being against their religion, I also see a high fear of what, and how, they are going to tell your children. What will their lives look like after divorce?

That's a hard question to ask yourself when you start down this path. Honestly, this can be somewhat paralyzing, and it's a huge factor in deciding whether or not you're going to pursue a divorce. I know personally, you have to be able to take inventory of how your children are going to handle the divorce and whether it's going to be the best thing for all of you. In the end though, if it is the best thing for you, it ultimately is going to be the best thing for your children as well.

This is the place that you could spend years going around and around, thinking that there isn't a "right time" to tell your children and you'll wait for a better time. The most important thing before even telling the children about your divorce is talking to your spouse. This is an opportunity to plan what you want to say, control what your ego is telling you to do, and stay calm throughout the conversation.

Another very common question I hear is, "how do I prepare myself for the reaction that my spouse is going to have?" You need to be prepared for the reaction because this is a time that all emotions are going to be heightened and emotions are going to be in a reactive state, rather than a proactive state. You might even find that your partner is shocked if they haven't been in therapy or gone to counseling with you, so it might catch them off-guard.

You have to understand that you are the person doing the telling. You have taken inventory and chosen that divorce is the next step for you. The person you are telling will likely not be in the same mental state that you are. From this you can predict that there's a possibility the other person will be overcome by emotion because they are not in the same place. I want you to be mindful of this if you are the one receiving or even the one sharing the news of divorce, I want you to put yourself in the other person's shoes. At the end of the day, it's essential to allow the space for emotions to be shared but please do not react and take them personally.

It's very rare that both partners come to each other at the same time and agree that divorce is the only option for mutual happiness. That being said, the acceptance and emotional process is going to be a journey for both parties. This is the stage where if you haven't already been in some type of divorce coaching or counseling, I strongly recommend that you seek outside support through this time. Coaching or counseling will help the communication process, allowing you to bring awareness to your emotions and help you to tell your children.

Paralysis happens when you are lacking a support system. I had to confide in a few key people to build up the support system I needed to plan out how I would tell my spouse and my children. I lived in a house under the guise of separation for TWO years before I found the right time to go forward with my life the way I wanted to. I wanted it to work out for my lifestyle's sake and my children's sake but deep down I knew that it wasn't going to ever work. Listen to your gut and go forth with the decision you make or years will pass you by. Rarely will throwing more time at a failing marriage result in anything other than divorce. Avoid falling into paralysis yourself by finding support, planning your difficult conversations, and staying grounded. You can always be a tone setter in your house, even during a divorce.

The Wholeness Journey

The message I want you to hear in this chapter is that it's important to understand it requires a lot of courage to be reading this book in the first place. I know you can relate when I say, "sometimes the right thing is not always the easiest thing." And so I think that it does require a lot of courage for you to move in the direction of happiness because it belongs solely to you. Believe in your life, value it, and then value it even more. Accept your path forward and know that you are not alone. This book has all the tools you're going to need to walk you through a smooth divorce and post-divorce journey. Everything here is what I wish I would have had in my post-divorce journey so I could have managed the stress in a more proactive and healthier way.

I'm here to help you through this storm because you and I both know, one person cannot make a healthy marriage, nor make the marriage work. It takes two, and if somebody is not committed to the marriage or relationship, then you are not going to experience the love that you deserve. I know you will take all the necessary steps to try and make your marriage work, but if you've reached a point where you want more, then your new life of self-love and transformation are waiting for you. Your next steps are not going to be easy as you begin the paperwork process of filing for divorce and working with your children to establish their new normal. But I can promise you this, all of the emotions you are feeling right now are going to be worth it in the end. Your wholeness journey is just beginning - let's keep going and walk you through the actual divorce!

CHAPTER TWO

What to Expect During the Divorce Process

Along with helping you move through your divorce with the most grace possible, I also want to provide you with tangible ways to make the step-by-step process easier on everyone, and your wallet. You may hear people refer to divorce as a business deal or a business move. Have you heard this before? While there is truth with this statement, the better way to approach your divorce is by seeing it as project management. The very simple nature of the term "business deal" implies that there is a deal going down and someone may end up losing or winning. Divorce is not merely a split of children and assets between two adults who fell out of love. For children, divorce is a reshaping of their entire reality in which they now see mom and dad separately and live in two different places for agreed-upon amounts of time. I hear business deal and I think of money right away. I can see people arguing over numbers while totally ignoring the other aspects that are at play. That's just my outlook.

Take a moment and think about what that term ("business deal") means to you. Does it bring up any images in your mind? What vibe do you feel when you hear that phrase?

Now let's look at a divorce from the standpoint of managing a project. In the construction industry project management is not about doing a deal or agreeing on terms that suit you best. Project management in the construction world is about getting something done the fastest with the lowest cost. You will probably hear this from me throughout this book, but a divorce is expensive. The cheapest divorces also happen to be the ones that get done in the shortest amount of time. Imagine I'm building you a brand-new house. Halfway through the project I come and tell you that your house is behind schedule and the budget is too low. How would that make you react? You'd feel stuck and at the mercy of added time and costs from me, your contractor. Divorce lawyers bill hourly and the longer your divorce carries on, the higher both parties' legal fees will go.

Let's go back to the brand-new house example. If you had been managing the daily construction progress of your home you would have plenty of control over the direction the project is going in. You would be solving all the issues that arise right away. You're there to make sure that the project is managed as well as it can be given the situations presented to you. Things will come up. You will get frustrated, emotional, fed up, and much more. You don't need to eliminate these emotions from coming up, you need to know how to deal with them and push forward to get the project done.

If you let the need to win at a business deal come into play, fear will take over, and your emotions will spiral further out of control. Your ego will take you down a completely different path than where you need to go. I want to be a realist and prepare you that undoubtedly your soon-to-be ex-spouse will be functioning with a strong ego. They very well may approach mediation and attorney disputes with a great force to "win" in the deal. Stay grounded and do not get sucked into playing business deals with emotional parties and lawyers. It will happen. I am certain if you can quiet the ego, and approach this time from a more peaceful state, your attorneys and your ex-spouse will shift towards you and quiet their egos as well. It will allow for the mediation and legal process to deliver quicker and more peaceful outcomes. So, let's pause and do this breathing exercise together before we get into the chapter details.

4-7-8 Relaxing Breath Exercise:

The 4-7-8 (or Relaxing Breath) Exercise, by Dr. Andrew Weil, was created to reduce stress, calm your nerves and relax your mind. It should be practiced at least twice a day, so it becomes a relaxing tool for you. The 4-7-8 breathing technique is easy, can be done anywhere and learning it early in the divorce process is essential so that you can nourish your mind, body, and spirit. This breathing exercise is a natural tranquilizer for the nervous system. You cannot do it too often.

This exercise is a favorite of mine that I still practice to this day. I avoided letting stress break me down when I wanted to quit many times throughout my divorce. I opted to pass on prescription drugs to deal with the emotion of my divorce and instead breathe with intention. For two whole years my nervous system was out of alignment, and when my stress hormones went off my breathing became shallow. Like the change from winter to spring, my health slowly degraded under the weight of holding so much pain inside. This was in the months leading up to finally making my decision to proceed with divorce.

Practice this exercise when you are dealing with a stressful event. You can increase the breath in through the nose from four to eight counts once you have practiced for a month. You will have this tool everywhere you go and the more often you practice it, the quicker your body will adapt and relax. Use this tool to ground yourself and maintain a positive mindset and controlling your reactions.

Exhale completely through your mouth, making a whoosh sound.
Close your mouth and inhale quietly through your nose to a
    mental count of four.
Hold your breath for a count of seven.

Exhale completely through your mouth, making a whoosh sound to a count of eight.
This is one breath.
Now inhale again and repeat the cycle three more times for a total of four breaths.

The Overall Process of Divorce

Filing a Petition

The first step in a divorce is to file a petition for divorce. Even if you and your spouse both are ready to move forward with the divorce, one person will need to file the petition. This is where you state the reason for the divorce, which can vary depending on where you live. I'm not sure but I would wager that "irreconcilable differences" is the most common grounds for divorce in this day and age. There are other options as well and those are best discussed with your lawyer. It may make sense for you to explore other grounds to pursue, and a lawyer can provide you with all the scenarios.

Temporary Orders

Temporary orders are what allow a divorce to play out using orders that act as temporary rules the two parties will need to abide by. Such orders include Child Support Order, Child Custody Order, and/or Financial Support Order. The court will grant temporary orders that last throughout the court proceedings of your divorce. In order to receive a temporary order, one party must request the order from the court. If you are the one filing the petition for divorce you would want to also file your requests for certain orders at the same time.

Service of Process

The person that files the petition for divorce must also file proof of service of process. This is a fancy way of saying that you are responsible to present a document that states you have given a copy of the divorce petition to the other party involved in the divorce. That should be your spouse's attorney if they have one at the time. Ideally you are going into your divorce with both parties on the same page. If not, you will need to officially serve the person with the divorce petition using an official process server. It's ideal to avoid serving your spouse with divorce papers in a public place.

Response

The person receiving the service of process must file a reply to the petition. This is where the grounds of the divorce that you've stated may come under scrutiny. It's best to work closely with a lawyer to understand how to start your divorce so that the response phase goes smoothly. The person who is responding to the divorce can dispute any claims made in the petition.

Negotiation

In Negotiation things like child visitation, child custody, division of assets, and spousal support are hammered out. The court can do different things to try and help progress this stage towards resolution by scheduling conferences, mediation, and even using social workers to audit the home. This will be one of the most challenging aspects of the divorce. Let your lawyers do the leg work here, and stay grounded in managing your project at hand.

Trial

Any issues that are not able to be resolved during the negotiation will move to trial. This will incur added costs and time to your divorce and is best avoided at all costs.

Order of Dissolution

This is the part of the process that officially ends the marriage and lays out the terms of the divorce. This can be done by working with your spouse for the fastest and most effective agreement through your lawyers or it can be done by fighting out in court and putting your future in the court's hands. The ideal situation is to draft the Order of Dissolution between your lawyers and submit it to the court. This will provide the fastest and cheapest divorce.

Children and Parental Sharing

With just over 50 percent of marriages ending in divorce, it's important to think about our next generation and how we handle the divorce process and post-divorce relationship with our children. I am inspired by the possibility that if you follow this book and use it as your guide, we can all create a positive ripple effect of happier, less anxious, and more well-adjusted and adaptable generations to come. That is grounded with the roots of family and love.

I personally know, one of the biggest fears with ending a marriage is how to tell your children and answering the big question of "why are you getting divorced?" If you harbor hatred towards your ex-spouse and choose to let your ego hijack the relationship, you will face unnecessary hardships with your children. You can be confident that it will make simply telling your children that much harder. Regardless of whether you're the one receiving the news of divorce or initiating the divorce, you'll be flooded with an array of different emotions, from anger to bitterness, sadness to regret. All of these emotions encompass the ego umbrella (it wants you comfortable!) and are fear-driven. I'm sharing this message with you because these ego-driven emotions negatively impact your ability to communicate. I know from experience, if you choose to release your ego and communicate with an empathetic heart and mind, then your children will indeed thrive in the end. Children will experience adversity in life. Here is the opportunity to provide a learning platform that we can all learn and grow from, while still continuing to love and find peace in our hearts.

I understand that you're probably thinking how are you going to embrace the fact that you have to tell your children that their mom and dad are splitting up and getting a divorce. The first thing you and your partner want to make sure of is that you're on the same page when it comes to talking to your children. This is an important opportunity to be an example for your children during this time. Your children are going to be observing you every step of the way, so work on having all the details in sync with one another.

If you are, however, at odds with your spouse or there is a breakdown of communication between you, then you must, and without hesitation, shoulder your portion of letting your kids know what is happening and why. You cannot control the emotions, and/or the reactions to them, that your spouse will go through. It's right now that you tell yourself you'll relentlessly commit to staying grounded as a leader for your children. At the end of the day, it's your duty as a parent to show your kids that a difficult situation is not something to fear, even if you haven't conquered or dealt with all your fears just yet.

As a parent, you want to consider your child's well-being as a top priority, but the bottom line is that both parents need to set aside their differences and collaborate together to make their children an equal priority. If you can help your children navigate this process, they can turn the magnitude of feelings and anxiousness they will experience and most certainly the sense of loss, into visions of opportunities and openness. Being able to be an example for your children, and being mindful of their well-being, will give them the tools to use in all future life challenges.

No matter what ages your children are, it's going to be unsettling to them, but above anything, children want to feel secure and comfortable, no matter how hard the process is going to be on them. Children usually just want mom and dad to be happy and not fight. They cannot even comprehend the immense challenge that divorce presents the same way adults can. Their burning desires are simple and in your hands.

In 2008 when the housing market crashed and nearly toppled the United States economy, and nearly the world economy, the ones who got the worst end of the deal were the average American taxpayers. Things like 401Ks and investment portfolios lost significant value almost overnight, while the people that were responsible ultimately made money. Again, we can bring back the idea of doing a business deal–like the actions that led up to the unprecedented housing market crash–or managing a project. Project management (i.e., better oversight of the actions banks were taking during the housing market crash) would have prevented the people who were not even involved from suffering losses. You have the power in your hands, even if your spouse isn't on the same page, to gracefully show your children how a person handles adversity.

I had a conversation with my kids that was open, honest, and age-appropriate. I told them I went forward with the divorce but that the actions that brought us here fall onto both parents. My message was very clear. I didn't sugar coat it. I treated my young children who were the ages of two, five, and eight at the time of our divorce with great compassion. My two-year-old and five-year-old twin boys were too young to comprehend what divorce really meant in just a conversation, whereas my eight-year-old twin girls could comprehend that divorce was a very scary idea. Because my children were so young, it required me to have ongoing conversations that would soothe their fears and worries about how divorce would feel for them. It wasn't until they were living in two different homes that they could begin to understand this idea of divorce. I used simple phrases like "I love you" and "I will always be here for you." I didn't make it about me. I clearly told them it's an adult situation and we both have our own views on our marriage. I never threw my spouse under the bus. I never told them the concrete reasons we divorced until they were older and could understand the situation more clearly as young adults themselves. I did this with preparation through ego management, understanding my intentions, and not acting on high emotions.

Research states that over the last five years, 75 percent of divorcing parents tell their children the news in less than 10 minutes. In this section, I'm going to walk you through how to be in the 25 percent of divorcing couples that talk to their children honestly, and safely prepare them for what is to come. Regardless of who initiated the breakup or what circumstance brought you to this point, you and your soon-to-be ex are still on the same team and should always strive to be, as parents. It's both of your responsibilities for delivering the news of the divorce together and in synchronicity.

Having clear communication is going to help you stay above the stress and fear of what could potentially come during this time. You know the marriage is over, and it is very likely that you both have a different idea as to why it's over. Remember, you are experiencing this time through your very own set of glasses and choosing to see what your brain is wired to see–it's all based on your love and your fear. For the kids' sake, try to understand this before telling them so you can navigate the conversation with the intention of doing so from a place of inner peace and love.

I suggest that you practice what you're going to tell your children and how much detail you want to share with them. You need a shared mutual plan and as many of the details, of how your children are going to be affected, as possible. Some of the high-priority things that you're going to want to talk over and discuss with your soon-to-be ex-spouse are:

- Where are the children going to live?
- Will mom be moving out or will dad be moving out of the house?
- Will you be staying in the current home or will both of you be moving out?
- If you're both moving out, where will you be moving?
- Will the children go to the same school or a different one?
- What is the custody arrangement going to be?
- How will you spend holidays, birthdays, and vacation time?

These are not easy questions to answer for anyone in a divorce. All that stuff I've talked about up to this point about controlling your emotions will be tested. You may be dealing with a difficult personality on the other end of the table. If I can get you to see and understand how to answer these questions calmly, then this entire book will be more than worth writing!

TIPS ON HOW TO TELL YOUR CHILDREN

Once you and your spouse are able to come to a consensus and, ideally, a mutual understanding of the plan, talking to your children together as a couple is the most critical part of this stage. Depending on the age of your children, you're going to want to talk in a quiet space where nothing needs to be done afterward. It's also best to tell your kids over a weekend when they have time to be home with both of you and begin to process the change that is going to happen. It's important during this time that you are available to them over the next couple of days. Allow them the sacred space to ask questions and encourage them to talk about their fears and concerns. The consistent message here needs to be that you are still a family and are going to be family even after the divorce.

It's important to revisit the discussion over and over again reinforcing the same messages talked about in the initial discussion. How they react today might be different than how they respond next week or next month; reassure them and address their concerns. Here is a look at what a conversation looks like: "Our family is going to look different now, but we are still going to be family," "We are going to have two different homes, but mom and dad still love you," "This has nothing to do with you, and it's not your fault," or "nobody is blaming anybody else."

The most important thing to portray to your children is that they should never feel that they have to be disloyal to one parent or the other with their love. This is not a time to put your children in the middle of your divorce. It's best for the children that you retain a calm presence together and have as toxic-free of an environment as possible.

Telling your children is never going to be easy. My children were two, five, and eight and all reacted differently; however, they responded age-appropriately. We had been separated for two years prior, still living under the same roof and sleeping in different rooms. My kids were young but they could still sense mom and dad were not together even though we were living under the same roof. Kids can feel our energy.

All divorces are different when it comes to talking to your children. What might work for your friend might not work for you. One commonality with any divorce story is that all children want what they are used to, familiar with, and accustomed to. Children will be resilient, but in the meantime, they want reassurance that their lives will still be "normal" (what they are accustomed to). Regardless of their age, it is important when you talk to them, to have it mapped out and let them know how it's going to affect them.

TIPS FOR COMMUNICATING WITH YOUR CHILDREN ABOUT GETTING A DIVORCE:

1. Let them know this is something mom and dad have decided after working on their differences for a very long time.

2. These are adult decisions between mom and dad that have nothing to do for their shared love for them and nothing to do with the children themselves. Let them know there is nothing they can do to turn the decision around.

3. Nobody is to blame anybody else or encourage the children to love mom or dad more than the other. They should never feel that they are betraying the other parent or needing to choose one parent over the other. Protecting your children from the pain and maladjustment is essential.

4. Mixed emotions are standard here. They will feel sad, angry, worried, and even curious as to what the future might look like. Your responsibility as a parent is to help your children process all these feelings and emotions.

5. Share the plan with them. Try to have as many details predetermined before talking with children. Who will be staying in the house? Who will be moving out and where will

they be moving to? If one parent has already found a new home to live in, plan to invite the children to come to see the new place. If one parent is looking for a new place, then include the children in the process of looking for a new home, so they can feel they had an active part in starting the new life. Share the specific custody plan as to when they will spend time with mom and dad. Ideally, you will all be together for sports games and school functions and possibly celebrations, but on a regular basis, you'll be sharing custody (more later on how to handle this topic gracefully). Try to reassure kids by sharing the day-to-day specifics of their schedules, because this is what is going to affect them the most.

6. Be ready for all different reactions. Depending on the age of the child, they may begin to act out at home and at school. Children need to be encouraged to talk about their fears and be reassured over and over again. Don't hound your children at this time but ask them questions every few days, like "How are you doing with the changes in our family?" "Did you feel sad when you thought of dad or mom moving out of the house?" Keep the communication going with your children.

I am not a licensed child psychologist, but I do know that continuing these conversations is crucial to how your child will adapt—not only to divorce, but how they will handle adversity later in life. If we allow them not to push their emotions down, then that is how they are going to handle challenging, emotional situations in the future. Give them ideas as to how they can healthily express their feelings, like drawing pictures, talking to friends or their teacher, talking to mom or dad or another family member, or merely giving mom or dad a hug.

Children will never be fully comforted through your words. It's not until they are living the life of two different homes that they will create an ability to self-soothe. It all depends on how successful the two parents are in creating the safe space of two

separate houses and how well they work together to provide
the children with a healthy transition.

7. Reassure your children that you will get through this together.
    For children, this may feel like the end of the world to them.
    They want to know that they will be okay and life will get back
    to a new normal. Maybe share examples of other families who
    are divorced, who are in a good place post-divorce. I found
    it really helpful to have my sister's children, who had gone
    through a divorce, talk to my children and let them know they
    would be okay.

    My children were young, and I still can recall them
    being happy when they found out Santa Claus would now
    come to two homes. Given the ages of my children, that was
    something that was important to them and relatable to their
    age. Depending on your kids' ages, they will worry over things
    that adults would never even think of. Be gentle with them
    and listen to their concerns. Sometimes simple things like
    celebrating holidays and having two birthday parties, in which
    they can celebrate with both parents individually, allows them
    to know that life will go on after divorce.

8. Showing emotion is okay. It is okay for children to see us cry
    and acknowledge that this is sad for the whole family. If one
    parent gets angry or mad and starts saying things that are
    upsetting to the children, the other spouse needs to rescue the
    situation and tell the children, "Mom or dad is really upset
    right now." "We are all really upset right now, and this is hard
    on all of us."

    Don't make the situation worse; be forgiving even if your
    spouse is not showing their best side, for the sake of the children
    who are feeling like their world is falling down around them.
    You need to make their world feel safe. Remember this is the
    most tumultuous time not only for you but for your children.
    Helping your children find their way back to a place of inner

peace and calm is just as essential as finding your own way to that place, and the only way to do this is by operating from your best at this time.

9. Treat each other with respect no matter how hard it is. Your children are observing and watching how you behave towards each other. Children can become embarrassed and scared in front of their peers because their parents are getting a divorce. If you treat each other poorly, this feeling of worry will increase and shame them even more. Try to co-parent with respect and compassion for the next weeks and months after the initial conversation. Work together towards trying to keep as many family routines the same or as close to similar as possible. In time, children will see that some things have remained the same and other things that have changed will become a new normal.

All divorces are going to be different, and your children are going to experience it differently, but the common denominator is the way that kids are going to show their reactions.

COMMUNICATION WITH YOUR SPOUSE DURING THE DIVORCE

If you haven't guessed by now, communication is everything in the divorce process. That's why we started talking early on in the book about putting the ego aside and remaining in a place of peace, to the best of your abilities. Communication is everything because if you have one person in the relationship operating from a position of ego, what the ego is going to do is make communication even more difficult for both you and your children.

When I say communication I'm mostly referring to the art of listening. Listening and hearing are two completely different things. If I have a newborn baby in my house that won't stop crying I need to really listen to what that baby is trying to tell me. Hearing is the act of, literally, absorbing the sounds of a baby crying. The difference here is that listening is active and hearing is passive. Beyond just being a passive trait for us, hearing is reactive. If you are only hearing your spouse talk about what he or she wants in the divorce you'll grow reactive as well. Listening is an art, and it needs to be practiced daily in order to use it to move through your divorce quickly and at the lowest possible cost. It's about not rationalizing the wants that you have. It's about really absorbing what your spouse has to say while equally clearly stating your intention to them. You want to be in a position of clarity so that when you communicate you are not adding fuel to the fire but rather holding your grounding force.

There will be many, many moments when your emotions will spike during a conversation with your spouse. He or she will be feeling their own versions of high emotions. It's potentially volatile even when it isn't. During my divorce, and when we were living together but separated, I was faced with anger, sadness, confusion and even guilt over what was happening to my life. I was in the infant stages of learning how to listen, process, and proceed with what my spouse was communicating to me, even when it was hostile. The reality is you may not always be at your best during the divorce process. That's why you need to have your intentions clear in your mind, and share those same intentions with your soon-to-be ex-spouse.

The last thing you want to resort to is having to communicate through attorneys. Have you ever sent (or received) a text message that may have been totally harmless but was read differently by the receiving party? When you have to talk through lawyers, or even through email, you will struggle to have grounded and meaningful conversations. Again, this will drive up the cost of a divorce and add time to the overall process. If you are dealing with someone that will continuously put roadblocks in your way to resolution, listening to them will seem almost pointless. But it's not. It's a practice for you to grow as a person even against the biggest odds: a divorce.

When we talk about narcissistic traits shortly, you will see that your tactics will have to change. I want to provide you with both the ideal avenue and the more likely avenue where one party is refusing to cooperate for the good of the whole. It is impossible to have healthy communication with a narcissist.

Healthy discussion is giving yourself the grace, space, and permission to "just be" during this time and to honor where you are at. It's a time to be fully present in your heart space and to speak with intention to yourself, your children and your spouse. This allows you to speak with truth and honor your feelings, so you're clear with your spouse. When you're able to master healthy communication, you're ready to diminish anger and resentment. It also allows you the physical space to create a toxic-free environment in the home. When two people set the tone for healthy communication, the entire house can feel at ease. This is ideal in a perfect world, but it is not often that both people will be able to practice this.

You want to be a healthy example for your children, just as I mentioned earlier in chapter one. You want to show your children that a divorce is the healthiest option and that ideally, you can maintain an even healthier relationship with your ex-spouse in a better way than when you were married. Controlling the conversation or behavior right now is not serving your highest good or well-being because you can't control the other person or their behavior. You can only control how you react to their behavior and listen to what they need to say. The ultimate goal here is to maintain inner peace within yourself and not react.

I know sometimes there are going to be moments where one person is being volatile or toxic but take this as a moment to stop, pause, close your eyes, take a deep breath, and not react to the behavior. Committing to being the bigger person is how you are going to change the energy and dynamics of the situation. Rising above will not only be healthy for you but the more you are able to stay in this place of calm and neutrality, the more your partner will eventually know that the name-calling, yelling, attacking the ego, judging or whatever it is, is not going to work anymore.

If you operate from a calmer and more peaceful place, as opposed to the emotional, negative, and disrespectful space that your partner is operating from, he or she is no longer getting the reaction that makes them feel they have control over the situation. If you both continue to operate from the negative place, I can guarantee you will never resolve any of the smallest, let alone most substantial, details because you are so focused on winning the argument.

It is healthy to say to your partner when moments like this come up, *I understand that you're mad, upset, angry. I understand that you have strong emotions and feelings; however, I am not and will not communicate with you in this way. I don't want to communicate from a place of anger. I want to have a healthy relationship with you.* The more you are able to consistently stand in this self-empowered space and reflect these words back to your partner, you are setting the tone for the course of your conversation and protecting your own spirit. Listening doesn't mean giving in to your partner. Listening is a strong quality to have, and you'll be much less likely to be persuaded to do something you don't want to do if you learn and practice active listening.

Once you develop a healthy communication plan with your spouse, it's time for you to develop a plan together of how it's going to be best for you to communicate after the divorce. Maybe it's emailing each other, perhaps it's texting, or communicating on a weekly basis. The point is to establish a communication plan that works for both of you, and that you're able to have neutral conversations and be an example for your children. Be open to the flexibility of changing the plan over time as both of you grow and respect one another. When emotions are high during the divorce stage, many couples communicate more effectively via email or text. In the post-divorce stage, time will likely heal your wounds and open both of you up to sharing a friendlier dialogue.

Surrendering to the outcome and the uncertain future of what everything is precisely going to look like is essential as well. If it helps, check-in with yourself and tell yourself again, that this divorce is a big project that you have been tasked with managing, without emotion.

The faster and smoother you're able to process the paperwork, the closer you and your family are to living a more balanced, happier life.

QUICK TIPS FOR COMMUNICATING FROM THE LIGHT:

1. Listen first. Don't respond and react. It is natural to want to react but don't. That is only going to fuel the fire because the other person is operating from a place of fearful emotion.

2. Breathe. Use the breathing technique at the beginning of this chapter.

3. Guide yourself back to a place of inner peace. State your intentions clearly to yourself. Identify the chatter that is happening in your head when your ego is talking. Are you arguing inside your head? Identify when your ego is taking over and resolve that chatter by clearly stating your purest intentions for going through with a divorce. This will bring you back to a state of inner peace naturally because you know what you need to do and why you need to do it.

4. Respond with love. Respond from a place of calm, peace and a tone that is happy and fueled with love. It is vital for children to see a calm parent who is confident and not trying to manipulate or control the outcome or situation

Child Support and Marital Assets

If there is going to be an argument or a discussion that is going to cause a reaction, it's going to be here, when talking about child support and assets. This is one of the most important topics that you're going to cover with your spouse, so it's imperative that you intentionally practice communication through listening that we just went over.

Marital assets are all the things or stuff that you've acquired throughout the marriage. This includes the house, cars, everything in the house, trust funds, 401K, investment portfolios, etc. This is what you pay your lawyers for. The more you fight with your spouse about assets, the more money you will pay your attorneys. Being grounded as you're heading into asset division by having thoughtful conversations with your spouse on who gets what and how the children will be affected, will save you massive amounts of money and stress with lawyers. Trust me, I know from my experience and that of others that this is easier said than done. I don't want to paint a picture of constant struggle and fights during the legal process of divorce but I'm also going to be real and let you know it will get harder before it gets any easier.

This is a moment when your ego is going to take over, fear sets in, your head spins, and you're ready for the fight. One of the greatest fears is that what you're receiving will not be enough, especially financially speaking. Can you relate? Trust me when I say though, child support is not a weapon, it is not used to cause pain for the other person. It's just a legal responsibility that must reach a level of agreement from both of you, depending on your current financial situation and whether there are single or dual incomes.

People get emotionally fixated on what they are supposed to receive, whether it be child support or alimony. I will tell you this, from most of my observations, the initial child support or alimony amount will change as life, career, and income evolves and changes over time. What you discuss and agree upon at the beginning of post-divorce will most likely not be the same as the years progress. Don't get paralyzed in this scenario and don't create a life that is going to expect this financial contribution to solely support you and your children. You'll read more in chapter six about your finances.

When talking about child support, it's best to start this conversation before lawyers get involved, so you're able to have a more level head and neutral conversation when the paperwork begins. I challenge you to start this stage with a simple acknowledgment that you both brought different skill sets to the marriage. You both have your strengths, weaknesses, and incomes. You are going to experience a loss because you all of a sudden go from having your children 100 percent of the time to now only 50 percent of the time (most states will award 50-50 custody to parents). Understand that you're not going to have every holiday with your children: it is a loss. Remember both you and your partner are feeling the same feelings, so be mindful of their feelings when you begin to strategize child support and custody.

High Conflict Situations

In this book, I want to give you the best scenario, but honestly, it's not always going to be the most pleasant journey. Divorce will test you and has the potential to bring out the worst characteristics in both of you. It will be a time of turbulent conflict, anger, fear, and sadness. These negative ego emotions can fuel you to behave in ways that are similar to the characteristics in somebody with a personality disorder. This typically happens because it's the longest lasting stress that you'll ever experience, aside from the death of a loved one. If you are not appropriately dealing with the stress and are not in a place of balance and neutrality, then it will drive you to a place of destructive, high-conflict situations.

When it comes to a partner who actually has a personality disorder, the law does not acknowledge personality disorders when custody agreements are being made, and whether or not someone with a disorder is fit to share custody.

Unfortunately, there are more times than not that high-conflict situations will occur in a relationship. A high-conflict person will show the following behaviors:

1. Quickly makes assumptions and demands

2. Makes demands that are inflexible and draws conclusions

3. Creates arguments from small things

4. Recruits family, friends, and even their lawyer to defend their position

5. Is willing to drag the conflict on for years

6. Is unable or unwilling to put the children's needs first, before their own.

I want to reassure you that there are steps to take that will help keep you emotionally and mentally sane and also protect your children. Your partner can be the most charming of people, putting on a show to the outside and even at the beginning of your relationship to have you fall in love with them. And then over time, their real personality begins to show and/or it might only start to come out when you enter into the divorce process because of all the stress. Even in a healthy "normal" breakup, most couples experience a lot of conflict, mostly in the first year, which is normal and to be expected.

The key to a healthy breakup and dissolution of the marriage is the ability for both people to let go of past issues, stop fighting and create a new life. Signs that you are not in a normal or healthy breakup would be the constant anger, resentment, and refusal from your partner of not taking responsibility for their own actions. They blame you for the marriage ending and continuously portray themselves as the victim. Their ill behavior during the marriage is what likely brought you to initiate the divorce. It takes a tremendous amount of courage to leave someone with a personality disorder but it is a necessary step to freeing your spirit.

This is a person displaying traits of personality disorder such as antisocial, narcissist, or borderline personality disorder. People with a personality disorder, especially thrive on creating chaos in their personal lives and have fears of abandonment, which make them even more resistant to the idea of somebody divorcing them. Narcissistic people have an inflated sense of self, lack empathy for others, and a deep need for excessive admiration, lack attention and poor relationships. If you are divorcing a spouse with a narcissistic or borderline personality disorder, you are in a high active mode already and trying to protect yourself and your children. Narcissists will not let you divorce them easily. It will be an exhausting journey, but a very necessary one.

It's essential to protect your own spirit through this process and stay in balance, mind, body, spirit. If you find yourself having a hard time balancing or working through the high conflict personality or situation, then I encourage you to dig deep within and find your strong inner warrior because you have to protect your children. I found my inner warrior, and you will find yours too.

QUICK TIPS, TOOLS AND TECHNIQUES FOR DEALING WITH HIGH CONFLICTS

The best thing to understand is that you will not change a person with a high-conflict personality. A good strategy of coping and dealing with the situation can help you come out on the other side as a stronger person.

1. Get a Good Therapist or Divorce Coach: First and foremost, this is going to help you reduce the emotional toll that this is going to take on you and your children. Post-traumatic stress syndrome is likely going to occur after processing so much abuse from your partner. So you need someone who is familiar with the personality disorder and who will be there for you in a dependable way to help you process the emotion. Living with a narcissist is damaging to your mental health, so you need a sacred space to process all the emotions you are feeling. It's also a safe space for you to process why you stayed in the relationship for so long and how you can change this pattern in your future relationships. I recommend that you meet with your therapist or coach more often than not, perhaps even more than once a week, if needed.

2. Make Your Attorney Aware: Make sure that your attorney is aware of the mental abuse. If your lawyer is not familiar with this personality disorder, you should get a different lawyer who is, or who can set firm boundaries with your actions. I

personally recommend using someone who is experienced with this because they'll be motivated to move your case forward rather than be manipulated and roped into playing games and racking up fees. Attorneys can easily feed right into narcissistic behavior because they get paid more money the longer the case is extended. So you need an attorney who understands these behaviors and will be driven to get through the process.

3. Set Boundaries: Plain and simple, don't give somebody with personality disorder access to you. If you do, you are their prey. If you don't have children, then cut off all communication permanently because there is no reason to communicate further. If there are children involved, try to communicate as much as possible through text or email, eliminating emotion in words, being precise and clear in the dialogue. Avoid reacting to them and be proactive in managing the tone of the relationship. This will allow you to feel like you are in a powerful position.

4. Don't React to the Small Stuff: A narcissist or somebody with a personality disorder wants you to engage with them and wants conflict. It allows them to dictate and control you. If there are small negotiations that you can let go of, do so. After all that you've been through with this person, starting a battle or engaging is precisely what they need and thrive on. So choose your battles carefully. Leave things like this behind.

5. Let Them Win: Or should I say, play the game and let them think they've won. It is exhausting to need to continually think and get into the same frame of mind as a narcissist. But you need to do so in order to protect yourself and your kids if you have children together. Narcissists win-always. They will not stop fighting until they have won. So give them what they need and let them think they have won.

6. Make "Me" Time: This time is so critical in maintaining your well-being through the divorce process. It is emotionally going to drain your mind, body; especially if you're divorcing someone with a personality disorder and high-conflict situation. Make your goal about finding your way back to inner peace and wholeness. A high-conflict situation will create internal chaos, so creating ways to bring back your inner peace will help keep you grounded.

Meditation is a vital tool that immediately can bring you back to a place of inner peace and center. Find a place, whether it is on the floor or at your desk, sit up straight, and close your eyes. Create a mantra (I am peace. I am love. I am strength), and repeat your mantra over and over again. Focus on your breath (use the breathing technique that you learned earlier) in this quiet space.

Wear something symbolic or have something symbolic always close to you, such as a bracelet, jewelry, crystals, or something that could be held in your hand, which reminds you of inner peace and love. I personally wore, during my divorce, a bracelet with words on it like freedom, peace, love, strength, wisdom, and journey. It was a leather bracelet that I could look down at and immediately be reminded of who I was in the moment. It allowed me to step into my light and greatness.

7. Don't Take it Personally: Your partner will make unreasonable demands on you. These are not your issues, not yours at all, so don't take it personally.

8. Create Boundaries: If you are not being treated with respect, you have the right to calmly say, "I am going to hang up the phone now," or "I'm going to walk away from this conversation." To set healthy boundaries, you must see the high-conflict person as a separate person with their own agenda. Get in

touch with your calm inner peace where you understand how you deserve to be treated.

9. Don't be Bullied: Bullying is just not acceptable, and you should immediately end any conversation. Don't give in to demands. A high-conflict person can be manipulative, using tactics to get what they want. They can be sad, needy, evoke pity or guilt, become angry and threatening, argue, be intimidating, and belittling. Don't take on their emotional state and say no to unreasonable demands. You are not responsible for them.

10. Create a Support System: I know everybody going through a divorce needs a therapist but if you haven't found one that suits you yet, do so now or seek out a divorce coach. A good therapist or divorce coach will help you navigate this situation and be a neutral sounding board for you. Friends and family can be great support systems as well. Have someone in your life to be there with you as you go through this stressful time.

DEALING WITH A NARCISSIST

During your divorce you may find that dealing with your spouse is clearly not going to be an easy task. Oftentimes, there are high emotions and people need time to cool down and collect themselves. That is a normal and understandable situation during divorce. On the other hand, you may be dealing with a narcissist or someone who is exhibiting behavior traits of a narcissist. During your divorce it's important for you to be able to read your specific situation and understand how to best deal with your it. This section is all about what a narcissist looks like and how you need to deal with them.

Narcissists often come into your life using charm and intelligence. They will show you a person that is exactly what you'd want in a partner. To put it another way, they are master manipulators. They will put on a show for you and play off your desires and emotions in order to get you to see them as an amazing, perfect person. They extend this behavior to your friends and family as well. It's a nefarious act of manipulation through displaying character traits so attractive to you and your closest family and friends that everyone puts them on a pedestal in your life, so to speak. I like to think of the phrase "if something (or in this case, someone) seems too good to be true, they probably are."

During divorce, if you find that you are dealing with a full-fledged narcissist you will need to employ a strong and consistent strategy to handle them. Remember, a narcissist lacks empathy and is a master of manipulation. This is important because if you are trying to engage a narcissist as if they are a normal person, you will drive yourself crazy. A narcissist will try to throw everything back on you. They will blame you for the smallest mistake and blow it out of proportion to prop themselves up in the eyes of others, including children. A narcissist will try to make you feel like you are unlovable in order to force you to stay with them, or be alone forever. The most important thing to know when dissecting the behavior of a potential narcissist in your life is that if you are constantly being roadblocked over even the smallest of issues, you are likely dealing with a narcissist.

Dealing with a narcissist is like trying to get light out of a black hole—it's not going to work, ever. A narcissist feeds on fighting and arguing. This is fuel to the fire for a narcissist, they need it in order to properly function. This is true because a narcissist's mind is flooded with the self-belief that they are better than you and you need them. A narcissist will not give in to you, much less reason logically with you. This is where I see most people fall into the trap of trying to deal with a narcissist through logic and basic reason. You must employ a strong and unwavering tactic to successfully get through a divorce of this magnitude. Of course, no narcissist is going to let someone leave them without a fight.

In order to beat a narcissist without also driving yourself crazy you must stick to only engaging with simple 'Yes' or 'No' answers. If you try, for example, to send a thoughtful email to a narcissist explaining what you think and what you would like to do, they will turn that into an argument. A narcissist will use something like that as ammo to fire back at you. They will not see that as a mature way to communicate or read it with an open mind. Narcissists are not often (or ever) open-minded. They will pick apart every point you make. They will criticize you any way they can. What they say won't even make much sense—they just have the need to twist things to make you look stupid or wrong.

In order to win against a narcissist you must be stubborn yourself. I'm not advocating for negative behavior on your part, but I am arguing for you to stick to one word answers as much as possible.

You must stick to little or no response.

Anything that doesn't require a response should be ignored.

You should only respond to Yes or No questions.

Never explain yourself.

If you agree to speak with a narcissist on the phone or in person you must remember that there could be a time when you need to simply leave the situation. If you are speaking with a spouse who is narcissistic over the phone and they start to get manipulative or critical, be stern with them. Tell them "If you have anything to discuss with me, please put it in an email" and hang up. At no point should you engage with a narcissist, no matter how absurd their comments become. Deal with a narcissist the same way you would deal with a child crying in the supermarket because they want a candy bar and you said no. Would you try and reason with a crying child? Of course you know that will not work and the child doesn't know any better. In most cases, that's the same way you need to look at narcissists.

HOW DOES THE NARCISSIST AFFECT CHILDREN?

- The child will feel like a puppet or accessory to that parent, rather than their own person.

- The child won't feel heard or seen because their feelings will not be acknowledged.

- The child will learn to feel the emotions of that parent and not their own, which leads to crippling self-doubt and inability to trust their own feelings.

- The child is valued for what they do for that parent rather than who they are as a person.

- The child will be taught to keep secrets in order to protect that parent.

- The child will learn to be there for the parent rather than the other way around, as it should be.

- The child will be taught that image is more important than living real.

- The child will grow up feeling not good enough.

- The child will not feel like he/she is good enough because they have never received any validation from that parent.

- The child will have difficulty with the necessary individuation from that parent as he or she grows older. They will continue to feel like they need to "take care" of that parent by stroking their ego or "feeling" that parent's emotional chaos.

- The child may grow up to feel unlovable by another because if their parent(s) couldn't love them, then who will?

- The child may either become a high achiever or a self-saboteur.

- The child is brainwashed in terms of how to feel, what to think, how to behave in ways to make that parent look good.

- The child will feel used and manipulated.

Utilizing these simple tools and knowledge with a high conflict personality or a narcissist will help you remain grounded and have energetic alignment. If you find that you are still looking for support, discuss the situation with a professional or someone who you know can handle a difficult person. Above all else, remember that your mindset and your plan going into divorce is what will keep you from drowning in the other person's personality issues. This book, a good support system, and your goals for a better life are what will get you through a divorce with a difficult person.

How to Deal with the Stress of Attorneys and Your Soon to be Ex-Partner

Divorce can be a release for some and a devastating blow for others. You may define it as a new and better beginning for yourself. For many people, including myself, divorce is the most challenging crisis you've faced in life, especially if you are divorcing a narcissist. The process of divorce itself is grueling emotionally, physically, financially, and spiritually. I want to help you and warn you at the same time: dealing with attorneys during your divorce can be one of the most challenging times in the whole process.

I like attorneys and have many friends who are attorneys. As you know, I did go through a divorce, so I have my own personal perspective to share with you of what the legal process looks like. The first thing I want you to know is that there is this heightened sense of emotion and that there are going to be many egos involved in this process. There are two lawyers and two spouses, which contributes to many dynamics in one situation. It's imperative to stay grounded during this time, and it comes down to really managing your expectations and your "wanting to win everything" in the legal process. If you begin to operate from a mindset of wanting to win, it makes the process that much harder and time-consuming. Because guess what, the only person or persons that make out when you want to win everything are the lawyers. You shouldn't give in to things that are important to you, but if you are fighting over everything, the lawyers will gladly let your divorce carry on as long as it needs to. They get paid by the hour and benefit greatly when two people would prefer to drag out these conversations of splits. The best lawyers want to move the case forward quickly for you; however, they need you to have that same mindset. I was lucky to have an amazing lawyer who had great empathy for my situation and her wisdom allowed me to move my legal case forward quickly.

The best mindset to be in is that of neutral neutrality and love. Neutral neutrality is when you walk in with fewer expectations of what the outcome will be so you can allow yourself to stay in a grounded state. Neither party will walk away feeling like they have won. When it comes to the legal side of a divorce, it's natural to come from a place of feeling that there's not enough and you're losing control of everything. When you are able to look at the other person during this time and see that they are driving the legal process from a place of fear as well, you will have even more compassion. You can shift your energy by not responding or reacting to the madness, and confuse the other person. This type of dramatic change will unconsciously move the other person into a more empathic state as well.

Everyone has their expectations of what they deserve from the life they've built together. Neutral neutrality is being open to an outcome that is going to benefit everyone as much as possible. No one wins in divorce, but that doesn't mean everyone loses either. If one of you sacrificed having a career in order to stay at home and raise your kids, that person is entitled to half the lifestyle. I see a lot of people struggle with what they are losing instead of focusing on splitting everything fairly and moving on. Even if you do get "more" in the divorce, you'll have to fight for it through lawyers and the court, which costs money. In the end you will both always lose if you do this.

I spent so much energy, time, and money on my legal process, trying to fight for what I thought was fair. And naturally, my ex-partner was fighting for what he felt was fair as well. It is in this part of the process where we create so much of our own stress. I spent the entire divorce process in a fight or flight state, flooding my body with excess stress hormones. At the end of my divorce I felt like I had been through a tornado. I was mentally and emotionally beat up! At that point, I could not wait to move on to my new life. I was not coming out of my divorce with a partner that was also ready to move on.

If I could do it all over again, I would have simply let go of trying to win on a lot of points. My ex made many realistic and unrealistic demands that he felt he deserved, putting me in a reactive state. He was operating from a place of fear. At the end of the day, the settlement was always going to be the same within the context of the legal process. Ultimately, if I had looked closer to see the volatility and toxicity that was coming from my spouse due to fear and his lack of control of the situation, I would have saved a lot of money. His energy prompted me to want more control over the situation. By sharing this about myself, I want to reinforce to you that if I had practiced the art of neutral neutrality, the situation would have been much less toxic and volatile. When you are raising children during a divorce, you want to minimize toxicity, conflict and volatility because the children will pick up on that vibe.

At the end of the day, the law is the law. Most attorneys are more than happy to let you continue to drag out your case and let your egos fight an uphill battle. Rise above this situation and keep in mind that we are all entitled or deserving. If you see that your ego is the only thing that stands in the way of resolving an agreement and putting an end to the legalities, then the sooner you can let your ego step aside, the sooner you are going to be able to move on with your life. It's really that simple.

The process then becomes about legal rights and you both can move on in peace. Ideally, you will be able to prep for this process with your partner before you come to an agreement with lawyers. If you're able to both look through each other's eyes to see an empathetic soul on the other side, then your legal proceedings will be the business transaction that we spoke about at the beginning of this chapter. Letting emotion come to the forefront of your legal business will only strain the process even more—shift your mindset to look at this as if you're managing a project because that's what it is. Have the empathy and compassion that I know you desire.

THE DIFFERENCE BETWEEN A DIVORCE ATTORNEY AND A MEDIATOR

Your legal proceedings can be done by a divorce attorney or a mediator. A divorce attorney will advise you on specific aspects of the law in the state that you reside. A divorce attorney will argue on your behalf during settlement negotiations and in court, if there is more than you feel you should have or be given. A divorce mediator, on the other hand, does not offer legal advice to either party, they are simply there to work with both parties and not take sides.

If you've been able to work together as a couple before seeking legal counsel and feel you can work things out amicably on your own, you can file what is called an "uncontested divorce," which will save you both time and money with court costs and any other mediator or attorney fees. An uncontested divorce, unfortunately, is very rare and more often than not, one party will begin the filing process and have their bags mentally packed, while the other spouse will most likely not be on the same page.

In a standard divorce, the two parties are represented by legal counsel. Collaborative law is an ongoing process, which means more time and more money. Mediation is often significantly cheaper because there are no lawyers involved. Mediation can be done in one day; however, it requires that both parties be totally transparent and show trust and good faith in the other spouse. If you feel your spouse is hiding assets or debts, or does not act honestly in their business dealings, then my personal advice is that you hire an attorney. I am not here to offer legal advice, only to offer advice on how to navigate through this time with more peace and less fear.

Mediation is ideal but, if you're like me, it isn't possible. It's your responsibility to keep this process moving quickly. My divorce process took nine months to complete. That's quick—most divorces take at least one to two years. I responded quickly to all matters that needed my input, instead of avoiding dealing with the issues. I would diffuse tense situations by not reacting, avoiding any back and forth between our egos. I kept my interactions with my spouse at a minimum during the process. My attorney helped me stay focused on the facts. When you're in the negotiation process with attorneys, negative feelings come up because you feel like you are losing control over your life and your future. That's why I want to emphasize that you need to find an attorney that you can trust to advise you towards a speedy, and fair divorce. Your attorney can help you reduce your fear of the unknown and help keep the facts and conversation in project management terms and not just as a business transaction.

QUICK TIPS AND EXERCISES TO STAY GROUNDED DURING THE LEGAL PROCESS:

1. Active Listening: When you are active listening you are able to see something so much more significantly. You can find compassion for the other person and look at their fears as the driving force behind what they are working so hard to negotiate on. This is not a moment to react. It is a moment to listen to what fear is being presented here. Ask yourself, *Is the anger driven from a lack of being in control or a need for a certain outcome? Is it fear that you will not have enough money? Is it the loss of identity or control over the time that you'll get to spend with your kids?* Listen to what the fear is here and see it with love.

2. Practice Peace through Meditation: Type in "Guided Meditations" on YouTube and lots of great beginner options will come up. Guided meditations are a great way to get started with a meditation practice.

3. Positive Affirmation Response: Acknowledge your partner's request in a positive and supportive way. Can you meet them on this request? You may not want to give up your kids every Wednesday, Thursday and every other weekend but your partner has equal rights to spend time with them, the same way you do. I know this request can seem scary and an immediate knee-jerk reaction of "no way" is the common response. However, if you can begin the process by making space for peaceful negotiations, that very same gift is going to come back to you in the process. It's your goal here to get through the process with less hatred and fear, and more love and peace. This is the best for your soul and for that of your

children as well. If you respond and communicate from a place of love and understanding, your partner is more likely to acclimate to this same form of communication. You will be able to reach a mutual agreement sooner and spend less money with attorneys.

4. Acceptance: At times you need to accept where your spouse is at, which might be in a place of anger and volatility. I understand this. Sometimes you need to recognize that this isn't going to be easy and you may be dealing with someone who has mental illness or addiction. If this is the case, you need to accept this fact and let go of control. You can't change their path—you can only change yours and your reactions. You want to be okay accepting a lot of different scenarios in your mind because you cannot predict the final outcome of your divorce. Run through a lot of scenarios in your head and the pros and cons of each. This will prepare you for the legal outcomes of the divorce and keep you from being blindsided by a certain outcome. When you can think of all the situations, you can see the good and the bad from neutral neutrality, and stay nonreactive.

Surrendering and Letting Go

Author Gabby Bernstein of *The Universe Has Your Back: Transform Fear to Faith* states, "Trust that your wounds are exactly as the Universe planned. They were divinely placed in your life in the perfect order so that you could show up for them with love and remember the light within." I believe that my journey led me to my ex, led me to my kids, and healing, to help me change my story and be the person I am today. I don't know for certain that I would be as happy as I am today without all the experiences I've had leading up to this point in my life. That's why I am a believer in learning to surrender and let go.

Now is the time in the divorce process that you begin to change your story. The power is within you to surrender and let go of the outcome. Now is the time to open your heart, and embrace the love and light you are beginning to create. It's a time where you are going to have to come to terms with your life, and your story is going to look different for a little while. The most significant change of all is most likely going to be your financial status and family picture. You're dividing everything in half with your soon-to-be ex-spouse. Of course life is going to look different! This is the perfect time to surrender to the Universe and accept all the changes that are going to happen within your family. Surrender and let go of your worries. Trust that you are evolving and moving towards living from a place that is more genuine and authentic. Trust that you have made the best decision for yourself and your children, and learn to get comfortable with letting things go.

The quicker you're able to accept this reality by surrendering, the quicker more doors and possibilities will open up for you. If you stay in a place of anger, resentment, judgment, control, ego-driven fear, and fear of not enough money, then you will remain in a negative space. Remember, that negative place will also affect your children. Negative energy is not what you want to carry forward with your children. You want them to have the happiest, and the best opportunities available to them going forward. The only way to do that is by trusting in God, the Universe, or whatever your belief is, that everything is going to be okay because you've surrendered and let go of control. I had to learn to be open to being guided by my internal compass, my quiet voice of intuition. In the beginning of my divorce I was so intense and wound up. I was overly focused on the fact that my life was transforming and beginning to look certain ways that I wasn't ready for yet.

My surrendering early on allowed me to feel better, and lighter when the process was finally done. You can fight as much as you want, but it will make your divorce longer, cost more, and will inhibit the growth you experience when it's all over. I tried this for a few months with no positive results! I knew I had to change what I was doing in order to facilitate a better outcome. I would have loved to have a partner who wanted the same. That simply wasn't the case for me.

I was forced to consciously make the decision to surrender and let go of the outcome I wanted.

Lastly, honor that your spouse played a significant role in your life. Let the anger, resentment and emotional feelings you have shift into positive and more appreciative energy because you have learned to surrender and let go. Give gratitude and thanks to what you had with your partner, and the beautiful children that you had together.

The Wholeness Journey

Everything is energy in this world. It's important to keep your vibration high and have trust and faith in the Universe that you are being guided by your internal compass towards what is best for you. Throughout this book, you are going to find the tools to embrace your inner warrior and spirit further, connect with your Divine God or Goddesses, and learn to love yourself first.

The internal shakiness that you felt at the beginning can begin to calm now that you are surrendering to God and the Universe. There is no reason to let the control of your ego cause unnecessary stress and erratic chaos in your body and brain. I will teach you how to welcome new experiences into your life, find your way back to self-love, and heal your way there. The quicker you can surrender, the faster you can heal.

CHAPTER THREE

The Reality of the
Divorce Sets In

The reality is simply this: You are going from a life with lots of certainty to a life with a lot of uncertainty. This is where I want you to embrace and love these feelings of shakiness. You have learned how to honor your fears, and you're learning to let go and surrender to what just transpired during the divorce stage. Hopefully, you are doing the exercises that we've been practicing in this book, to allow yourself to come to a place of acceptance. You don't need to stay in the place of bitterness and resentment because it will eat you alive in the post-divorce stage. This is a time where you're going to experience the transitional feelings of your new lifestyle. All of a sudden, you went from having somebody that had your back, shared your life, and was going to be with you for a lifetime; to a life with a big hole of unknown. The vast changes you are feeling and navigating are all new waters. You're on your own, making decisions on your own, and settling into a new phase of life.

This is a time that you want to surrender and find the gift in every stage that you're going to experience from here. This is not going to be an overnight transition—you should want to welcome in this flood of different emotions. You are processing big changes, you're going to feel the unique moments of freedom and the excitement for a new life, but there are other feelings too. The sad feelings are important to take in as well, which will lead you to feel like you're on a roller coaster. Stop and love where you're at today, always reflect and ask yourself "Have I grown? Am I in a better place than I was a week ago, two weeks ago, two months ago, six months ago?" In every phase of this journey, you will be evolving, growing, and healing, so it's essential to find the gift in each step. Express gratitude in where you are this moment because it will help you progress to new levels quickly.

Two Homes

The ideal goal that you want to strive for is to be consistent and on the same page with your spouse. You both just went through what was, hopefully, an amicable experience...or not. If you didn't, then likely a traumatic experience. If you have children, the communication between parents does not end after the divorce. The most significant thing I can say to parents is to be as consistent within the multiple homes as possible. Stay consistent with how things used to be and/ or with the new routines and ways of doing things in order to put your children at ease. The more consistency you have with routines, the more predictability you'll establish, even in separate homes. This greatly helps your children function day-to-day. However, with this similarity and consistency, I also want to emphasize that you can't force your ex-spouse to have the same routines as you. If there is something that your ex-spouse has implemented into their life and home, that is up to them.

My ex-spouse and I had very different rules in our homes. For example, I remember my kids would go to bed later at his house when they were young, and it used to bug me. At the end of the day the advice that I would have given myself then, is not to control this situation because that is his life now and his home and I have to respect that. In a perfect world, you want to make these lifestyle decisions, such as bedtimes, homework, and extracurricular activities together as equal parents of the children. In the real world, you will face situations where you and your ex-spouse act differently as parents. You're going to have different rules for the kids, priorities as a parent, and structure within the two households. This is a great time to go back to your practice of surrendering control over what is happening in your ex-partner's home—within reason of course. You cannot control what happens in your ex-spouse's home the same way you can in your own home.

Of course, if there is behavior that is putting your children's safety at risk or compromising the health (mental, emotional, or physical) of your children, you must take legal action. Please do not get this confused with different parental rules or routines that you don't agree with. That is going to happen. Issues with children's safety are very serious and should never be taken lightly. Use your best judgment when assessing what is unsafe and what is just a different parenting choice for the children.

When you have two separate homes and two parents with their own independent routines, you also want to make it your responsibility to not "trash talk" the other parent in order to persuade your children to take sides. This is a terribly selfish thing for parents to do because this diminishes your children's self-esteem. You have to be mindful that children are 50 percent of you and 50 percent of your ex-partner. When you trash talk your ex-partner, you're really trash talking your child as well because they're half of both of you. That might be a hard thing to soak into right now, but if your ultimate goal is wholeness, this is an unhealthy place to put yourself and your children. You also don't want to have your children settled in the middle of a situation between you and your ex-spouse because this puts an unnecessary burden on them. Your children are innocent bystanders of the divorce. Let them heal on their own, your feelings are yours, and you need to heal them on your own as well.

Kids want to feel safe emotionally, so give them that safety through your grounded actions and routines. They are going to be observing you during this time and will begin to draw their own conclusions on how the home feels. I made a great effort to provide my kids with a home that felt warm, comfortable, and literally normal for them each time they stepped inside: things like adding flowers on the kitchen counter, making fruit or snacks available, and making sure the house was clean and very organized. These small daily efforts gave my children, when they were with me, a sense of calm and peace in my home.

You may feel (or factually know) your ex-spouse is trying to persuade your kids and even fabricate stories to turn them against you. This is indeed the ugliest thing that a partner can do, and some people will behave this way because at the root of it all, is merely their fear driven by their ego. And narcissists, who are very toxic people, will use their kids as pawns (puppets) to turn them against the other parent. Avoid allowing yourself to sink to the lowest level possible and make your children choose between one parent or the other. The behavior of a narcissist would be perfectly in line with trying to put down the other parent in front of your kids, or simply trash talking your ex-spouse in an effort to validate yourself as the better parent. In nearly every divorce, your kids are not going to be remotely interested in loving one parent over the other.

If your ex-spouse chooses the path of diminishing you as a parent, it's your job to stay in a place of light and avoid reaction. The only souls that are damaged by this are the children's, not your ex-spouse. Think back to how a narcissist operates. A narcissist will continuously try to bait you to fuel their own inner fire. You may be thinking that this won't happen to you in the post-divorce but I can assure you that this happens more than you'd like to believe. You need to be prepared for it by being the mirror of love and neutrality with your ego silenced. Your kids will always gravitate to unconditional love: it is authentic. Eventually, as your children grow older they will see this toxic behavior, if it persists long-term, and drift away from the narcissistic parent and towards the authentic, supportive, and loving parent.

I remember observing my kids in many situations, reluctant to show me love when my ex-spouse was present. I experienced this in spectacular fashion for years after my divorce. During sporting events and school functions, or really anytime out in public, my ex-spouse was highly driven to distort the image of the relationship we had with

our children. This was meant to make me look like less of a parent
to outsiders. For example, my children were taught to ignore me in
public, glare at me when they were with him, and always hold onto
him to completely banish me as if they had a real distaste for me
as their mother. I felt this was his way of showing our kids that he
was good and I was bad. They would be rewarded for unknowingly
displaying hurtful behavior towards me in public and silently scolded
if they would acknowledge me. Obviously this was incredibly difficult
for me to deal with as not only a mother but also just a human being.
Even though I was crying on the inside when I witnessed this behavior
(always in public) being encouraged on my children, I knew that if I
wanted my children to grow up with love I had to be that driving force
all the time. I never allowed my internal pain from these experiences
affect the energy, direction, and vibe within my home. My home was
a place of love and grace and it was always felt when my kids would
walk in. I share this with you because I want you to see the big picture
for what it is. It's about how you hold yourself regardless of any and
all pain hoisted on you and your children through your ex-spouse. In
the end, and as your children grow, the true nature of the situation
will show itself to all those involved, and that is why you must move
forward with love and grace within your home, for your children.

I encourage my children, to this day, to love both parents equally.
You can never control what the other parent communicates to your
children, which is even more a reason to be an example of what
healthy, loving behavior looks like. Today, my children are teens and
young adults who have come through some confusing years with an
enormous capacity to love and see things for what they are. If you find
yourself in a compromised position like this, never scold your children
for actions that they don't understand. Avoid doing anything to make
them feel bad because the root does not start with them. They were
simply put in the middle of a volatile situation. I advise that you not
even address this type of situation with your children. I know you're
probably thinking, "why would I not address this with my children?"
Because it's a time to love them harder—they are in the middle of a

situation that should be worked on as adults, and they are receiving messages from a very inept parent. Keep living the example of love and your children will soak this in.

A parent's (or any adult's) affection should not come with demands or requirements of any kind because these aren't genuine or from a place of unconditional love. The way to show your children more love is back under the roof of their sacred, safe space. Say to your children, *I am happy you are home; I hope you enjoyed your time with your dad or mom; I missed you when you were gone, and I love you; I am always going to love you no matter where you are at, and it is okay to love both mom and dad equally.*

LAYING THE FOUNDATION OF FRIENDSHIP WITH YOUR EX

The communication between you and your ex-spouse will need to shift into a conversation of being friends, ideally. Good communication is the intention here and begins with respecting the other person's words. This is the art of being an active listener. What you're learning is to give yourself the space to start the healing process. Provide space for the healing energy that is now between you and your ex-spouse, so it's safe to share and hear what they are requesting. This may not be the easiest thing, especially if you were in a marriage that was filled with a lot of tension when you split up. Honestly, this will be a hard transition. Picture this, you and your ex are able to have an adult conversation where you are able to look each other eye-to-eye and acknowledge that the marriage and relationship you had together was hard. But this is a new transition and time of growth for both of you. You can transition into a cordial and friend type of relationship regardless of whatever crap you just dealt with…you can come to the table and just be, without the baggage of what happened. Embrace this idea—it will take time but make this your goal. Visualize it. This is easier for *you* to do right now because it all comes back to quieting the ego. Your ex-spouse might not be able to do this as quickly, so be the mirror for them. Remember, don't react and remain the higher person and example they need. They are going through a healing process as well, even if their behavior isn't in line with actually trying to heal and move on.

There are key mindset goals you want to embrace and a few important steps to move, slowly, towards friendship with your ex. Tell yourself right now that this may take YEARS to achieve, and that is perfectly fine (and normal). Rome was not built in a single day, and genuine friendship with your ex won't be either. Honestly, it may never happen. The best mindset to harbor is that one day it will happen, or simply that it could happen. Even that is enough for you to move on with your life without harboring feelings of anger and hate towards another person. Years from now you can live your life knowing that you would, one day, like to be friends with your ex-spouse.

I want to paint a realistic picture for you on how you can pave the road for an eventual friendship with your ex-spouse. I'm going to assume, because you have this book in your hands right now, that you are willing to be the champion for this potential future friendship. That's a huge step that most people struggle to take. I want you to take a moment to acknowledge yourself for being that person!

The very first thing you will need to do is set the tone of friendly dialogue between you and your ex-spouse. This means not fueling a fire of anger at any time, like we've talked about. This means being a nonreactive person who understands that tensions will rise and fall as the years of post-divorce progress. When tensions are high, it's your job to be an anchor of peace and to diffuse the tension by not reacting to it. Do not try to force your ex-spouse out of your life if you have children together. That will not benefit the children in any way unless the children are in harm's way. Friendly dialogue means that you avoid any judgment, name-calling, accusations, or backlash. Again, I want you to play the long game here. If you are dealing with a difficult person then you need to revert back to 'Yes' or 'No' answers only until the tension dies down. Trust me, it will die down over time. Once you feel that tensions are low, you can begin adding in new ways to pave the path to friendship with your ex-spouse.

Transition to Friendship Exercises

The question of "How could I possibly transition this into a friendship?" isn't going to be an easy one to answer right away. Time heals all wounds, and time will help this question get answered within the context of your divorce. In this exercise, I'm going to lay out the best way to plan your friendship even when the idea of friendship may seem entirely hopeless.

First, I want to bring back the idea of project management when it comes to your post-divorce life. Project management during the divorce is a better mindset than "it's a business transaction," so embrace that same mindset in your post-divorce life as well. Good project management does not have high emotions, and this will help you remain stable during all communication in post-divorce.

I'm going to lay out the big picture path to friendship, or at the very least decent communication with your ex, in a few easy steps. Friendship with your ex-spouse is different than dealing with your ex-spouse. You want to come from a place of positivity when you communicate with them. What I mean by that is that you want to share things about your children or yourself with them. You want to begin laying the groundwork for spending time together when it makes sense. For example, if it's three years after your divorce and you feel ready to celebrate your child's 10th birthday together at the local bowling alley you can take that initiative. You will need to be completely independent of the outcome when you put yourself out there like this. If the talks revert back to ego-driven, fear-based arguing, then let them go for now. Plan to revisit them at a later date if the energy between you two feels right. That time may never come again, or it may come again in a few short days or weeks. You never know.

HERE IS A BREAKDOWN OF WAYS TO EASE YOUR RELATIONSHIP TOWARDS FRIENDSHIP:

1. **Email Communication:** It is very likely that this is already how you are used to communicating with your ex-spouse. I don't want you to think of this as just sending messages because you will need information or answers from them. Start with email as it is the most formal. You want to stick with formal communication if you have had a rocky past either before, during, or after your divorce. Email is still communication, and healthy communication at that. It's also the least investment on your part because it's more project management and less friendship. That's why it's the best place for you to start. Email your ex-spouse with an update on your life or something that has to do with children. Start with email and establish positive, grounded, friendly communication here before moving to the next steps. Find something you feel comfortable sharing via email, write it up with a positive undertone, and see what happens. That's as simple as it gets!

2. **Text Message:** This is similar to email, of course, but it's more personal. It's more personal because we all have phones these days and the messages tend to come right to us. Most people will see a text message right away, whereas an email can go unnoticed for hours or days even. When you move from email to text message you are putting yourself in a more vulnerable situation and thus you need to make sure your relationship is ready for that investment. Texting will result in more short messages back and forth, unlike emails, which are typically lengthier and more thought-out. For you and your ex to get to a place of texting can take years, but if you feel like it's the best way to establish positive communication, go forward with it as your primary way of chatting. Texting is a hugely positive step towards an eventual, and authentic friendship.

3. **Phone Conversation:** I want to be very clear that any form of communication is not meant to reignite a romantic relationship with your ex. I mean that especially when I bring up phone conversations. This is all for the sake of healthy, positive dialogue towards friendship. If you feel comfortable enough to plan children's birthdays, holidays, or other events over the phone with your ex-spouse, then you are on a great path towards healthy friendship. Avoid long conversations just for the sake of companionship. Spark healthy phone dialogue only when you have details that need to be discussed. Let phone calls be purposeful and friendly for the sake of eventually getting in the same room together for the sake of the children.

4. **Sitting Together at Events:** There will be times when your children will have functions that you will both, naturally, be attending. Things like a school performance, extracurricular activities, and functions are good examples of when you can spend real-world time with your ex-spouse. Simply sit in the same area together to support your children as a family unit. When you can accomplish this, your children will feel a seriously powerful sense of support in their lives. It's a massive step to see mom and dad in each other's presence. It will make a world of difference if you can achieve this for your children. For that simple fact, it's entirely worth the effort to work towards this. I have always made a point of sitting together with my ex-spouse at events. It has and always will be about my kids.

5. **Plan Events for the Children:** This is the last step I'm going to bring up for this exercise because beyond this, your friendship will simply need time. If you have spent time with your ex-spouse in the real world together then you can begin to make plans for the children together. Planning a birthday party or spending the holidays as a family unit will often take years to work up to. That's okay! Celebrate the fact that your children

will feel a massive sense of relief when they can have mom and dad host Thanksgiving or their 16th birthday together. Think about that in your mind right now. You may have even been the child of divorced parents and can relate to the positive emotions that amicable family events would have brought (or did bring) you as a child. It's clear that being able to have a family unit together again, even though mom and dad have moved on from a romantic relationship, is a net positive for children. This is your end goal.

Whether it's at the beginning of your post-divorce phase that this happens, or it's five years later, after continually seeing, hearing and watching you maintain a non-reactive state, positive growth can occur. Whatever form of communication and the frequency that you agree and share, maintain that consistency because it is what a good friendship looks like. Consistency in communication, no matter what stage of the process (email, text, family gatherings) you are at, is a key metric to how strong your friendship will be.

I encourage you to visualize this before you either meet your ex-spouse in person or before you reach out to contact them in any way: *Imagine how you would communicate with your best friend and how that person is the most critical person you would want to share something with or seek advice from.* I know you might not reach out to your ex-spouse for help or guidance right now but visualize them as a friend even before you ever email them. I want you to embrace the beautiful energy of what and how a real friend looks like and feels to you. Put that intention out before you text, call, email, or make any contact with your ex-spouse.

I can promise you this—if you're able to release what happened up to this point and make the energy shift to thinking of this friendship as the most critical friendship that you ever create, you will have so much abundance come into your life. Your healing process will be that much quicker and you'll move into the beauty of your new life with less stress weighing you down.

SPIRITUAL SACRIFICES

Taking this new life alone and empowered, you're going to see a difference in your ex-spouse's communication style and how they operate their home. Know that it's not in your space to worry about them, you have to let go of your ex's outcome. It can be hard to accept that your ex may or may not be in the same financial position, career space, or on the same level emotionally as you. You may think you need to rescue them emotionally or financially, help them create a new home, control how they have a relationship with the children, etc. because you see that their current life will lead down a path of self-destruction. Know that in this new stage of life, it's not your responsibility to save them. It's your responsibility to be the light and healthy mirror for them, so they are able to rise and meet you where you're at, instead of the other way around.

There will come a time though that you're going to have to make spiritual sacrifices. These are the necessary sacrifices we make as parents, for our children, when we are called. Yes, you will have signed legal documents that said there are financial responsibilities, but sacrifices will come when your ex-spouse can or cannot do what is required because life has happened. Spiritual sacrifices might come in the form of getting a second job because your ex might be out of a job. It could mean your ex has addiction problems or suffers from depression and/or other mental illnesses that prevent him or her from creating a better life. For example, for you to pay the orthodontist bill, you might need to get a second job because your ex isn't able to follow through on their half of their agreed-upon responsibility. It may mean that you no longer share custody and you must raise your kids on your own. You don't want to be a doormat, but sometimes you're dealing with an ex-partner who cannot rise to the occasion of his or her responsibilities.

These are sacrifices that you must make along the way. Don't get attached to the papers and decisions you made in front of the attorneys because they are likely to change based on how life goes. Often changes will be minimal or evasive but know that part of the post-divorce process includes these necessary spiritual sacrifices. If you stay in a place of resentment over this or hold a grudge, it will only pollute your spirit and trickle down to your children's souls as well.

I personally hold sacrifices near and dear to my heart because I was there and had to live this. What was agreed on paper in my divorce was not the reality of how life was supposed to look like. The sacrifices that you might have to make are not going to be easy. That's why they are sacrifices! In fact, most of these spiritual sacrifices are very hard. I found myself raising five kids on my own financially, physically, emotionally, mentally, and spiritually, all because my ex didn't believe enough in himself to create that same abundance. Whatever your situation becomes, remain brave and believe you can fill the largest pair of shoes with great courage. Always try to find gratitude and love for these difficult situations. Spiritual sacrifices can even end up paying dividends if you have a positive mindset. The spiritual sacrifices that I made blossomed into some real gifts in the form of enhancing my character strengths. It's spiritual growth for yourself—if you choose to see it this way.

You can't control what is happening in your ex-spouse's world, you can only put your energy and focus into your own path and invest the time and energy into being your best self. My inability to control my ex-spouse's path was one of the hardest things I had to learn after my divorce. We all evolve at different paces, some evolve further than others, and some don't ever grow. It's essential for you to be extremely mindful of your own capability, and let go of the things you have no control over. This creates less fear and stress in your life without a doubt.

Redefining Friendships

You might be surprised by the way you will be treated by friends and family after your divorce. This might not be the first thing you think about, but I promise you that it will be evident in your life. These reactions may be both good and bad; supportive and unsupportive. In the beginning, once friends know you're going through a divorce, you will find they will want to know more of what's going on and be there for you to lean on in your time of pain. Once the post-divorce came for me, I wish I had someone that would have warned me things would shake out a bit differently than when I was going through my divorce. Divorce still has a negative stigma, albeit much less these days.

You'll find that some friends all of a sudden, in the few months after your divorce, will begin to feel very uncomfortable and distance themselves from you. It will have nothing to do with you at all. They are afraid that it's going to be contagious and could happen to them, or they simply may not like the divorce stigma. A newly single person can pose a big threat to somebody who is not secure in their relationship. Some friends will even feel uncomfortable because they think they have to choose between you or your ex-spouse, so they decide it's better not to be friends with either person; therefore, there are no hard feelings.

I personally found that in a couple's world, divorced women can make other women feel very uncomfortable with their marriages because there is a level of being a threat. I have had many female friends share this same experience. This is a double standard in my opinion. Divorced men are less threatening to couples. I recall my attorney saying to me, "Women are much harder on other women. Women expect other women to rise to the occasion of multitasking work and career, cook, clean, laundry, primp, work out and always look fabulous. Whereas a man throws in a frozen pizza for his kids and we feel the need to celebrate his success as a single dad."

There is a mindset that you have to cultivate that your tribe of friends is going to change and that's okay. This allows you to have the opportunity to begin the beautiful journey of seeking friends and building a tribe that is accepting of you for who you are. Best of all, you're going to build a tribe of friends who are of like-mindedness. This was a tremendous opportunity for me to really let go of some surface friendships and immerse myself in friendships that made me feel safe and supported. Take inventory of your friendships at this time. My married girlfriends (and their husbands) that I knew from raising our kids together have always been the greatest foundation of my tribe. I expanded my tribe with new friendships too. My divorce allowed me to focus on nurturing both the old and new friendships, and really appreciating these friendships in my life.

I found there was an excellent opportunity for me to expand and find other divorced women as friends because there was a level of understanding of what we had gone through. There was empathy and support for me in those friendships, which I so desired in my post-divorce. It was also nice to create a circle of single friends who had free time and were looking to create fun and new experiences. This might not be what you expected to hear, but I told you that I was going to share all the in-depth details and things you needed to know in the entire divorce and post-divorce journey. It will be hard but sometimes necessary to let old friends go if they are not feeding you in a positive way. It's how you'll create space to invite new friends in who better understand who you are today and can enhance your path to healing.

An essential piece of advice I've given to my friends and clients is that many divorced women and men are not as warmly welcomed and accepted into the social circle. My other big piece of advice is this: don't take it personally. I remember I told a friend that her circle of friends would change, and it was shortly after her divorce that she didn't receive an invite to the annual Christmas party she had always attended. She called to tell me, "Sharon, if you hadn't prepared me for this, I would have taken it so personally." Some people feel really uncomfortable with the idea of divorce. Divorce feels icky to them, and they don't want to be around something they fear. Please, please know that this is their feeling and not yours. This will be hurtful and hard to deal with at times, and I will not downplay those emotions at all, but you can own it at the same time. Look at it as a great opportunity to weed out those that don't support you and find true, real friends that have your back no matter what.

A true supportive friend is somebody who is there for you when you get knocked down, and they're also happy for you when you're up. That is an important distinction. I learned that I had many true and supportive friendships as I was going through my divorce. One of the greatest gifts to come out of my divorce was discovering what a true friendship looks like. True friendship is a friendship where you feel safe to be vulnerable by opening your heart about your situation. A real friend is there for you when you are sharing all the fears, pains, or even small adjustments you are going through in this new, post-divorce life. A supportive friend is not judging you, and they are accepting of you no matter what. You have to remember that friendship is a two-way street where you're offering something to them as well because you don't want to be just using a friendship for your own good. That would be a one-sided friendship. But when you're going through something big, like a divorce, a friendship might seem to be one-sided for a while.

Rebuilding the Identity of Yourself

I've already talked about the flood of emotions you're feeling, like gasping for air and finding stability from one hour and day to the next. You might feel joyful that you've made it through the storm of the divorce and when you enter post-divorce, you feel like you are done, and can move right on with life without healing. When you end a marriage, you lose a big piece of your own identity. One moment you are feeling on top of the world and a whole new excitement for life, you feel independent, may want to date again. The next day can be a complete reversal of your emotions. You will feel a sense of loss, aimlessness, depression, fear, unhappiness, and loneliness.

Can you relate when I say your sense of high will come from wanting to date and celebrate your new life? But the sense of loss will come from the fact that your identity was wrapped into the identity of your ex-spouse? You and your ex-spouse would be invited to parties together, you would go to dinner together, share the parenting of your children, share your income(s), and even establish the give and take of roles in the home. Now everything is falling on your shoulders. There will be times when you feel a more substantial sense of aloneness and will be overwhelmed, often when you are sitting alone or when your kids are out of the house. I remember trying to figure out how I was going to do all of this on my own now.

I still remember I had a sincere desire to fill the empty space and sense of loss that I felt. I didn't want to be alone or sit with my thoughts in silence. I was guilty of this in the beginning. You'll naturally want to fill this empty space with everything else other than feeling alone and the sense of loss, and shakiness. You'll want to jump right into filling this space by staying busy and doing new things all the time, and perhaps go on dates. Honestly, that alone time and sense of loss is going to be suffocating. The suffocation would personally flood me with different emotions like fear, the lack of control, high levels of stress about the future of being alone, never finding another partner, not being good enough to do the things that I wanted to do now, finances...I'd go through these moments and say "Oh my God, I can't."

The feelings of aloneness, worry, and stress would hit me harder when my kids would be gone with my ex-spouse. I really struggled with loneliness during this time. Nobody could have prepared me for this type of loss. You will go from being with your children every day, experiencing the love of being a mother or father, to now only seeing your children 50 percent of the time. That loss of time can feel truly unbearable. All of a sudden there was quiet time when I had nobody but myself, and I could do nothing but think. My identity was wrapped up into being a mother. I've always had a career in my life, but my identity as a mother was much stronger. Looking back, this was valuable time that I learned to sit in the quiet space and acknowledge all the fears that were coming up. When the shakiness came, I had incredibly strong urges to run from it by inviting my girlfriends to go out for drinks, go out on dates, or go to dinner. I had to fight powerful urges to escape my thoughts. To put it another way, I had to learn to accept that the Universe has a plan for me. In the alone time, that's when you connect to true healing. All the fears that were coming up were all my holes, and my inner map that was vibrating with the need for self-reflection and self-love.

I came up with a new identity by telling myself I am so much more than a mother. There were many additional parts to my identity outside of just being a mother. The quiet time, or loneliness, allowed me to internalize that my identity was not so one-dimensional. I came to realize that I had so many different aspects to my personality that were attractive. I spent that alone time falling in love with myself because it was all I could do! There was no one else around.

When you see how many aspects you have to your identity, the creative energy inside you starts to flow more freely. The future will immediately become bigger and brighter. I had to go back to the drawing board and peel away the layers that made up my identity. I found that I am comprised of so many beautiful layers that I became in love with my alone time. It was no longer a burden to be alone. It was a blessing to be able to understand who I was and what magic I can create in my life.

Sometimes you have to literally stop all other things and go down a rabbit hole to fill your inner basket with love and begin to process the emotions you're feeling. Your internal map is trying to give you directions. It's necessary to use this time for what it is. It's personal time that you may not have had in YEARS! Your old identity is no longer you, which simply means you have a lot of holes that need to be filled with a new story of you. Personal, quiet time is foundational for your healing to advance, and for you to rebuild your social life, your dating life, and you home life.

One piece of advice that I loved receiving and I want to give back to you right now is not to hurry this process along or skip over the grieving process. You must grieve. A lot of people come out thinking "I'm going to get through this divorce and three months later I'm going to be back out in the world and be okay." Whatever the case is of how you got to post-divorce, there's a great deal of grieving that needs to take place. The best advice someone gave me was to just plan on two years—two years of doing nothing but healing and lots of introspective work. The grieving process is healing and it's critical for you to acknowledge, forgive, and love yourself. Here I am 12 years later, and I look back on who I was two years after my divorce, I think *oh my gosh, I had so much growing to do even after the two years.* I genuinely believe that stages of grief can come in and out of your life, even years or decades into your post-divorce.

STAGES OF GRIEF:

1. **Denial:** This was my favorite stage. I moved through my greatest storm (divorce) by going on and pretending to the outside world that all was the same and perfect with my family. I lived like nothing had happened. I should share with you that my grieving process began two years prior to me filing for divorce because of a traumatic event that happened in our marriage. I spent much of my time in therapy over those two years, focused on whether the marriage could be healed and also opening my eyes to see that my marriage wasn't the picture I was portraying to the outside world. Grief may well begin earlier for you too as you process through emotions.

    Denial is your brain's defense mechanism of protecting you from being too emotionally overwhelmed. It acts as a buffer to shield you from the immediate shock of pain and loss. The loss that is felt at the end of a marriage can be so great and terribly difficult to digest. Even if the divorce was your decision, it can be hard to believe and accept. Denial allows you to block out the painful emotions that are going to follow in the post-divorce stage, even months and years later. It's a useful coping mechanism for as long as you can refuse not to face reality.

    I allowed myself to float in and out of denial for quite some time, which allowed me to digest the painful emotions that brought me to want my divorce. I spent two years in denial about my unhealthy marriage before even filing a divorce. For me, I had to work through letting go of my idea of what a marriage was supposed to look like. I had created a story that looked good to the outside world even though that story wasn't going to be possible in reality.

2. **Anger:** Once reality sets in that you're in post-divorce, and literally your entire life has changed, many people become angry. I personally would transition from denial to anger for quite some time. You may be resentful towards your partner for things they did or did not say, you may even be regretful of your own actions.

   This is a time when you are focused on what you "hate" about your partner or the things you are feeling guilty about. This stage is full of fear, judgment, blame, disgust, and a great sense of the loss of control.

3. **Bargaining:** In this stage, you are coming to terms with the decision that you made—your divorce is final. You may have felt this stage in the divorce proceedings. Often times, it is a last-ditch effort to undo or repair what has been done or press the brakes and stop the crazy feelings you are having. If you are or were the person that left the marriage, it is during this stage that you realize you are either making a mistake or you are doing the best thing for yourself. You must remember that your ex-partner is also going through the bargaining stage as well, so it's a time to be mindful for yourself and your ex-partner.

4. **Depression:** Debilitating sadness becomes your companion as you realize that your marriage is no longer. Many upsetting decisions and significant changes are taking place now in your new life of post-divorce, which leads to great sadness. You have had to determine what the split of assets looked like, who has custody or who would be moving out of the house. There is the loss of friends in this stage, you are feeling a withdrawal from going to events because it is really difficult getting used to going alone. You can find yourself spending weeks, months, and even years after your divorce floating in

and out of depression, feeling ashamed and wanting to isolate yourself from the world around you. Having this book in your hands right now will be a driving force towards healing if you are stuck feeling pain like this.

5. **Acceptance:** In this last stage of grief, you come to accept your divorce as part of your life now. I recall feeling there was a great light at the end of the tunnel. I was able to move through adversity and embrace the guidance and support of others along the way. This is the stage where a lot of what you are reading in this book will help you ground your emotions and energize your spirit again.

   I practiced letting go of negative emotions and opening my heart to a sense of inner peace and wholeness. For me, there was a loss that stemmed from an idea of what I couldn't create with my partner. But once I accepted that feeling, it was the best path to move on, and that's when I felt a great sense of relief.

I experienced all of these stages throughout a two-and-a-half-year period before leaving my divorce but then also in the post-divorce phase. Once I was able to process and accept that I was ready to create my own path, I knew deep within my soul this was the best decision for me. You cannot outrun this phase or period in the post-divorce journey of healing. You must sit with this terrifying and uncomfortable period to grow and figure out who you are and who you want to become. I hope that this book will allow you to process through this stage of grief and identity loss in less than two years. Being in the moment and allowing yourself to feel is the most powerful thing, aside from healing, that you can do for yourself. Use this time also to see your own gifts and beauty, lean into and hear your intuition, and quiet your ego. This will bring you to self-love and silence the deep fears of abandonment and loneliness.

Emotions Exercise Check-In:

In the grief process, there are many emotions, so it's important to be mindful of them and not push them down. I'm going to encourage you to "check-in" with your feelings on a daily basis. This is an important practice to start doing daily. This is an exercise that you can do with or without your journal, but if you want to track your reflections, I suggest you use your journal. Ask yourself the questions below and reflect on the emotions that come up for you.

How am I feeling today?
How do I want to feel today?
How did I feel today? (Reflect on this question towards the end of the day)

Money and Economic Realities

The immediate reality of post-divorce is consistent across the board—people are going to feel a huge "lack of"—lack of money, assets, and status. Unless you had an unusual amount of wealth, your economic level will decrease, and you will definitely have to make adjustments in your living standards. This is a huge process you are going to need to work through, just like the loss of identity. However, now is the time to acknowledge and surrender to the fear of a lack of resources. When I say surrender what I really mean is deal with the reality that there is going to be fear around money and other important assets. Surrendering to the fear inside you simply means pondering all possible outcomes given your new situation, and then determining what your life would be like if that fear actualizes. In most cases, your fears and the reality of those fears, were they to come true, are not the same. Usually, the reality is far less scary than the ideas we let run through our minds.

Strong and smart men and women don't rely on their ex-spouses for their long-term financial status. Accepting that there will be a reduction in your lifestyle, especially in the interim, is crucial. Make the appropriate lifestyle changes that will help you stay within your means. We will go into greater depth about money in chapter six but for now understand that for the interim, after your divorce, things are going to change financially. Every day you wake up and every night before you fall asleep, internalize that you are a strong person, and that strength inside you will guide you down a path of abundance because you know how to deal with fear!

I've watched it happen time after time. I see, mostly women, sit back after their divorce with no drive to earn their own income because they have money coming in from their ex-spouse. The truth here is that getting comfortable after your divorce is going to plague your growth in the long term. Regardless of what your immediate financial situation looks in the first few years after your divorce, things will change. Money that was once being paid to you may start to dry up. If you have been coasting on a solid income that your spouse is providing, or plan on meeting someone new who can support you long-term, you are essentially telling the Universe that you don't want any growth. If I see this type of thinking with clients, I nip it in the bud right away. Happiness comes from pushing yourself and seeing the fruits of your labor come to fruition. I want you to get excited about the new possibilities that you can draw into your life by committing to supporting yourself and your children as much as you can, with little to no outside help, in the long term.

You need to look at creative ways to bring in additional money, including making spiritual sacrifices. I see people coming out of their divorce and facing the harsh reality that their ex-spouse may never work or be able to contribute to the financial responsibility of their children. Honestly, in the beginning, that thought alone is paralyzing. At the end of the day, it doesn't really matter what your ex can or cannot contribute, signed or didn't sign during the child support agreement. My advice is to hire a financial planner and an accountant after your divorce so they can help you map out a 10-year plan, a budget to stick to while you get through the immediate post-divorce stage and help you get on a realistic track of spending. It will feel overwhelming to think about this right now, but I can tell you, don't stick your head in the sand and ignore the financial planning that needs to be done. This will help you feel at ease later. This is a time for you to start looking at where you're at, look at your goals, and think about how you want your life to look. Knowledge is power here.

Ignoring finances, with the hope that you will be able to get by, can be one of the most significant mistakes you can make. I have seen over and over again people ignoring spending and hoping things will be okay, but eventually they feel the financial strain catch up. Successful people, post-divorce, are the ones that hit the financial issues head-on and know what they need to do for themselves and their children. They seek the support they need and know there is nothing wrong because they are reaching out for help. They are not ignoring the situation or waiting to meet somebody who will take care of them. They take matters into their own hands and develop a plan from the beginning. Where there is a plan, there is a vision for success. With success comes self-confidence and internal financial wholeness.

I was a real estate broker at the time of my divorce, having success representing home buyers and the sellers. It was a nice income, but I realized I would need to be more creative if I wanted to create the new life that I was envisioning in my head. I used my real estate background and love for homes to sell my home and settle into a smaller home that I knew I could make improvements on, making money by selling it two years later. I would sell that home and get a much bigger home that I knew I could transform and again sell it and make money. Moving from home to home and using my love for real estate made it easier and quicker to rebuild myself financially as I made great strides with each home. At the same time, I bought a barre business and had 20 instructors working for me. I worked grueling hours, waking up at 4:30am many days, seeing the details through, teaching classes, being present at the studio, keeping the books accurate, and getting to know clients and knowing their story.

I sold that business after five years and went back to school for nutrition and health coaching and then on to functional medicine.

Since then, I've worked with many people on living healthier and happier lives, and many regarding divorce. Today, I'm an author, coach, entrepreneur, real estate expert, restaurant owner, and full-time mother. It all started at realizing that my financial status had changed, so I needed to make adjustments sooner, rather than later, to have the long-term success. I knew that my financial situation was short-term, and I would make that money back and more. I think it is so important to remain a student of life, curious and ready to rebrand yourself on your path to financial success.

The Wholeness Journey

At this point in your journey, it's going to feel erratic because obviously so much has changed. I mean you've gone from living in a home with your partner and children to your children not being with you 100 percent of the time now. Of course, your divorce is officially final. I understand all of it. You're going to feel the stages of grief and feel that your whole world is coming crashing down at times.

However, it's time to regenerate yourself and recharge your batteries as you go through the post-divorce years because you are meant for bigger and better things. It's time to hone in and expand your deserve-o-meter, your inner guidance system of assessing what you deserve out of this life. Your deserve-o-meter is here to help you reassess what is important now and what are your realistic steps in your journey to self-love and wholeness. This is an easy tool and energy to tap into when you are feeling out of balance or when things are feeling out of control.

Surrender to the outcomes. You'll hear me say this again and again and again. Part of your wholeness journey is not to lose yourself or wrap yourself up in the self-identity and loss of money. You can't allow yourself to stay in that energy. This is the very beginning step of embarking on a new life alone, confident, and feeling independent on your own two feet. Life is about the ups and downs, the highs and the lows; so honor all the feelings of guilt, loss, and the transition of having two homes that your children have to live between now. This new life is for you to embrace the gifts that are being shown to you during the emotional lows and grow from them, fill your holes with love, and expand your newly rediscovered deserve-o-meter. What you deserve in this life is a choice and your choice only!

Deserve-o-Meter Exercise:

The deserve-o-meter is here to help you get in touch with your inner desires, worthiness, and what you feel you deeply deserve in this life. You can come back to this exercise whenever you feel you need it, but once you begin to do it often, it's literally something you can do while you are out for a walk, on the train home from work, or taking a shower. The first couple of times that you do this exercise, allow yourself the space for introspection. If you desire to create a sacred space, have calming meditation music on in the background, candles lit, and your journal by your side. I absolutely encourage you to do this. Once you have done this a couple times, you can begin to practice it outside of your sacred space and tap into the energy of your deserve-o-meter. A sacred space is helpful, just like a mantra, but they're tools to help you with your initial practice of mindfulness. Let the need for having tools go as you dive deeper and deeper into this book, and your new life. You can access the benefits of these exercises anywhere, at any time of your choosing. For now, it helps to have a dedicated practice as you learn and see the benefits of these exercises!

Step 1: Create a Sacred Space

This is one of the best parts if you ask me—I want you to create a sacred corner or area in your home, just for you. This is the area you can retreat to in times of chaos or when you just need to check-out for five minutes of quiet time. Bring together your favorite candles, plants, pictures, whatever you feel called to put in your very own sacred space.

Step 2: Sit in Front of the Mirror

In your sacred space, for this deserve-o-meter exercise, I want you to have a mirror. It can be a handheld mirror, or it could be a stand-up mirror, whatever you have is perfect. This is going to begin your mirror work. I want you to sit in front of the mirror and start to look into your eyes and ask yourself "What do I deserve? What do I desire?"

A lot of thoughts, feelings, and emotions are going to come up, you may even feel uncomfortable at first. It was probably not very often up until this point in life that you may have intentionally stopped and looked at yourself in the mirror. Whatever is coming up for you, know that nothing is right or wrong, you are feeling what you are meant to feel.

Step 3: Visualize your Deserve-O-Meter

Write the date in your journal, so you are able to come back and reference this and see your growth. Awareness of your deserve-o-meter is going to be the key to your growth here. Now close your eyes after you've looked into your own eyes for at least five seconds, begin to see your desires surrounded by love and light. You see a glowing white light around yourself...

What else do you see at this moment? Write it down in your journal—begin to create a picture of your deserve-o-meter because this is the energy that you are going to hold onto and embrace when you are feeling stressed and overwhelmed. Get specific with your details. What do you want your life to look like? Your deserve-o-meter is all love.

Step 4: You Are Worth This

Know that you are worth all of this. You need to create a new frame of reference for who you are now, single and living a new life of post-divorce. However, don't let "divorce" be your story, it's time to let go of the story and make a new story for yourself. You've got this, and I'm here every step of the way with you!

CHAPTER FOUR

The Universe is at Your Fingertips

Divorce rookie and epiphany of emotions—that's where you're at right now. The epiphany of emotions is a beautiful experience because two worlds are colliding. The first is that you are now undergoing a new life, your post-divorce life of living and earning on your own. The second is that you are grounded and a strong person—I hope you get that from this book if you don't have it already. You are deserving of a big and bold life. You are a strong person who knows how to carry themselves through the good and the bad with your head held high. With these two worlds colliding, you will have "Ah Ha" moments, when the realization of what the bigger lessons at play actually were. These moments are born from hard work, pain, and most importantly, your ability to push past them. It's almost like there is a bigger plan at play for you, set out by God, or the Universe, or simply by the way things in life usually go!

It's critical to cultivate a mindset that will get you through to the other side. This is a long-term game, not something that will change overnight. It's easy for me to tell you that the Universe has your back, to trust in God, and everything will work out. But the reality is you cannot truly internalize these ideas unless you experience them. The experience of having these "Ah Ha" moments, of seeing the Universe or God reward your hard work, is what will change you at your core. Divorce is here to teach you everything: life lessons, responsibility, discipline, patience, awareness, love, respect for self, and the power of your mind.

Law of Attraction

I fully believe divorce was one of the best investments I've made in my life. I look at all the money, assets, and fees I lost in the divorce as my initial investment into myself. Everything I have learned, and who I have become since my divorce are the dividends I am (still) being paid. I want to repeat that again so you can understand my mindset now as I look back on my divorce ten years ago. The overall money spent (including assets split and lawyer costs) was, quite possibly, the best money I've ever spent in my life. That's a massive statement for me to make, and if you had told me that ten years ago I would have laughed in your face. It was not my best investment because it got me out of a failing marriage. Instead, this money was the best investment I've ever made because it brought me the biggest epiphany of my life thus far. That is that the Law of Attraction allows us to take our visions, dreams, and deepest desires and turn them into reality.

I'm a believer that the Law of Attraction is a giant photocopying machine. It's photocopying all our thoughts, feelings, and emotions. In other words, your thoughts have great power in creating your day-to-day experiences. Your thoughts create your experiences. Your thoughts are one of the only fundamental things in life that are always in your control. For me, this epiphany was hugely empowering as I began to create a strong, healthy new life for myself and my children. The thoughts that you run through your head will create belief patterns that will be played out in reality. You are what you think, and it's really that simple. Your emotional intelligence (intent, behavior, reactions, impact) helps focus, plan, and execute your reality. One of the biggest reasons I have for writing this book is to illustrate the power of using the thoughts in your head to reshape your reality. The power of your mind is the number one factor that will determine the future in your new life. I couldn't have created a great story for myself without understanding the Law of Attraction. It's like a secret weapon that's really not so secret anymore.

I remember in my relationship with my ex-husband, my thoughts were always ones of fear and worry, waiting for the next shoe to drop or the next blowout to happen. I always felt the internal shakiness in my heart and in my gut. My thoughts were surrounded by doubt and negativity, day in and day out. I saw it all play out right in front of me with my interactions with my ex-husband. Negative energy was flowing around me because I was consuming my thoughts with fear, ego, judgment, and worry. I had no idea of the Law of Attraction at this time. I didn't know that what you think, feel, and see would come back to you like a mirror in real life. Today, I practice the LOA in every aspect of my life and I can plainly see when I am not.

Everything is energy; worry attracts more worry, anxiety attracts more anxiety, anger attracts more anger, fear attracts more fear, and unhappiness attracts more unhappiness. If you are willing to accept that fear and negativity will breed more fear and negativity then you can also accept that love and positivity will bring more of the same into your life. Aristotle once said, "Happiness depends upon ourselves." It's an internal process in the reprogramming of your mind, to consciously create the environment and energy you desire and deserve. Happiness is an inside job, so is love, peace, tranquility, and wholeness. Your thoughts are the key to harnessing your own energy. Even as I say those words out loud to myself right now, I feel that I have this amazing super power that I can use at any time!

In order to feel joy and happiness, you must change the way you feel inside. You cannot control someone's actions and behaviors towards you, but you can control how you react to it. For me, it was understanding how to use the Law of Attraction in my relationship with my ex, and managing to keep my emotions in a positive state no matter how negative the communication. The Law of Attraction is always working for you because the energy to change is within you.

You don't have to go seek something or someone out to tell you what you desire, it's already within. You are attracting in every moment of your life. If you feel the laws are not working for you because you don't have something you want, or your post-divorce emotions are getting the best of you, realize that the laws are responding to those exact thoughts. You either attract what you want, or you attract the absence of what you want. The laws are always at work.

The way I use the LOA is by first aligning my intentions and goal with my thoughts. The biggest thing I have to do once my thoughts are congruent with my intention is engulf and feel the emotion of what it's like to have achieved that goal. For example when I sold my last house, even before it was put on the market, I internalized the feelings of a smooth and successful deal. I felt the emotions of what I could then invest those profits into for my children and myself, and that further compounded the positive, strong, successful energy that I needed to make any of it reality. Had I worried that the sale would be stressful, or that the market wasn't perfect I would have invited, unknowingly, that energy into the sale of my home.

You ultimately create the mold, and the Universe fills the mold based on what your thoughts are asking for. In order to have the capacity to manifest and create, you must begin to align yourself with your intentions. You are not only attracting the experiences or "things" you want in life, but deep down you are attracting the energy of the person that you will soon become. That is an important distinction to make. It isn't about getting stuff or having great experiences all the time. It's about who you are as a person, and how you interact with people every day that will ultimately bring positive or negative experiences into your life. Use your thoughts as the base catalyst for having a more positive than negative energy in your life. That is what is most empowering and exciting about the Law of Attraction.

I saw this work to my advantage when it came to my career and finances, and I didn't even deliberately know what I was doing at that time. I felt determination and empowerment by my ability to do "life" on my own. In my head I had a few key things I wanted to get done after my divorce, to put myself in the driver's seat of my new life. First, I wanted to sell my house to help make up the financial loss of the divorce. Second, I wanted to immerse myself in my physical practice of barre by making it my new career path. I had no idea about how I was going to accomplish any of these goals at the time though. Within the first two years after my divorce, the power of visualization started to make significant impacts in my new life.

My children were emotional about selling our house because it was a part of who they were. I knew that there would be challenges in selling a house that had so many memories in it. I visualized that my children would transition smoothly from one house to another. I felt the feelings of having completed a successful and stress-free sale. I internalized that the act of moving wasn't going to be painful or hard. Everything about making a big change for my children and myself could have been stressful and hard, but I played out the opposite outcome in my mind. That doesn't mean there were no difficult moments. It means that I didn't let the difficult moments infect the positive thoughts I was harboring in my head.

Intentional Visualization Exercise:

The Law of Attraction is not a magic wand that you can use to get things that you want in life. The power of the LOA needs to come from your burning desire to enact real change in your life. I want to share a simple exercise that I have used every single day to create a strong sense of calm and control in my life. Using this three-step process every single day, with intention, I am able to cultivate a sacred energy that continues to guide me down paths I cannot see in front of me. I have had so many "Ah Ha" moments over the years that I continuously reinforce how valuable and powerful using the Law of Attraction is. If you can commit to a daily visualization practice you're going to have the same type of positive benefits. Once you have your first experience or

"Ah Ha" moment using this exercise, you'll never be able to let it go.

Step 1: Visualize

I've talked about the power of my own visualizations, so I want you to embrace the power of visualization as well. An easy way to start with visualizing and combining it with the power of the Law of Attraction is to simply begin. I want you to take three to five minutes to visualize yourself having a new day filled with gratitude. The purpose of this visualization is to see the results, changes, and/or healing that you desire before they happen. Get comfortable in your favorite position and make sure there are no distractions. This could be done as you are beginning your day or before you fall asleep at night. Avoid focusing on the amount of time you are doing this. Visualize the current, or following, day being full of gratitude. There is no right or wrong answer here, and you can't visualize incorrectly. What does gratitude look like for you? How does a day full of gratitude feel? What things are you noticing that you feel grateful for? What does it feel like to have lived a day with more gratitude throughout it? Visualize the things that are important to you. Things like enjoying your kids, even if they are in a bad mood. Or feel gratitude towards eating a great home-cooked meal even if you aren't a great cook.

Step 2: Give Thanks

The second layer of this exercise is to give thanks for the day you've had or the previous day, depending on when you are practicing this exercise. If something happened during the day that you wish you had done differently, replay it in your mind the way you wish it had played out. Feel how things would feel had they gone exactly the way you wanted them to. Give thanks again, and continue to replay this event until you are able to embed a calm, peaceful place of gratitude for the lesson and growth it gave you today. Reprogramming the brain will help you consciously create responses from a different place in future events, such as a place of peace, gratitude, and wholeness.

Step 3: Prepare for Tomorrow

Before you fall asleep, after giving thanks for the present day, tell yourself "tomorrow is going to be the most amazing day." Visualize yourself and the future in a bright white light of love and happiness, then repeat this phrase to yourself five times. By doing this, you are setting the intention for your day tomorrow, telling the Universe that you believe, mentally, physically, and emotionally that you're going to have a great day. This energy will help you sleep peacefully, help you see the vision you have for tomorrow, and feel the positive energy that it brings.

Visualization and mindset work takes practice and repetition, so the more you are able to practice this exercise consistently, the more you will be able to quickly apply the principles of LOA in other areas of your life. Remember, everything you believe is a thought, which keeps going into the Universe and is mirrored in others' emotions and/or behavior.

Quantum Physics

What is quantum physics (QP)? Quantum physics for me is the energy we put out in the world. Your energy tells your story. Bad energy and good energy can both be felt by the people around you. When my energy slipped, it was almost always caused by something I could not control.

Quantum physics is the ability to control real-life outcomes by using the power of your thoughts and your energy. The outcomes in real life are either fueled by positive or negative thoughts, and to be even simpler than that, good energy or bad energy. This differs from the Law of Attraction. Quantum physics is based on energy, whereas the LOA is based on aligning your thoughts with your intentions and actions.

In the quantum physics world, life is not happening to you, but instead, you are responsible for creating the world that unfolds around you. This is how energy flows (positive or negative), and affects how you see the world within your mind. Are you angry, fearful, bitter, resentful, depressed, or jealous when you think about different situations? Do you tend to see the good and the positive in situations with great optimism, even if it might be hard to overcome the ego to stay in this energy? Your energy is the fuel that many of your thoughts need to send out messages to the Universe, and then the Universe sends back that energy and manifestation of what you are looking for. If you hold onto internal thoughts that sound negative, for example, "I really hate him/her; How could he be so entitled and malicious?; How could she cheat on me and expect me to pay her alimony?; I am not good enough; I can't do this; I am a failure; Nobody will ever love me again." These are all thoughts that are based in fear, and continuing to wallow in them will prevent you from rising above.

I remember thinking if I was able to make the Law of Attraction work in some areas of my life, what would it be like to have LOA and the power of quantum physics work in *all* areas of my life? Especially relationships because I saw how much stress the post-divorce relationship with my ex was causing me. I knew I was responsible for a lot of it because of the energy I was putting out and the reaction that I would always have to his behavior. I started to literally shift my energy and begin to deliver positive energy back to him. I knew positive, non-reactive energy was going to be received differently than the negative energy I was creating when I was in reaction mode. I only hoped that it would eventually help him shift his energy as well. And it did. Two people are responsible for ongoing negative interactions. We all have the power within to change the energy (vibe) by choosing more positive thoughts towards another person. I think the important thing to mention here is you can never control how someone else reacts to you or the behavior and energy they deliver to you. You can control how you choose to receive it. If you are consistently receiving negative energy from someone, you have the power within not to react, and you can choose not to let their negative energy towards you affect you or bring you into their dark space. This takes practice but one I still practice often.

I never want to meet someone at their energy level because I am putting myself in a potential situation to absorb negative energy. Today, I go into all situations with my energy at a high and positive place so that whomever I interact with can absorb that energy. Many people are also giving off a high, positive energy in life already but that is not always the case. I know that when I practice visualizing my day (using the exercise we discussed before this section) I can pre-program my energy to be at a positive level before I interact with anyone that day! I use my understanding of energy and quantum physics to shield myself from low or negative energy people. Even the simple act of smiling or greeting a stranger is an act of lifting someone else's energy up to your level. That is empowering and exciting!

Inside my home I create energy that is nurturing and positive by not falling into the pitfalls of negativity. I want my kids to feel positive energy when they are around me because they will carry that energy outside of the home and use it to become stronger people as they grow up. You might have an ex-spouse whose home is not a place of positive energy. This negative energy can be as simple as a messy or dirty, overcrowded, unstructured home that makes kids feel stressed out and unsettled being there. My children would instantly feel a loving and warm vibe the moment they stepped into my home and much of that was because my home was a clean, structured and a peaceful environment. That transition to a positive home energy lifted significant stress and weight off them, without them even knowing it. They just felt better. Had I been one to trash talk my ex, the energy in my home would have certainly not felt strong, supportive, or positive at all. You need to understand that you control that energy by your thoughts and actions. Can you see how powerful it is to hold a positive, high energy inside yourself?

When you give power to negative thoughts, you are adding fuel to the fire and will continue to head down a very unhappy path. You are the master of your own energy fields, and you have the power to reprogram your brain out of the darkness. Changing your thoughts and emotions is going to change the experiences you have with other people, the experiences you have in your career, with your children, your finances, and even your spirituality. In essence, bringing in new, more positive emotions to your body expands your energy and begin to fill your holes with wholeness and balanced, healthy wellness.

YOU ARE WHAT YOU THINK

Your thoughts are one of the most powerful tools you have at your disposal to enact change in your energy and the energy felt by those around you. Dr. Joe Dispenza, scientist and author of *"Breaking the Habit of Being Yourself,"* and several other books, inspired an easy to understand explanation of QP. "When you combine a clear intention with an elevated emotion, you move your brain and body from living in the past to living in the future." Our brains are naturally wired for a fight or flight response in intense situations. This is actually a gift from our brains, through evolution, that serves to protect us by highlighting potential threats in the environment. It is the power and innate ability we have within ourselves that gives us control to change our thought patterns to positivity, inner peace, love, courage, etc. It takes a conscious effort to rewire your brain to think and see things this way.

It takes different groups of neurons in the brain from the knowledge we've gained in past experiences to be seamlessly pieced together to create a new vision with intent. When you begin to fire new neurons in different combinations and connections, you begin to change your mind. This is also true when you are forging new pathways and ways of thinking, which is called neuroplasticity. Neuroplasticity is the brain's ability to reorganize synaptic connections, especially in response to learning and life experiences. Think of neuroplasticity as building muscle in the gym. If you do 100 bicep curls every day your biceps will gradually become stronger and stronger, of course.

In 2012, I suffered a significant brain injury from a high-speed ceiling fan when it hit me in the head.

My brain was swollen inside my skull.

I was told by numerous neurologists that my only option for recovery was to rest my brain for at least 12-18 months. I was running a business with employees, raising five children as a single mother, and still healing from my divorce at the time. My circuitry was thrown way out of whack which caused brain fog, severe fatigue, and delayed my response times.

There was a constant cloud over my head that hampered everything I was working to accomplish at the time. I became fed up with all the doctors who said that there was nothing that could be done to move past this injury. I simply refused to accept that. I became fed up with western medicine and started looking for someone to help me from a holistic and functional medicine standpoint.

I found my way to a functional neurologist and on day one of my assessment—which was three months after my accident—he told me that I have a serious injury. He laid out the truth of where I was at right now, and that there was a path to recovery.

He was the first person that allowed me to feel relief that I could come back from this injury. A functional neurologist often heals any type of a brain injury through eye exercises and other brain exercises.

The eyes, I learned, are the gateway to the brain, and the method that I would eventually use to heal myself from this injury. It's scary to think about this now, but had I accepted that my brain needed 12-18 months of rest and nothing else, I believe I would have permanent damage from the accident. This was another experience that reinforced creating the life I want through my intentions and actions, using neuroplasticity of the brain. I set my intention on healing myself no matter what and I eventually found a way to do so, without surgery or drugs.

Whether it's coming back from an injury like I was or changing your daily patterns to align with your true intentions, your brain's circuitry needs reason to change and achieve long-term results. With my injury, I went through eye exercises every single day for months until I knew that I was completely healed. With your life, starting right now, you can change just one habit to rewire the way your brain interprets the world around you.

If you wake up every morning and go through the same routine and experiences that you did yesterday: see the same people, go to the same places, your external environment will turn on different circuits of the brain causing you to think and feel equal to all that you know and experienced yesterday. If you believe your thoughts have anything to do with your health or your destiny, then you are absolutely right. As long as you're thinking the same way, you keep creating the same line, over and over again, day in and day out. Thoughts are the language of the brain, and feelings are the language of the body.

How you think and how you feel create your state of being. Most people's cellular and energy level is defined by their past—not by a vision for the future or new possibilities for life. The brain and body only know to keep firing the old circuitry of the past and feeling old emotions of the past. Wayne Dyer tells us "The single most important tool to being in balance is knowing that you and you alone are responsible for the imbalances between what you dream your life is meant to be and your daily life habits that drain life from that dream." Your spiritual energy must be driven by your love to live in wholeness, and it all begins with your mental energy matching your desires and behavior.

If there's one thing I want you to take away from this book immediately, it's to become aware of your thoughts, your mindset, and your energy. It's imperative to create a daily practice of being mindful of your thoughts and how your energy matches those thoughts.

It will affect how others interact with you and how others are going to go about their day. For me, I also love creating amazing energy in my household because I'm responsible for creating an uplifting environment for my children. They are observing me and feel my energy, so it's essential for me to set a tone of good health, mindfulness, and loving energy in the home. As my kids have grown into teens and young adults, I am told by many people that my kids all have a positive and high vibrant energy as well. One of the greatest gifts of QP is that energy is being delivered all around us and it begins in the home. If you're able to have a positive example in the home for not only you but your children as well, everyone will carry forward a level of high energetic vibration that is an example for others. It's a ripple effect that resonates throughout your home.

Forgiveness

As a coach who has worked with many clients in their post-divorce life, one of the most common roadblocks I deal with is how to work towards forgiveness. Forgiveness is one of the most fundamental actions that you need to embrace in order to move through your new life with positivity and mindfulness. My goal for you is to practice and embrace the action of forgiving someone, not for their sake but for your own personal well-being.

Forgiveness does not mean that you need to forget what someone has done to you and just move on with life. That's not how you heal from what has happened to you and what needs forgiving. The best cure for battle wounds, such as divorce, is forgiveness.

You need to forgive in order to heal and you can't heal without forgiveness.

You create your own suffering when you stay in a place of not being able to forgive. It's a necessary stop along the path of the wholeness journey. You can't speed up the emotional feelings to forgiveness because you will have to feel the emotions to come to this point. Some people think that if you choose to stay in suffering and forgive the person who hurt you, then you're saying, whatever you did was okay. But let me tell you, that's not the case.

Forgiveness is understanding and having empathy. It's the power to free yourself from the emotional turmoil you've experienced. Trust in yourself, and the Universe, that your journey to wholeness and self-love is pure. Why would you want to create your own suffering because that is what it is when you allow yourself to stay in the energy of not forgiving. Part of forgiveness is opening your heart, your spirit, to grow and most of all, working through the hardest forgiveness, which is with yourself. Forgiveness will restore your trust and connection with the Universe and self-love. When you welcome the energy and emotion of forgiveness to your ex-spouse, you are sending a path of light to them and being the light in yourself: you are releasing the burden that you have been carrying for them, as well as within yourself. We can't heal along our journey without this piece. When you are finally able to come to a peaceful place of forgiveness for your ex-spouse and yourself, you're able to invoke more compassion and empathy into your life.

We must forgive ourselves, which is sometimes the hardest person to forgive. We also need to forgive our ex-partner, our friends who may not have shown the support that we needed, and even our family who may not have said the right things. You must forgive, it's that simple.

There are enormous physical burdens to being hurt, believe me. When your body is in a constant state of anger, it puts the body into a "fight or flight" mode response, releasing excess stress hormones into the blood. Stress hormones are than converted into sugar, and excess sugar leads to weight gain and inflammation which can lead to disease. When you're able to process your emotions effectively, forgiveness can improve your overall health and reduce negative feelings of fear, anger, tension, depression, and fatigue.

The barrier that you will face is that you will feel you deserve to stay angry for what happened because you were wronged before, during, or after your divorce. Forgiveness allows you to rewrite a new story for yourself. That's the goal we are really after!

Forgiveness and Self-Reflections Exercise:

There is no right or wrong time to step into forgiveness, but the most important thing I want you to understand is that you want to have an awareness of your emotions. The power of journaling can be incredibly healing because you are able to see how and what you were feeling each day, week, and month, of your journey through a divorce. Even if you progress slowly through your healing process you will be able to see a progression in your thoughts, emotions, and feelings.

Grab your journal and use the questions below to begin your journaling practice. There is no time limit to how long you need to journal, just let your emotions flow onto the paper with ease. What I am most interested in is having your build a consistent practice of self-reflection, and there will be more exercises like this in the upcoming chapters. If you can learn consistency in your self-reflection practice, you will decrease the time it takes for you to navigate your own map to Wholeness. Take a moment and answer each of the questions below with as little or as much writing as you feel necessary:

- *What are the emotions you feel in this moment towards your ex-spouse?*

- *What are the emotions you feel for your role in the marriage ending?*

- *How would it affect your life to forgive yourself for the divorce?*

- *What emotions come up when you think about forgiving your ex?*

- *What does it feel like to forgive your ex-spouse and their actions?*

- *What are the obstacles in your way that are hindering you from forgiving your ex-spouse?*

From my personal experience of going through the path to forgiveness, I can say that you're going to experience serious pain. The pathway, the journey through pain that led me to forgiveness, was led by a man that gave me many amazing lessons along the way about myself and about other people. Open your eyes to what forgiveness feels like to avoid keeping yourself in a victim state. I know it's really easy to stay in a victim state, It's natural to feel like a victim, especially when you don't think you are at fault for what happened. Your ego wants you to feel like a victim in order to protect you from letting bad things happen down the road. We all do, because we all get hurt. If you are able to look at the beautiful lessons that are beyond the victim state, and forgive the times when you were hurt by anyone, you will move towards wholeness much faster.

Being the Artist of Your New Story

Being the artist of your story, especially in a new story, must start with positive thoughts. We've talked about how the Law of Attraction and quantum physics explains that our thoughts are connected to the energy we put out into the world. The energy that you put out into the world is absorbed by everyone you come into contact with. What I want to show you now is the importance of having positive thoughts flood your mind in order to dramatically change your story for the better. Your story is one that is incredibly exciting because the main character is you AND you are an editor at the same time. With the power of positive thinking you can influence the direction your story goes. My turmoil gifted me with the eyes to create opportunities for myself because I could see the aches as opportunities to grow, and as stepping stones to what I was really meant for in my life.

Wayne Dyer, author of the well-known book *Your Erroneous Zones,* says "Co-creation is cooperatively using the energy from the invisible field of Spirit. It is perfectly balancing your in-the-world calling with the pure energy of creation. You emulate this creation field by being as much like it as possible. This involves your willingness to contemplate yourself as a being of balance attracting the conditions you desire to produce." Even in the gutter, you can look up at the stars and choose to see positivity no matter what is happening around you.

Divorcees tend to get stuck in a mundane life before they even reach the energy of forgiveness and new positive goals. They are just existing with no vision. They get stuck in a lot of fears and let their fears become more significant as time goes by. All of a sudden, they find themselves three years after divorce still in the same fears, nothing improving or on the horizon, and repeating poor coping mechanisms. This can lead to things like addiction and drinking, just to get by from day to day.

I want you to embrace your ability to become the artist of your new life. It's very rare that someone who thinks and lives positively also struggles with drug addiction or alcohol abuse. If you embrace that, as an artist there are no rules to what you can create for yourself, you'll allow negativity to dissipate much quicker.

Will the new life you're creating consist only of rainbows and butterflies?

No.

Of course you will still face the ups and downs that come with life. The main difference that I want you to embrace is that as those ups and downs come and go, your dreams and goals will only get stronger and more vivid. Think about your dreams, vision, and desires like colors on a paint tray. Each color will play a role in the finished product, and each brush stroke of color represents a positive thought that you put into the Universe. If you painted with no direction, you would struggle to ever create a finished product. Every artist has a vision in their mind, and as the artist of your new life you are the only one who can see that vision. The ups and downs of life, just like small mistakes in your painting, can be fixed or ignored. The final product is your dream and yours alone. With positive thoughts feeding your ability to paint the masterpiece of your life, you cannot fail.

I've painted and repainted my life a number of times since my divorce. I like to say that my first painting took five years to create after my divorce! I needed five years to practice and hone my skills in order to have my first "final product." I used everything I learned in that process to go on and create bigger and brighter masterpieces—or life experiences—for myself and my children. I wanted to be a stay-at-home mother of five kids and have a career at the same time. I felt the feelings of having this in my life long before it ever happened. I put positive thoughts out into the Universe (my brush strokes!) and eventually that painting was finished. I was able to work on my own schedule and be home when I wanted to be there for my children.

I wanted to have multiple creative income streams to support myself with and to provide my children with savings and investments well into their future. I knew I didn't need to settle for just one. The positive thoughts that I put into the Universe showed me the path to believing I could do real estate, run a fitness studio, coach people on health and wellness, invest in a restaurant, and still be a mother.

There were many times in these examples that I allowed doubt to creep in and throw a shadow over my dreams. I would think "this isn't possible" or "this is too much for someone like me." Eventually I knew I could either settle for what I had or force myself to continue thinking positively. I came back to my artist mindset and painted over the doubt with all the different colors I had on my tray. It's great to dream big, but it's even better to overcome the doubts that accompany big dreams.

Become the Artist Exercise:

Creating goals is what got me through self-doubt and fear in the years after my divorce. I was in a situation as a single mom of five young children at the time, and I remember people looking at me saying, "Oh God, it's going to be tough." The more I looked inside myself, the quicker I found myself saying, *No, it's going to be beautiful.*

I can recall having lunch with an old friend immediately after my divorce. He looked at me and said, "Wow, five kids huh!" I can still picture us at this table and my response to him was so loud. I can remember hearing myself talk as if I was speaking into a microphone. I continued to describe to him what my life was going to look like. I told him I was going to create a life of ease—a peaceful, happy and abundant existence. At the time, it was anything but this but I refused to get swallowed up in that darkness. When I spoke of how my life would look, I could already feel all of those positive emotions that aligned with my future vision. I was feeling the emotions of living the life I imagined prior to ever achieving it. I could already see the picture in my mind that I wanted my life to look like day-to-day, and even months and years later.

I knew it was going to take some hard work to get there. That hard work had to match up with the visualization of how I wanted life to be. You must have your emotions in sync and feel balanced in every aspect of your vision. One kid, two kids, five kids. It really doesn't matter. What does matter though, is you have the power to create an easy life or a difficult life. It took years, but today I have an easier life than my friends who are married with two kids, and I also created a much easier life than any of my divorced friends with one or two kids. I created the vision and you can too.

I picture a life of ease with abundance in every way, not just financially, but with the freedom to welcome changes, and allow the best growth for my family. I want to pass along that power to you starting with a tangible exercise. As you learn to plan out your new life using positive reinforcement of your self-identity and your goals, you'll discover that making things happen *for* you and not *to* you is a better way to live!

Mindset and visualization are vital to obtaining positive outcomes in your life. The emotion and the visualization work together in one support unit to increase your likelihood of success in everything you do.

All of this didn't happen for me without first getting in touch with my mindset and verbalizing my goals. This exercise is going to help you get in touch with all the areas of your life and create goals and/or visions for each one of them. In each category below write what you feel in your heart right now. Think about the specifics within each category and put your intention on what you want to achieve. There is no right or wrong answer for this exercise, which allows you to write anything that comes up.

I do encourage you to think more about the emotions or feelings of what you want instead of material items or "things." For example, under "Finances," the first thing that I would write is "I want to know in my heart that my family doesn't have to worry about money. I will have multiple income streams working for my benefit. There will be an abundance of money for my children's future education!" The difference here is that I'm writing about how I want to feel and not about things I simply want. You are more likely to accomplish these feelings if you accept that at this moment you might not know the "how" but you know your "why". How things will shape out in your life is far beyond your control.

Your ability to tell the Universe what type of life you want to be living through the way it feels is a better path to actually feeling the success and abundance you deserve. Give it a try now using this table in the book, your journal, or a separate sheet of paper!

	Goals, Visions, and Desires
Love + Relationships	
Finances	
Health + Wellness	
Spirituality	
Parenting	
Work + Career	
Life Purpose	

If you need help getting through any specific categories in this exercise, use these questions to spark ideas:

- *What would bring you joy?*
- *What do you now want?*
- *What does this category mean to you?*
- *What do you see in others that you want for yourself?*
- *What would be the most ideal situation, even if it's not realistic? (This question can be helpful to reverse engineer what you desire from the very best outcome you can imagine.)*

Once you finish writing, take five minutes to soak into each one of them. Think about them, see them, imagine how you feel, think about why you want what you wrote, and be okay knowing that you don't need the "how" right now. Harness all the energy you can from each desire and goal. Bring each vision and goal into every aspect of your life by thinking about how it will affect not only you, but also the people in your life. Be congruent within your mind (what you think), body (how you feel), and spirit (why you have the desire). All three of these are important because they send the same message out into the Universe. If I wanted to have stability in my finances because it would make my ex-spouse or old friends jealous I would not have congruence. Everything you desire must stem from a positive and meaningful place within you.

The Wholeness Journey

The power of the Law of Attraction, quantum physics, forgiveness, and the power of thought goals, all working together in one sync Universal system allows us to come out of the darkness. This is a defining moment, right here, to claim at this moment that you are ready to open yourself and your soul, to the power of what the Universe has for you because you can create whatever you want in this lifetime. You now have awakened the feeling, the emotion, and the positive energy to create it. This is your life now, and nobody else's. The Universe is here to meet you where you are and be there to support you when you need it.

PART ONE - DIVORCE COACHING TIPS

Consider this scenario: Your spouse tells you that they will be pursuing custody of the kids full time and they want custody of the kids every Christmas Day and Christmas Eve. You have been married for nine years, and you are both equally active in the children's lives.

Reaction 1: React with Vengeance
You react emotionally saying, *"How dare you, You will never get away with this—you are a selfish, irresponsible asshole. My attorney and I are going to retaliate with a vengeance. You will be sorry for this. You will never get away with this. I will ask our children what they think about this. I will tell our children what you are trying to do."*

Reaction 2: Breath work
Breathe…
You take deep inhales…
Deep exhales…

My breath work is 5-7-8 counts.

You breathe deeply through your belly for five counts, hold your breath for seven counts and then a loud audible exhale for eight counts. This breath work should be incorporated into your daily practice, as of today.

This breath work resets your autonomic nervous system and settles you into a calmer state. Once you have calmed your breathing, you can calmly discuss with your spouse. *"I am sorry you feel this way. I understand that you love the kids and don't want to miss them, but I love them too. I think it is important for their self-esteem and self-discovery to have love and healthy relationships with both you and me. I would imagine that you must feel this same way. Can we discuss this again when we are both less upset?"*

Take Away:

The first reaction stems from a place where you haven't identified your feelings, and you are reacting from heightened fear of loss of control and time with your children.

The second reaction immediately disarms the other person. The second reaction is a more intentional and mindful one, acknowledging both your partner and your own feelings. They are reacting from a place of fear. The fear can be stemming from the loss of power, loss of identity, loss of love. Your partner is expecting you to react with the same emotion that they are giving you. When you shift the conversation from an attack to a conversation of empathy and respect, the other person is disarmed. The natural reaction from them is to then shift with you.

It may not happen on the first attempt, but trust me it will happen. You can control whether or not the conversation goes down a positive path or a negative path. The first reaction is our knee jerk reaction and is most often seen throughout the divorce process. Both parties are in a highly emotional reactive state.

This coaching tip is a vital tool that will hijack the conversations and communication process to a healthier and more productive state. You and your ex-spouse will be able to maintain control over the outcome, rather than giving that power to attorneys, which in the long run will mean more money spent on their fees. That type of behavior will set you and your spouse on a path that will take so much time to repair in the post-divorce stage.

The Beauty
of Healing

PART TWO - GET GROUNDED

As you draw towards closure in the divorce process, there is a pretty good chance you're feeling beat up mentally, emotionally, and spiritually. In order to step into healing with an open mind and heart, you must accept and leave behind any decisions that were made during the painful divorce process. Nobody usually feels like they have won as they finish the tumultuous process of dividing assets, properties, child custody, etc. In the majority of cases, you and your ex-spouse will both feel like you have lost.

You have just consumed a new reality consisting of more responsibilities, less income, less time with your kids, and a daunting journey of doing it on our own. Accept the situation as your new reality now, or as soon as possible, in order to move on to building a better life. In fact, get excited about the fact that you GET to pave a new path for yourself. Who knows where it will lead...

Now that you understand what mindfulness is and how to practice it, use it to ask yourself, "*Is this emotion serving me or is this emotion stemming from my fears and worries regarding my new life?*"

As you heal, it is important to create an environment for yourself that allows you to heal spiritually, mentally, and emotionally from all that you've endured. You want to protect the body from stress by thinking positively and with goals and dreams from here on out.

Create a self-care routine that allows you to feel nurtured during this time. Self-care practices are also self-love practices. Your life has changed so quickly, and inevitably you are going to feel so much more additional stress, which is why we want to practice self-love.

Let yourself feel all of the emotions that will arise during this phase. You may find yourself all over the place emotionally. You'll feel like you're on a high one moment, so excited to have your divorce behind you and get on with your new life; and the next moment you may be so low, depressed, and scared to death to start a new career, worried about paying your bills or feeling the loss of time not spent with your kids when they are living with your ex-spouse.

CHAPTER FIVE

Getting Real with Self (Love)

By now, you can see that you are your own best listener, friend, guide, and inner warrior. Before diving into new relationships you have to learn to love yourself again. This chapter is about self-love lessons and principles for you to be aware of and use in your daily life. *The Wholeness Map* is all about bringing you back to self-love, to have true, deep, and connected love with yourself and in all relationships.

You can't be fully present on your journey to wholeness if you are living in the past with negative emotion. By using the beginning chapters of this book, you are able to lay the foundation for genuine healing and understand that the past is no longer serving you. In order to move forward, you have to embrace your self-love and fill your holes of pain, hurt, and abandonment with wholeness, gratitude, and love. In order to do this, you must change your story.

Humans have the incredible power to change their story at any time. For me, it's hugely empowering to know that I can recreate my story anytime. In the past, I was telling a story to myself that had pain, blame, anger, sadness and inauthenticity in it. I continued to give this story power over me and allowed it to hold me back from the many joys I desired in my life. I was a prisoner to my own creation. One of the biggest and brightest "Ah Ha" moments I had, came when I realized that all the mental energy I was using to continuously tell myself the old story, was the same amount of energy I would need to create a new story.

I didn't need my old story.

I was never broken.

Everything I needed to make the changes I wanted was already inside of me. All I simply needed to do was transfer my thoughts and actions towards creating my new story! When I made the decision to empower myself through detaching from my old story, my life changed dramatically and quickly.

Let's begin with a grounding exercise to tap into your gifts and gratitude. This sets us on the right path to changing our story. I have spoken of the power of gratitude and having a mindset of gratitude, so we are going to follow our talk and continue this practice because without gratitude we can't soak deeply into self-love.

Gratitude and Gifts Exercise:

The gratitude practice we are going to walk through is specifically a bedtime routine because it's normal that humans will only review a day or praise themselves when they have a positive day. But what about the other days? It's important to reframe the misfortunate and mundane days because they are opportunities to evaluate and really recall the valuable lessons and blessings that came from each one. Soaking into gratitude starts to release the urge to jump into self-sabotage and negativity the minute something does not happen the way you planned or envisioned. This type of practice heals and transforms your consciousness as it will show you the wholeness that lies within your heart and soul.

Some days will be easier than others. On those "other" days, you might have to search harder for the gifts that stem from your life lessons and find personal gratitude. If you are having one of those days because let's face it, we all have them, it is okay to keep things simple and be grateful for the fact that you have a roof over your head, your health, had a hot shower, had a nourishing dinner, and you're lying in a bed that is providing you a restful sleep. The small things are just as healing, and provide stability and growth on days that aren't so easy. And even sometimes the best gifts come from the ones we don't even recognize, so those hard days and simple gifts are just as valuable. Additionally, in the face of adversity, this simple practice of gifts and gratitude will allow you to count your patience, wisdom, and courage, alongside all the other gifts and lessons you experience.

Gratitude Practice

1. Choose a time of day that works best for you that you can consistently do this practice. All you need is a 5-10 minute time slot in your day for this. Consistency is the key here, so make sure it's a time you are usually free. Often, mornings, before meals, or at bedtime are good options.

2. Think about the last 24 hours of your day (or the amount of time since your previous practice). Remember all the things that happened and pick 2-3 that you are grateful for and why. Write them down in your journal, in your phone notes, or on a piece of paper. These can be anything, no matter if they are big or small, good or bad, etc. A few examples are:

    • *I'm grateful that I was cut off while driving because I had a chance to reflect on why I became emotional over it.*

    • *I'm grateful for my son/daughter getting a good grade on their homework because it made them happy.*

    • *I'm grateful for getting to bed on time because I wanted to stay up and watch a show but knew I needed to wake up early.*

There is no wrong answer with what you can be grateful for. Find the moments that stick out in your mind and think about why you are grateful for each one. Be as descriptive as possible. Say them out loud for an even bigger effect! Look for moments that are deeper than just simply positive experiences. My first example about being cut off while driving isn't really what most people call a positive experience, but I was able to go inward when it happened instead of just reacting. For me, and for you, that is always something to be grateful for!

As you get more experience with the exercise, you will get better and faster at reflecting on what you are grateful for. Even better than that, however, are the benefits you will get throughout your day, when you are not doing the exercise. As you think and write, daily, about what you are grateful for, you will become more aware of what is happening for you in life. I see life as happening *for* me every day instead of life happening *to* me. Embody that mindset as you cultivate it because it will accelerate the growth and abundance in your life. Celebrate when you find gratitude in what most people would call a negative situation. Cherish the moments when you become aware of your emotions and positive outlook. Establishing a daily gratitude practice will bring peace to your mind and eliminate unwanted stress in your body.

Self-Love Lesson One: Hello and Goodbye to Self-Sabotage

No matter how perfect or successful your life has been in the past, we've all gone through times where we get in our own way. Usually when you get in your own way there is something that has recently happened in your life that you didn't want and/or expect. This is life whether you like it or not!

Getting bottled up by negative emotions and existing with no vision or goals, is sabotaging yourself and your spirit. A life like this becomes a continual habit, and there is no interest in finding the joy, love or higher truth that you are meant for. When you stay in this energy, you live a reactive state, with more stress and less trust that there is a bigger plan for you. You may or may not live a spiritual life, that's not important for being your best self. That being said, no matter how religious or spiritual your beliefs are, for the sake of this book trust that there is a higher power. You can even think of your best self as that higher power if that works better for you. Embrace the spirit deep within you to shift your thoughts and say goodbye to self-sabotage now and any time in the future.

I remember when I was living in a reactive state, and I was forced to shift that energy because it was literally causing disease in my body. It literally took the Universe knocking me down by getting me continuously sick to get me to trust that there was a better way of living. For me, living in a reactive state and not seeing gratitude and abundance in everything continued to keep my body in the "fight or flight" state. I was raising a family of five young children, getting through a volatile divorce, and trying to rebuild my life. Self-sabotage seemed to be around every corner because I lived with too much fear of the unknown and very little trust in any higher power.

I used to self-sabotage myself when I would react to things my ex-spouse would do (or not do) that I didn't like or agree with. There were small things that I could have "let go" the need to control, but there were also big things that were so difficult not to have an emotional reaction to. For example, when the kids were younger and spent time in his home, he would get them to bed later, whereas I would get them in bed early at mine. If this would happen too often I would fall back into reactive and negative thought patterns towards his behavior. There was nothing I could do to change it! Yet I still let it affect my state and take me out of my positive mindset. The big things encompassed moments of lashing out towards me that seemed to hinder my parenting at the time. There was always that black cloud lingering over me that someone was trying harder to sabotage my parenting efforts than supporting and aligning our efforts together. I was self-sabotaging my ability to grow towards my goals and desires because something out of my control was getting to me.

Another area I see self-sabotage often is when I see someone looking for someone else to support them—either in the divorce process by getting more money—or in a new relationship. This is common in a lot of my female clients who have not worked in years because their job in the marriage was to raise kids. I absolutely think a spouse in this role should be compensated after the marriage is over, but think of it as a means to get by while you create an even better life. Many of you will need to rely on your ex-spouse for financial maintenance and child support because you chose as a couple that one of you would stay home to be the caretaker of your children. And that is okay. But, take an active part in being a contributor to your financial success. I don't think you will ever feel empowered sitting back and relying on him/her to provide your financial stability. That will never feel good. I think it is important to create a secondary income with a job or career path that fuels your soul, giving you more confidence and a sense of accomplishment. If you are looking for someone to take care of you financially you are sabotaging yourself by telling the Universe that you don't believe you can support yourself. The Universe will always hear exactly what you tell it!

Can you think of one instance recently where you've been pulled into a place of self-sabotage by something that happened to you or something someone said? Take a few moments and reflect on that to come up with something from your life.

Another common act of self-sabotage is not being able to forgive yourself for what has happened in the past. I've worked with many people who hold onto guilt or shame over their role in their divorce, even years after it's over. You must accept that forgiving yourself is an act of self-love that is completely necessary if you want abundance and happiness. Even if you screwed everything up, and weren't present in the marriage while it was falling apart, you must forgive yourself. Sit with, and truly feel, that guilt and shame in your body. This is how you acknowledge the emotions in order to put them behind you. You can either get over that guilt and shame now, or you can wait until you're old and dying because no matter what at some point you will face it.

Self-sabotage occurs most often when you are not being real with yourself. It's the result of your mind, body, and spirit not working congruently towards what you really want for yourself. I'll give you an example. Imagine you desire to create a second income stream for your family using social media and blogging. If you don't put time and effort into how to get a website, create exciting content, or learn about online marketing, you'll never actually get off the ground! If your thoughts are not in alignment with your actions, you will tread water in the same spot until eventually you tire out and your goal drowns.

The opposite of self-sabotage is being able to step into the space of growth through taking action. You reap all the rewards I'm talking about when you take more action in what you think and do each day you wake up. When you take action on your positive thoughts, and trust your intuition that it's the right action to take, you're setting an example for yourself and for your children. The more you can provide a toxin-free and loving environment and positive energy for your children, the more they will be able to follow along with the self-love lessons, consciously or unconsciously. This helps them heal their spirit and soul as well. It's a gift for all.

Self-Love Lesson Two: Awareness is Your Roadmap

Awareness is the number one key to every shift, evolution, healing, and transformation that you desire. Awareness is your ability to recognize where you're currently at and work from there without judgment or ego. The opposite of awareness is ignorance, which will cripple you during divorce if not addressed. In order for any real change and healing to happen, you must first develop awareness of how you feel, react, engage, and cope with all that you do. Awareness is seeing where you are in your journey and accepting it. If you can tell yourself, *I'm in a volatile situation with my divorce and I will remain calm, grounded, and positive no matter how much fear I have,* you will fortify the strength of your awareness every day.

The second part of awareness is being aware of where you want to go and what you want to achieve in your life. I was extremely aware that I wanted to create happiness within my home, so I would always have fresh flowers in my kitchen. I could feel the positive energy from a bright and colorful kitchen and that fortified my awareness of the future I was creating. After my divorce, when I was dealing with a lot of fear, I used to buy flowers every week for my kitchen table where I had dinner with my family. Doing this helped me remain aware of how I wanted my state to be—calm and collected no matter what was going on around me.

Awareness is noticing when your job is causing stress.

Awareness is being tuned in to how your body feels.

Awareness is asking yourself: *Where am I at today? How do I feel? What is on my mind?*

Awareness is a skill that can be developed and strengthened.

In divorce, you need to operate from a high level of self-awareness at all times. I often see people get stuck in a victim state of mind because they are unaware of how they react to tension, unaware of what energy they are putting off, and unaware of how they are feeling each day. Your awareness of your day to day feelings is usually the hardest to cope with AND the most important to develop. If you can understand how you are feeling each day, you can begin to make progress on the underlying cause of those emotions. That will lead you towards dealing with your true emotions much quicker than being a victim and not accepting reality the way it is.

In order to develop true self-love, you must be aware. Self-love isn't an accident, it's a practice. If you are a basketball player you want to be aware of your strengths and weaknesses without any ego so that you can develop your skill set. That is how you become the most complete player possible! In divorce, I want you to become the most complete version of yourself. The more aware you can become towards your weaknesses, the faster you can work on improving them.

EXPECTATIONS

Expectations are complex, often invisible to the naked eye, desires that do not serve us. Unfortunately, we all have them. Expectations are like a poison that has no odor, color, taste, or feel. I want them to sound scary! If you want to fear anything in life, fear your own expectations. Expectations infect every area of our daily life. They can creep in without you even noticing and throw you completely out of whack. Before we move any further, I want you to do a quick check-in. Ask yourself right now "How do I define expectations? Do I have any expectations?" Let's see what your own opinion and analysis is before we talk about expectations.

First, I want to give you a different view of expectations. In business, expectations are everywhere and they are completely necessary. You need expectations in business or the free market economy would fall apart. But...we have a different name for expectations in business and how they are set. In business, expectations are contracts. Think about that for a moment.

Corporations use contracts in order to ensure that certain deadlines, scope of work, and costs are agreed-upon beforehand. If it were not for contracts, there would be no accountability between business partners. They are completely necessary and foundational to our economy.

In life, however, expectations mostly lead to pain and disappointment. Expectations that you place on others, or that others place on you, have no contractual obligation in real life. I'm not talking about business anymore. I'm talking about what can happen if you expect someone in your life to do a certain thing or act a certain way. When you place an expectation on someone else you set yourself up for fear-based reactions and emotions. Expectations pull you away from center. They take you out of a positive mindset and thrust you into fear or confusion.

"How could he/she not do that for me?"

"How could they do that to me?"

"Why would they say that about me?"

All these questions, and many more, that we ask ourselves in times of pain stem from unmet expectations.

It's of paramount importance that you rid yourself of expectations during divorce. In my divorce there was a moment when I finally gave up on my expectations and focused all my energy on what I desired, and what I could control. I was in a toxic divorce and there were many times that I would spiral emotionally out of control because I wasn't aware of my expectations.

As I started to gain higher awareness in my daily life, I was able to pinpoint my expectations and deal with them before they had a chance to not be met.

Early on in the divorce process, I would often place expectations on what I would get and what my ex-spouse would get. Of course, many of my expectations were not met and that was inhibiting my ability to stay positive and focused. The moment when I realized my expectations were damaging to my healing, I become focused on rooting them out. I became better at dealing with unmet expectations instead of dwelling on them.

Children often have no expectations other than having their basic needs met. They make assumptions more than set expectations because they don't know any better. You want to help your children set healthy and positive expectations during and after divorce. This is especially important when stepping into the post-divorce stage because of the expectations that children might have with living between two homes. Set expectations for your children that one parent–you–may see tremendous growth with your career, finances, spirituality, and life because you have painted a beautiful canvas of intentions, goals and a vision for your life. Their vision and goals help diminish their fear, even if the other parent is stuck in fear.

The parent that is living from a deep place of fear has not opened to the awareness and vision to see what fear is doing to their life. Set an example for your children by eliminating the expectations you place on your ex-spouse. It's essential to prepare the children for what to expect with how each individual grows and evolves differently and at different rates, physically, emotionally, and spiritually. If you react and become angry when your ex doesn't meet an expectation, you are not setting the right example for your children.

Children tend to have fear for the parent that isn't doing as well as the other parent. They may gravitate towards wanting to take care of that parent. This is a time to honor the feelings your child has but tell them to picture what their parent's life could look like in his or her best state of living and the endless opportunities they could create. Encourage them to visualize and see the space they desire for their parent to step into. Encourage your children to envision, with intention and positive thoughts, both parents living beautiful, happy lives.

Your awareness of what you expect of others is the key to growth in your post-divorce life. Trust that your intentions are being communicated outward through your positive energy. That is how you let go of expectation. You must learn to trust in yourself. Whether you believe in the Universe, a God, or anything, you must have trust that everything will work out. It can be that simple. It is that simple.

You are responsible for yourself and must trust in your soul, picture what you want, and always have the internal compass and trust in the Universe that you will get there. A big part of my post-divorce life has been achieving and celebrating small wins. The truth of the matter is, the small wins didn't seem that significant at the time, but now, looking back on the last ten years, I see that my big "wins" happened as a result of allowing smaller achievements to "snowball" together.

One thing I hear a lot through my coaching clients is, "I thought that my divorce would be the thing that finally made me happy." But a big, life-changing event like divorce or a break-up isn't always going to bring immediate happiness or a carefree life. For me, it brought a lot of stress, pain, and fear over the first few years. I stressed about money and if I could make enough to support myself and my kids. I stressed about where I would live and how I could make up the money I lost when we split marital assets. I stressed about how my social life would change.

The things that can lead to stress after a divorce or life-changing event are usually hidden until they are standing right in front of you. I wanted my post-divorce life to be full of success and happiness! Who wouldn't? When you are in a bad situation in life, the grass is always greener on the other side.

I set out to make small changes and let them compound over time. I bought a house and started to fix it up. I read books about intention, the Law of Attraction, and how to focus on what matters to me. Even something as small as reading a new book is a win! The small changes lead to bigger changes.

I would have thought it impossible for me to go through a significant life event like my divorce then turn around and achieve all these things I wanted to achieve. It took time, and it took healing. Divorce, along with other major life events, can bring a massive amount of happiness into your life, but it's not the event itself that will be the catalyst—it's all the things that you do AFTER the event that will make a world of difference.

Awareness Exercise:

This is an easy three-step exercise that you will do whenever you feel like you have an expectation of a certain outcome. This exercise will train you to operate in your daily life independent of any and all outcomes! Use this as often as possible to increase your level of awareness.

1. Write down exactly what you expect, who is involved in this expectation, and why you expect this. For example "I expect my ex to share the costs of our son's football pads with me. I expect this because he is always helping our son with football and he wants him to play football. The costs are not too expensive. It's fair that we split these costs."

2. Now, write what you feel if this expectation is not met. Why do you feel this way? For example "I will feel angry

because it's only fair that we share unexpected costs like this!" or "I'll feel confused because I thought my ex would be totally fine sharing this cost!"

3. Finally, write down the possible solutions, in detail, to this expectation not being met that only you can control. For example, "I can pay for the full cost of the equipment and my son will get to play football. He will be so happy that he gets to play football!" or "He will not be able to play football and that will hurt him. All his friends play football and he loves the sport."

The goal of this exercise is to understand and accept only the outcome of things that you can control. The more thinking you can do like this, the more awareness and control you will have over your thoughts and actions.

Self-Love Lesson Three: Leave Judgment at the Door

Judgment exists with a low level of awareness. Most often, judgment of others stems from something we want to change about ourselves. The first two self-love lessons we talked about in this chapter are crucial for now understanding judgment. If you can spot self-sabotaging behavior in yourself and others, you will not need judgment. If you become aware of expectations and your actions, your ability to let go of judgment can happen rather quickly. And I repeat, letting go is a practice! That means the more judgment you become aware of now, the more judgment you can let go of, faster, down the road. Judgment is bad for communication during your divorce. Judgment of other relationships will infect your mind and create more negative relationships for yourself. When you judge others, your children will see this and absorb that energy from you.

I used to judge women who would serial date after their divorce because I didn't agree with it. It would bother me and stay on my mind far longer than it ever needed to. Why was that? It was because I saw serial dating without taking time for yourself after a divorce as wrong or not the right thing to do. I had the expectation that everyone needed time to heal. In reality, that's what I needed. That's what I knew was best for me.

My judgment of serial daters only worked to inhibit my ability to heal myself from my pain. Instead of staying grounded and focused on my positive energy and vision I was thinking about how other people date! As I learned to accept their actions as their own choices instead of "not how I would do things" I felt a lightness to my energy. It felt really good for me to be able to see that need for judgment dissipate for the first time. I realized that my ego was using judgment to protect me from "bad" ideas by judging others who made those choices.

There is certainly not one way to do things, including healing from a divorce. As I realized and embodied the energy that the Universe would take care of me no matter what, I also realized the Universe would take care of others too. That change in mindset helped me commit more fully to putting out the most positive and intentional energy. Today, I always make the effort to center myself if judgment arises. Leaving judgment behind allows me the internal energy needed to cultivate compassion for others.

If you look back on where you were a year out of divorce, two years out, five years out, there is a pretty good chance you will see continual self-growth. You'll look back say, "I have come a long way!". You are going to have judgment come up, in all shapes and sizes, even in ten years when you have a whole new life compared to now! That's okay. The growth that you have seen does not eliminate your ego, but rather it increases your awareness and control of it!

You'll be surrounded by friends and peers that are going to be ahead of you in your journey or might be slower on the journey to healing. Some people will have deeper scars financially or emotionally, depend on child support, and/or have career obstacles; which can put them in a deeper place of fear than others. Divorce can land people upside down, and how each person deals with their situation is a learning experience in itself. The one thing I tell myself is that we are all doing the best that we can do with the tools that we have.

A big part of the self-love healing process and lesson of judgment is to learn how to find your groove and happiness in being alone. There is a big difference in being alone and being lonely. I know it's uncommon to want to be alone and live a life of loneliness, but we do need to find peace and comfort in 'alone' energy. If you are okay with being alone with yourself, even if there is discomfort, you are on a beautiful path to wholeness.

Judgment Exercise:

Take out your journal again and use this exercise when you feel judgment come up. If you have the opportunity to write when the moment comes up, please do so. If not, you can practice mindfulness and ask yourself these questions quietly in your mind, to reflect. The biggest lesson to learn about judgment is the art of reflection and getting in touch with your inner self.

When you feel that you have judged someone or you have the feeling that judgment is coming up for you, reflect on these questions:

What triggered you within to want to judge someone else?
What are you not owning or not seeing within yourself?
What are you projecting onto others, that you wish you desired?

Self-Love Lesson Four:
House of Cards

I see so many people step out of a divorce and into this illusion of a "house of cards," which I define as "living in a false image and persona."

A house of cards is creating an image of how you want people to see you from the outside world, looking in. To truly step into self-love and awareness, it takes living genuinely and authentically. A house of cards supersedes almost all other feelings and emotions. A house of cards focus is on what others think and how you can compare yourself to others. If you don't know by now, this is not going to be a healthy way to move forward in life for your mind, body, and spirit. A house of cards is an image that can change in a minute, and if you literally picture a house of cards, then you see it can be blown down easily. It's not the type of house you want to be building in the long term.

What I desire for you to create is a house made of bricks. A house of bricks is a sturdy foundation that takes, love, care, and attention to heart. It's a house that is built from the inside out. This is a metaphor that I know you can relate to. If you are working on controlling your emotions, building self-love, and listening to your voice of intuition, than you're going to communicate to the world and the Universe that you are building a house of bricks.

We are all guilty of trying to create happiness from the outside looking in, such as buying a new car, building a big house, and accumulating unnecessary jewelry, clothes, you name it. Once the thrill of buying the new shiny object wears off, sadness, self-sabotage, anxiety, etc. comes back and it's not translated well in your body, nor with your children.

There are going to be disappointments in life, there are going to be setbacks, and challenges. Be aware of all of these with your emotions and thoughts. It will help you move forward with the strength of a house of bricks. Be in the now, embrace life, good or bad—that's living real.

Your children are going to experience the same, but we can't sweep in and save them from all the stresses and anxieties of their lives. So life's challenges are opportunities for both you and your children to grow. I used to say to my kids, *sometimes it isn't always pretty, there are going to be problems, but you know what we're going to do…we're going to live real, not brush them under the rug, and we're going to learn from them.*

I told them in all moments of life, big or little, good or bad, there are opportunities for us to find a gift from the situation. In the long run, you'll be living a great life of realness, and you'll be paying it forward for the next generation.

QUICK TIPS ON HOUSE OF CARDS:

1. **Emotional House of Cards** - Feeling the emotions of a falsified exterior world and not living in connection to how you really feel. For example, it felt like I was an actress in my own movie. I wasn't happy in my marriage early on, and especially the time leading up to the divorce, so I got caught up in creating a fake image, and matched that in my emotions. Often times, some of us stay in our marriages even though we are unhappy. This creates a false image to the outside world with the intent that if it looks good enough to the outside world, then it might begin to feel good on the inside. This is a classic example of not being connected to your emotions and letting your "image" beat out your happiness.

2. **Physical House of Cards** - Living a life outside of your means and "keeping up with the Joneses" type of energy and standard of living. This is relevant after a divorce when you feel you still have to create the perfect image and act as if everything is okay. Living in the right neighborhood, driving the right cars, and living in a beautiful house with a white picket fence is like your "costume." It's getting caught up in the way things look, rather than portraying a life of real happiness and living parallel with what is inside of your means.

The process of allowing a house of cards to fall apart and turning it into a house of bricks comes from doing these exercises. It comes from living more authentically, and in order to do that you must take a close look at yourself in the mirror. If you live in a house of cards, you will not be able to move forward because your love for yourself is not the most important thing in your life. You will care too much about what other people think of you.

The hardest part for me was finally dealing with the image I had created. When I finally accepted that I needed a divorce, my house of cards was blown over. And it was incredibly liberating. Before I let go of my need to hold onto a past family image, I felt no freedom. I had created a prison for myself to live in. My growth path completely changed when I accepted my situation and began to build my house out of bricks.

Everything from there on out had to have substance and had to be real. I was real with my kids, real with my ex, and real with myself.

My new house of bricks started with me owning where I was at in life. I knew that a house of bricks was what my kids needed from me. In building that house of bricks from within, I was able to be real with myself first, and let others see that from the outside. I built a bright, loving home on the inside and eventually that brightness started to shine outside.

I want to share my process for identifying and removing the masks that I was wearing (and at times still do). This is an exercise you do in your journal, when you have a few moments of quiet. I like to start my day with my journal and what thoughts I want to hold in my mind for that day. I suggest you add this exercise into your repertoire. This will help you build your house of bricks in a shorter period of time. We all wear masks. There is no one person who hasn't projected some false or inauthentic image to the world at some point in their lives. The important question is not "*Do you wear masks?*" but rather *can you remove the masks you wear?*

Removing Your Mask Exercise:

1. *Think about where you are in your life right now. Without any judgment, identify a mask you have worn lately, to the outside world. What have you projected to people (family, friends, or strangers) about yourself or your life? Write this down and say it out loud to yourself.* For me, during my

separation period with my husband I was consumed with running. I was running miles and miles every single day. I was running because I was consumed with how I needed to make my physical body look a certain way and it was the only way I knew how to manage my stress. I wore a mask that portrayed my physique being my identity, and that I am always in great shape. I know this is a mask because, even though I enjoyed running, I was running to escape my deepest scars and emotions. I also needed to look a certain way to fit into the image of how my life was supposed to look.

2. *Next, identify what this mask was offering you?* In my example, my mask was validating myself only when I looked a certain way. I felt I had to always run, even when it was potentially harming my body from exhaustion, because I needed to be validated by my social circle. This mask was offering an image of feeling and looking great, and being in shape even though on the inside I needed to deal with a deeper path to self-love.

3. *What does your life look like if you remove this mask? What would happen if people saw you without your mask?* For many people the simple act of getting a divorce is one of the biggest masks they can remove! I used to protect my family's image to neighbors and friends. But once everyone knew my spouse and I were getting a divorce, they knew that I didn't have the perfect family household. With my excessive running, when I started focusing on internal healing like meditation and new exercise, I felt a sense of calm because I was finally addressing the deeper issues of what I was running from.

4. *Lastly, what is one or two positive outcomes of removing this mask?* When I removed my mask of needing to have a perfectly in shape physical body, I started setting a better

example for my young girls at the time. They no longer had to see me worrying about how I looked externally, and instead I showed them the importance of actually feeling great from within. I have focused my energy on letting beauty begin internally which always transcends externally, and that has been absorbed by my girls who are now young women. If you are wearing the mask of having a perfect marriage, one benefit of removing that mask is that you can actually begin to work on the important things like finances and building a house of bricks. There are many benefits to removing these masks and opening yourself up to vulnerability.

Self-Love Lesson Five: Release Your Masks

There are stories that you create in your mind that take over your insecurities. Over time we begin to develop masks to hide from those insecurities. The masks are disguises or facades that we all wear!

Our masks keep us in a weakened state, by not allowing ourselves to grow and build an authentic lifestyle. The masks that people carry with them are similar to living a lifestyle like the house of cards. When you are able to see that you are living a house of cards, it becomes easier to look at your masks in the areas of wealth, finances, relationships, career, etc. and then remove them. It's important to do so because without masks hiding who you really are, you can take leaps towards your dream life.

These disguises are built out of childhood insecurities, or trauma that you've experienced over a period of time in your life. You may only now, post-divorce, begin to recognize them but they have been with you for quite some time. These insecurities can run very deep in your psyche, and that makes your brain want to hide them from the outside world as much as possible! It's very scary allowing people to see who you really are, so masks offer some protection from that. However, over time it will feel like you are so far disconnected from your heart, your center, and true self.

Before and during my divorce I had many feelings of *"I am not good enough," I am not smart enough," "I am not pretty enough," "I am not skinny enough," "I am not deserving enough."* I was running from self-love because I had such intense emotions and masking the things I needed to work out seemed like my only option much of the time.

For me, I was over exercising and focusing on my external appearance because I felt that I was not worthy of being loved unless I looked a certain way. I think this is a common trap that women fall into. I see a lot of people mask their true financial situation. This is a common mask and it shows when people buy expensive cars but struggle to save money. People will buy toys they do not even care much about in order to mask what their life looks like.

It's not the easiest thing to do - look your insecurities, masks, disguises, or whatever you want to call them, in the face. On your journey to self-love this is a crucial stage you're going to have to work through. In the end, to make things simple, all the masks and insecurities are your ego's natural defense system. Your ego loves to live in your mind and fill you with masks that only appear to serve you.

When we wear masks, we find ourselves searching for love and acceptance by means of "validation," "validation," "validation" from others.

Vulnerability is a real gift that you can share with yourself, no matter what stage of divorce you're in, where you are at in life, or what life events you've experienced up to this point. Remove your masks because only then can you move into your inner sacred world. Only when you remove a mask(s) can you can ultimately build a true connection with yourself and others. A true connection with yourself must begin with being honest and vulnerable about where you are in the present moment.

QUICK DEEP DIVE INTO OUR MASKS

- Possessions Mask: Placing material possessions above anything else, always seeking and desiring the next shiny, luxury thing.

- Emotional Mask: Repressing emotions such as insecurities, health, the fear of money; having the lack of connection to our feelings and emotions.

- Intimacy Mask: Not expressing an intimate emotional connection with someone; afraid to be vulnerable and connect.

- Physical Mask: Thinking your self-worth and self-love depend on the look of your physical body; obsessing about exercise, your weight and how you look.

- Career Mask: Hiding the strength, focus, and drive for career advancement. Afraid to fail so why try.

- Know-it-All Mask: The person that feels they know everything and has all the answers, lacks the ability to say "I don't know…"

- Victim Mask: Holding onto pain and always feel and portray "poor me."

Self-Love Lesson Six: Create a Tribe

Creating and cultivating a tribe that can grow with you over the changes that are happening in your life is the most soulful feeling. This is what I want for you. One of the greatest gifts in the world that came from my divorce is the power of like-minded friendships. This time allows you to see who your real friends are and who is someone that may not be right for your tribe.

I remember friendship was an unexpected challenge for me when I first went through the separation in my marriage and then my post-divorce. Working through this challenge allowed me to open my eyes and see that a handful of true friends is better than 100 acquaintances. It was not easy for me to experience the loss of some friendships that were tied to my ex and/or my marriage but it was completely necessary. As I look back on that time in my life, I see that there was a subtle change happening in my social circle that gave me the boost and support I needed to get through my divorce. I was creating a tribe of people that, through our shared experiences in life and love, could understand and relate to me without judgment.

Remember when I said earlier in the book, you will come to understand who your true and genuine friends are during tough times - well it's true. In reality, you're going to find that you may only have a handful of true friends...and I want you to be completely okay with that potential reality! Honestly, you may discover that you only have one or two, and that is no different than 10 or 20.

I like to say, "your vibe creates your tribe." and going forward, that's the mindset you'll learn to cultivate. It's okay your friends who you thought were friends, don't turn out to be friends. Your new vibe is going to give off an energy that the right people will be attracted too. That is how you want to build your tribe! It all starts within you and that's a universal message throughout this book that even resonates with your social circle. If you have never had a friend before, in your entire life, it wouldn't matter going forward. Your past is not your future, and you past relationships have no effect on the relationships you'll be forming. The only thing that plays a major role in creating your tribe is the energy that you house inside your mind and body.

It's so important to surround yourself with like-minded friends that share the same energy, ambition, strength, and goals. The best way to find these types of people is to, slowly, become that type of person yourself. Low energy people will attract low energy friends who are not on the same trajectory as you. In your post-divorce life, you will have highs and lows that can affect your state or energy. The key is to come back to the exercises we've gone over in order to reinforce the desires, goals, intentions and dreams you have for yourself. Doing that on a consistent basis will put out an energy or vibe that will attract people who care about the same things!

Let's stop for a moment and take inventory and see what your tribe looks like. These are people who you want to invite, welcome, and manifest to come into your life. You can either do this with your journal, or you can reflect in your mind.

Create Your Tribe Exercise:

Take a moment and think about the friends and people that immediately surround you and also the people that you feel would be categorized as acquaintances. This is your opportunity to remove low-energy, toxic-energy people, as well as people who don't support you, perhaps judge you behind your back, and/or don't reciprocate the love and support you desire.

Ask yourself these questions as a starting place and then begin to chart low-energy friends on one side and beautiful people on the other.

- *Are you being left out of parties?*

- *Are people curious about your single life and creating drama about how hard it is?*

- *Have you been consciously left out of the "inner circle?"*

- *Do friends invite you out for coffee or tea dates just to genuinely see how you are?*

- *Are the friends around you wanting to hear more about drama than real life?*

- *Do they create gossip with others about your story?*

- *Are people spreading stories or rumors about you behind your back?*

- *Can you trust your friends?*

- *Do you feel you're being judged?*

- *Do you feel people are questioning your decisions and judging how you live life now?*

Unsupportive Friends	Beautiful Friends & People

**If you find you don't have a lot of people on the beautiful friends' side, use the space to write your manifestations and desires for certain qualities you are looking for in a friend.*

Divorce drums up all different kinds of feelings and emotions in people. It's impossible to predict what will happen AND who will be by your side to support you through it. You need to own the energy that you are putting out into the Universe. Without this ownership, you will bounce around between friendships and struggle to cultivate the meaningful tribe of friends that you'll need. Your vibe is the only thing you can control! You can eliminate complaining, obsessing over the same topic, trash talking other people, or any low-energy behavior of your own by paying attention to positive things in your life. Complaining is the most common form of negative energy and many times we don't even realize we are doing it.

Have you ever been around someone who complains as a form of conversation, even when the conversation feels positive? Do you notice when someone brings up negative topics instead of positive ones? I believe we all have dealt with, or been friends with, people like this. Let's call them energy vampires. The easy way to quickly determine if a friend is a good fit for you anymore is if you always feel drained or exhausted after spending time with them. This is one example of an energy vampire. People are not born as energy vampires, they are developed. You may have had a time in your life when you were an energy vampire! It's part of being human.

I want you to remember that energy vampires can change, and grow, to become part of your tribe down the road. If someone isn't building off your positive energy now, cut them loose. Make sure you acknowledge, however, that at a later date they may have grown and transformed their vibe as well. At that point, they could be a positive addition to your tribe. Your tribe of warriors can look different in different parts of your life. Your circle of friends ebbs and flows but your tribe of warriors will have one thing in common, they all support each other equally and add to the vibe of your tribe. That's how you allow your tribe to organically fill up with amazing people who are meant to be in your life.

When I was redefining my tribe of warriors and inviting relationships into my life, I always saw the same vision. The vision was my best friends and I celebrating over a beautiful home-cooked meal, and a few bottles of wine on the table. I focused on the collective vibe at the table and how it felt to be a part of that tribe. I have different tribes of friends and my friendships have grown in abundance these past 10 years. I have learned how to be a loyal and supportive friend in return for these gifts of friendships.

I still use this exercise today because I believe that it also helps my tribe stay together! I love visualizing and feeling all the good energy that comes from being with real friends who have your back. That's the tribe you will create!

You want to keep in mind that very close friends, as well as family members, are trying to create appropriate boundaries and support to both you and your ex as individuals. Family might even be too close to your situation and be conflicted about the relationship as they used to know it. Meaning, they might not be sure how to be supportive with both you and your ex "separately" anymore, so they distance themselves from both of you entirely. Or they might have a strong opinion or judge the way you are navigating your post-divorce. Create the space with loved ones that need more time to process your divorce and can give you what you need, not what they need. I found that reaching out to people who had been through a divorce, or a significant loss, to be some of the best resources for finding meaningful friends. My tribe was equally made up of married friends and divorced friends.

If this vision helps you as well, please use it and replace the details with what helps you most. Make it as beautiful, powerful, soulful, and as energetic as you desire. Your tribe is holding the space for you to succeed and be happy, just as you are for them. A truly supportive tribe carries energies of love, encouragement, courage, strength, perseverance, patience, and kindness. Be open-minded when visualizing your tribe.

HERE ARE A FEW IDEAS ON BUILDING YOUR TRIBE OF WARRIORS:

1. **Lean on Family:** If you have a close family member or members, lean on them for support. Our families can offer unconditional love and support, especially in times of pain and hurt. You may even have a family member who went through a divorce and can provide the most significant support to you because they have been in your shoes. Family members are great to lean on especially in the beginning when you might need help and support with childcare and making it through this transitional period. Family can also help advise you on future roles that you're taking on from your ex-spouse, like finances and investments, and all the other responsibilities of what use to be a two-person household. Don't be afraid to ask for help if someone in your family knows about this area and can help you. If your family doesn't live nearby, embrace interconnectivity and technology, which makes communication much easier these days. There are so many apps such as FaceTime, and video calling platforms that can connect you with family at the click of a button.

2. **Take Comfort in Old Friends:** When life goes upside down, taking comfort in your old friends that understand you, know how to comfort you, and most importantly help you realize that not all is lost, is so important. Your old friends knew you before getting married and can, therefore, give you appropriate advice to suit your personality and your situation.

    I remember taking comfort in my old friends who helped me remember who I was before I was married. Sometimes we lose ourselves along the way, in our roles as spouse and parent. Getting together with old friends can be a reminder of who you are. Getting together with old friends made me laugh again and remember the person that I was and that I still had within me. They helped reawaken my true self. I think being with old friends can help you find your way back to you again, especially if you are feeling lost and alone.

3. **Embrace New Friends:** Meeting new friends through current friends, or colleagues that you work with and haven't hung out with before are great ways to find a support network. New friendships inject positive changes in your life, and it's something exciting to look forward too.

    I often looked for other divorced women to build relationships with; divorcees want to find other divorcees for the same reasons. Everybody wants to build a support team, so put yourself out there. You may find yourself with better friendships now than what you were able to have during your marriage.

    Many of us lose ourselves in a marriage because our lives are consumed with carpooling, cooking, shopping, taking care of our spouses, and more, that we often leave behind the need for nurturing intimate friendships. You likely focused on friendships with other couples during your marriage, and the dynamic of those relationships might have now changed.

I loved meeting other divorced women and men and creating friendships to have somebody to go grab a drink with, have a wine night with girlfriends, take an adventure into the city for dinner, take bike rides on a beautiful afternoon by the lake, etc. Enjoy this time and embrace new friends that are around you waiting to be your friend!

4. **Discover External Sources:** Joining a divorce support group, religious group or online community are all great ways as well to find a community of support. In addition to making new friends, you can seek out support groups for people going through a divorce in your local area. Hearing other people's experiences will bring you comfort and let you know and feel that you're not alone in this journey. Outside sources create an environment that family and friends may not be able to provide for you. It is also lovely to receive an objective opinion from people who don't know your spouse or weren't involved with you as a couple.

5. **Find Fitness Pals:** Another great way to meet single friends is by doing something healthy for your mind and body. Whether your jam is weight and strength training at a club, cardio, yoga, barre, tai chi, CrossFit, or competitive sports, what better way to connect than having a common thread for health and wellness? You release amazing hormones while you exercise, which makes you feel good and happy. You always feel so much better when you're able to exercise with somebody who enjoys it as much as you do. This is also a great way to show support to someone when the exercise is physically and mentally challenging–sharing in the joy of getting a personal record or running a half a mile more than usual is expansion and growth for both of you. This shapes and grooms you to be stronger individuals on your own path and journey.

Self-Love Lesson Seven:
Energy & Chakras

We just went over how your vibe plays a key role in the tribe of people in your life. In this section, we will discuss how energetic alignment and chakras can transform the vibe you put out to the Universe. I am going to use chakras in this section because chakras are a way to represent different parts of your body. This separation will help you in looking at what parts of you need the most attention in your self-love practice. I'm more interested in teaching you how to go inward and find where your weak points are than I am in getting you to believe in chakras. I love the meaning of chakras, and they've helped me through my divorce and more, but you don't need to hold that same belief. The most important thing is learning how to use the ideas behind chakras as a tool for coming out of your divorce and building a beautiful life for your family.

Alignment within your mind and body creates a very strong vibe (and misalignment, a weak vibe). If you are not aligned in what you say, think, and do, you will struggle to find traction in making changes in your life. In your body, you need to also have that same alignment to steer your energy down the path you want to go. In order to have alignment in your body and mind, you need to be consistent and check in with yourself. You need to find out what needs attention and what you already have synced up with your intentions. The different parts of your body are fully interconnected, more so than most people think. In order to create the most positive change for yourself, you need to make sure you have the best alignment within yourself.

ENERGETIC PROTECTION VISUALIZATION:
Set your energetic protection intention by calling upon your highest self to create a beautiful invisible protection of bright white light around you, from head to toe. Visualize the invisible shield being a

gatekeeper of sorts, the gatekeeper to your energy. You can see this as a person, object, or thing–you may name the gatekeeper person, object, or thing if you desire. The exact vision of how you see your gatekeeper is up to you, kind of like the ego that sits on your shoulder. There is no right or wrong here, just create a visual that you can come back to quickly and that you resonate with. Then you can call upon your gatekeeper anytime you need them to close your energy off to prevent leaking and/or to protect your own energy. You can say:

"Thank you for closing my gate right now (insert name, if applicable)."

For me, I visualize the white light surrounding me and protecting my energy. I call upon this visualization when I need to protect my energy.

Setting the intention and asking for help to protect your energy can change and shift your energy in an instant. This is helping you create loving boundaries for yourself and your energy.

Chakras

You may or may not have heard of chakras before. When I think about my energy, I am using chakras as a tool to find out as much about my energy as I can. They are considered our "body energy centers." Chakra is a Sanskrit word for wheel, also referred to as the natural energy system in the body. You'll often see chakras represented as circles for this reason. There are seven energy centers, or chakras, in the body, and when your energy is carrying love, positivity, and goodness, your energy flows smoothly and freely through those seven areas. However, when energy is blocked or trapped in one area, it can lead to illness, pain, discomfort, mood shifts, and more. Again, whether or not chakras are your thing is not important. What is important is to understand that your energy can get "stuck" in different areas of your body. You may feel great and powerful in one area but completely lacking in another. There are ways to fix all these issues!

That's why we are talking about chakras.

Understanding the basics of your chakras and how to stay in balance and release those blocks will help you to stay in a more connected state of being, and with a much higher vibe.

CHAKRA ONE: ROOT OR BASE CHAKRA

Located at the base of the spine.

It's your foundation and represents your internal life-force, natural instinct, being centered and grounded, self-protection, and courage.

When this is out of balance, you can feel not centered, have heightened anxiety, feel fearful about family, money, career or independence; experience back problems; and feel constipated.

CHAKRA TWO: SACRAL CHAKRA

Located at your lower abdomen.

This represents your physical power, emotions, sexuality,

When this is out of balance, you can feel a loss of appetite, low sexual desire or libido, loss or purpose, and perhaps painful sex and blocks around pleasure.

CHAKRA THREE: SOLAR PLEXUS CHAKRA

Located at your upper abdomen, near the navel area.

This is where your intuition is located. It's also where you tap into your authority, confidence, drive, self-worth, digestion, and achievement of goals.

When this is out of balance, you have a lack of self-esteem and will, you can feel fearful, unable to trust your intuition, and have liver or stomach problems.

CHAKRA FOUR: HEART CHAKRA

Located at the center of your chest.

This represents your personal power, emotions, your positivity, happiness, love, and the ability to feel your emotions and to be loved.

When this is out of balance, it causes emotional instability, and you repress the feelings of happiness, joy, love, and inner peace.

CHAKRA FIVE: THROAT CHAKRA

Located at your throat.

This represents your ability to use your voice, express yourself, and communicate clearly.

When this is out of balance, you can feel shy, inexpressive, depressed, and have throat infections, get sick, have coughs or colds that prevent you from speaking.

CHAKRA SIX: THIRD EYE CHAKRA

Located at the middle of the forehead.

This represents your insight, intelligence, wisdom, and your ability to focus.

When this is out of balance, you may feel cynical; have a lack of focus; headaches and eye problems; lack creativity and imagination, and the ability to make wise decisions.

CHAKRA SEVEN: CROWN CHAKRA

Located at the crown (very top) of the head.

This represents the connection to heaven and your highest spiritual self (oneness).

When this is out of balance, you can feel a lack of inspiration and disconnected from God, the Universe, Spirit, your higher power, and self.

Be mindful of your blocked chakras, as the unaddressed energy can navigate its way into other areas of your life. Using all the tools you just learned in this chapter can help you stay in balance and above all take care of your physical body. Your physical body is what is here with you and what you have the power to nourish and cleanse. Love yourself and honor the energy that needs to be removed.

CHAKRA CLEANSING RITUAL:

1. Sit in a comfortable sacred space with no distractions. Begin to focus on your breathing and center yourself into your body.

2. Say to yourself, quietly in your mind, three statements:

    "My body is not everything I am."

    "My emotions are not everything I am."

    "My thoughts are not everything I am."

3. Once you are grounded into your own energy, place your left hand on your heart chakra and your right hand on your solar plexus chakra (navel, power center). Feel the warmth of energy start to flow through your hands, into your body.

4. Visualize yourself in your protective energetic bubble of beautiful white light. Visualize a bright, golden sun showering its light on you from above and ever flowing around your body. Feel its warmth and love flow in and out of your hands, and then begin to work its way through your seven chakras, starting with your root chakra.

5. As the light moves through your chakras, quietly in your mind, say to yourself, "I release in 100 percent love and light, what no longer serves me."

6. Continue to visualize this golden light, making its way up your body, through each chakra, reaching the crown of your head, to form a beautiful bright pillar of strong light.

7. Say one last time, as you see the bubble of white light and strong pillar of light through your body, "I release in 100 percent love and light, what no longer serves me."

8. Immerse yourself in the calm, peaceful energy of your cleansed and balanced chakras and when you are ready, no rush here, open your eyes, leaving your left hand on your heart and say, "Thank you, I love you."

Call upon your higher self, God, the Universe, or Spirit or whatever higher power you believe in, to help you protect your energy and release negative energy when you feel it. You'll be tapping into more of your chakras and energy as you make your way through the rest of the book.

The Wholeness Journey

The main goal I want you to take away from this chapter is to give yourself permission to experience healing and acceptance of self-love. You now have a tool kit full of ways to take charge of your self-love practice. Put your mindfulness to work and start creating these self-love rituals and intentions for yourself. None of these lessons and practices take a lot of time out of the day, and in fact, they can be done even in the height of stress and chaos to help bring you back to center. This is the beginning of becoming more highly acquainted with your spiritual being and watching your inner warrior, your inner light and love, grow and thrive. The first step to true healing and transformation begins with dating yourself–self-love. Let's journey on this together because your best lover is right within!

CHAPTER SIX

A Real Look at Your Money & Finances

What is the subconscious money issue that holds you back from moving forward with divorce? This question does not have one single answer. The answers to this question are driven by each individual situation that is leading to divorce. Divorce is a painful process that brings with it a lot of stress. What is more painful, though, is what led you to getting a divorce, or making the decision to actually go through your divorce. We get stuck in not moving forward because we tend to focus on what we have or don't have, leaving us feeling vulnerable and worthless financially. This chapter is going to walk you through step-by-step how to spiritually reach financial freedom.

Money Mindset

Money is one of the biggest roadblocks that holds people hostage in an unhealthy marriage.

Why?

Based on many people's experiences, it is almost always fear. Fear of not being able to "make it." The moral value that we give money is the mask of our "standard of living." The fear of a lack of money is keeping many people hostage in an unhealthy marriage, one that is not serving either person. Literally, it is serving no one except the pocketbooks. However, the fear of what a new "standard of living" could be making them even sicker than the unwelcomed toxic relationship that they were in. See the picture…

I commonly see people let this fear drown out their opportunity to create and manifest the life they desire. But we can all put money to work for us in many ways. We can tell money to do what we need it to do for us.

What does this mean to you? Let's go deeper.

First, be extremely honest with yourself about the reasons why divorce was the best option for you. As painful as it might be, remember the reasons that led you to see how you were in an unhealthy, physically unsafe, or mentally abusive relationship.

Second, once you have the reason or reasons that led you to think about getting a divorce, or maybe you're going through a divorce presently; ask yourself the following two questions:

1. *Has money been able to solve (make my relationship a happy one, a safe one, or one that is not mentally abusive) my current situation?* Most likely, no…

2. *Has my current "standard of living" been able to remove the unhealthfulness, physical or mental abuse from my expired relationship?* Most likely, no again.

Take a moment to think and reflect over these two questions. Only you know what the true situation is with your spouse. Think about all the people affected by a divorce and take that into account, especially if children are involved. It's not supposed to be easy to answer these questions. These two reflecting questions are going to open your eyes to the next step: the step where you can work on removing the perceived value of money, and see that you can do this–that you have within you the resilient seed that will help you get through a divorce. The resilience that will make you stronger each day to find solutions to your own life, with your newly defined standard of living, and with what is important to you.

Early in life I learned that money was already printed, so all I had to do was to go get it. Okay, that's easier said than done, of course, but also completely true. That truth gave me the power to learn to reset the way I look at money. The method I used to get the "already printed money" was by working for someone else, working for myself, and investments. But I knew that I wanted to have not just one of these income streams...I wanted multiple streams of money flowing into my life. I started implementing mindfulness exercises (like in the previous chapter!) to tell the Universe what I desire. That may sound corny, but it's the truth of the matter. Here are the mantras and intentions I use to shape my life to welcome more income:

Money is moving all around me, all the time.

There is an infinite amount of money available.

Money is just waiting for me to acquire it when I please.

Money works for me, I don't work for money.

I'm in control of how much money I earn.

Just like in business, one has to have a business plan, or personal budget plan that tells money what to do. It ensures one is aware of and realistic about all income or potential income, and all of the expenses going out. I use a personal budget as my driver to work harder by tapping into my inner desire to obtain creative ideas on how to make more money! I love solving the problem of how to obtain more of the already printed paper that would add to in my life.

A personal budget can be overwhelming, depending on the amount of details one uses to capture its intended plan. At the same time, a budget can be freeing and liberating. When you don't have a budget, it often sounds scary or intimidating to take a close look at your financial situation. In divorce, this is one of the most daunting things to come face to face with. That fear, which causes a ripple effect of stress to other areas of your life, is normal.

I want to be a strong voice for you right now and tell you that it isn't as scary as it seems. Develop a budget before you ever make an investment, purchase, or go through a divorce, and you will see that the fear holding you back is much smaller than the potential value going forward.

We are going to dive into: (1) what is a personal budget for divorce; (2) how to develop a plan that you can tailor to your individual needs; and (3) identifying an accountable friend from your tribe that can assist you to show up and be present in your new situation and life. These three things will put you on the right track if the task of a budget feels scary or impossible today.

Let's recognize that you have made it this far. This is not an easy process, nor should anyone try to paint it as such. The journey of divorce involves the intention of getting divorced, the emotion that it leads one to feel, the different behaviors that it can make us take out on ourselves or on others. The impact it can cause on others, especially children, make it a big life decision. Even a kind, successful, and mindfully aware individual is not exempt from feeling emotions of pain, sadness, and sorrow. Honor where you have been in the process. Honor where you are now in the process. Set your intention on where you want to go in the future.

Money Mindset Breathing Exercise:

Let's together take a few deep breaths, using Dr. Andrew Weil's breathing exercise we practiced in chapter two. You will use the exercise to reflect how you would like to move forward in the next month, next year, and even in the next five years. What would you want your life to look like in a month? What kind of supportive people would you like to have around you during this first month? Are they currently available in your life, or would you need to resource elsewhere to find them? Do they align with your new direction and offer you positive reinforcements, kind and honest feedback when you might not know what to do?

Find a place where you can sit comfortably and relax, away
from ample lighting, TV, computers, cell phones, tablets, and
anything that can be a distraction for the next three minutes.
Once you are there, softly and gently close your eyes.
Exhale completely through your mouth, making a whoosh sound.
Releasing what no longer serves you.
Close your mouth and inhale quietly through your nose to a
mental count of four.
Hold your breath for a count of seven.
Exhale completely through your mouth, making a whoosh sound
to a count of eight. Releasing what no longer serves you.
This is one breath.
Now inhale again and repeat the cycle three more times for a
total of four breaths.

Begin this money mindset breathing exercise, specifically
for your own personal time and space, to declare what you
want in your life, and depart from what no longer serves you.
If you need more than a few minutes, then honor yourself
and take as much time as you desire.

Develop a Plan

Part of developing a plan is to become organized in what you are
making a plan for and how you are making a plan. The hardest part is
adjusting your behavior and mindset around how you treat and work
with your money. For reference, winning at the money game is 80
percent behavior (mindset) and 20 percent actual application (money
management). This means what you do with money and how you
manage money isn't the number one focal point. It's the mindset and
power of how you think about money that I want you to transform!

The two main plans that you will need to work towards are a short-
term plan and a long-term plan. In the short term, you need to have

cash available for what is happening in the next 1-3 months as well as foresight into your 3-6 month monetary needs. For example, things like monthly bills, housing costs, children's needs, and car payments are common examples of things in the short term. Your short-term money mindset needs to be very realistic and practical. This isn't the time to cross your fingers and hope you can win the lottery. The short term, especially during your divorce, is often where most people experience high levels of stress. During or before a divorce, the thought of lawyer costs only adds to the stress you might be feeling. That's normal, and almost everyone who's been through a divorce can relate to this added cost.

Think about the position you are in right now—what type of short-term needs do you need to plan for? You don't need to write anything down yet, rather sit and think about what you've got on your plate. During my divorce, I had to get real with myself and make immediate changes to my lifestyle in order to cope with the fear I was experiencing. Remember that shakiness we spoke about in the beginning of the book? I had to force myself to get comfortable with the uncomfortable reality I was living in. Events, shopping and all the stuff that I used to love to spend money on had to be put on the back burner! I let the fear, or shakiness, wash over me during this time. Instead of going places during my free time, I forced myself to stay at home and sit quietly with the fear in my mind.

As I look back now, allowing the fear to, in a sense, "settle" within me gave me the power to overcome it. When it comes to fear, money is often the most crippling offender. As I became more comfortable with the fear of having less money after we divided assets, my short-term plan started to materialize. By not avoiding my fear, I was able to tackle the short-term budget plan head-on and without extra, unnecessary stress. Never avoid the fear around getting real with your financial situation, no matter how dire it may seem. Accept that you are afraid because your life is changing! Even better, get excited about taking complete control over your life by creating a short-term plan.

Long-term planning is just as important as your short-term plan, but the long-term plan allows for exciting opportunities as well. In your long-term plan, you can get creative by completely owning what it is you want in life! I wanted to plan for my kids' futures and the cost of raising them. I wanted to have multiple income streams. I wanted to be my own boss. I wanted to be able to live in a bigger house! I desired to travel with my kids at least once or twice a year. I had these goals and many more floating around my head, and that was very motivating. The only problem, and I especially see this with divorced people, is that they never take the next step by actually planning for their long-term goals. If you are telling the Universe "I want to have a five bedroom house in a great part of the city!" and you truly feel the emotions of what that would be like to have, that's a huge positive. The only thing missing here is the action step. In order to prove to yourself that what you want is possible AND to show the Universe that you are ready for it, you need to take action steps to manifest it. One of the first steps to attracting your dream house is by creating a realistic long-term plan.

I want you to look at your long-term plan just like an investment. If you can see attaining your long-term goals as a real return on investment (ROI) you will be more inclined to stick it out until the end. All the time, energy, intention setting, visualization, saving, and so on that goes into getting the ROI is the investment itself! For example, when I want to sell my house and buy a new house I invest hours upon hours of time creating a plan. I invest my mental energy into feeling what I want, and feeling the positive energy of getting it. I invest my energy into visualizing the end result. All these investments compound over time and the ROI is always much better than what I imagined.

We are going to walk through some preparation work for you to get organized and feel connected to your money management and planning in the next section. You're going to want to take out your journal, paper, or use a note on your computer, to take inventory of your financial spending. When you're taking inventory, you're going to be looking at all the areas money is present in your life, from both a giving and receiving standpoint. While developing your plan, you are also going to take inventory and assess your abundance goals. Earlier in the book, I mentioned that abundance does not just mean money; however, in this case, and for this chapter, we are going to look at financial abundance specifically.

Developing this plan will significantly decrease your stress and feelings of fear around your money. If you also desire to do this money work in your sacred space, I invite you to do that. Take a few moments to ground yourself and calm your mind before you move forward by going through the exercise below.

MONEY PLANNING INVENTORY:

Sit in a quiet and comfortable space. Close your eyes and take three deep breaths. Use the power of the "I AM" statements to ground your energy and focus your attention on love and abundance. Repeat these statements. Write them down if you desire and say them as affirmations throughout the day and/or when fear arises during this planning exercise.

I am abundance.
I am courageous.
I am perseverance.
I am creating a new center around money.
I am abundance.
*I am focused on creating a new story about perceiving money
    and making money.*
I am attracting money right now.
I am creating a stream of money into my life.
I am abundance.
I am letting go of all fear around money.
I am creating money every day.
I am abundance.

Now let's begin!

1. Reflect, identify, and write down all possible sources of income, including child support (however, pretend that it's not guaranteed), alimony (same as child support), employment, self-employment, investments, inheritance, and gifts.

2. Reflect, identify, and write down all possible expenses you have, your children might have, and any other dependent you have (i.e., caring for an elderly parent).

3. Reflect and reevaluate if what you are currently doing could be done differently, at a lesser cost. Think about current utility services, grocery shopping, clothing, etc. (for example, you might not "need" cable TV but could use a lower cost video streaming service that allows you a similar experience). This might require you to do small amounts of research to see what other options exist at lower costs.

Part Two of your money planning is going to expand on Part One and create abundance goals for yourself. The abundance goals that you will create below are for you, and they are about you! Stepping out of a marriage and into your post-divorce life, there is a feeling of empowerment. Everything you create from here on is because you had the will, desire, and drive to imagine it AND do it. Setting abundance goals is an opportunity to use many of the things we discussed leading up to this chapter. In order to create authentic abundance goals you need to remove your ego's voice. You need to set your intention on what will bring you the most joy. You will get to use the Law of Attraction by embodying the emotions of what it is like to already have what you want. You'll need to give off the energy (quantum physics) that you already have everything you want. You'll need to stay positive in your mind by manifesting positive thoughts in your mind. This is a really exciting time for you! When you start to see the Universe work for you, you'll see how powerful all these tools really are.

In what area(s) of your finances do you desire to see abundance presently, a month from now, and six months from now? Think about your short-term needs (bills, rent, necessities) and set abundance goals for how see yourself. For example, you can set an abundance goal of having a second stream of income flowing in your life within six months. That's a fantastic abundance goal. Another great abundance goal is to take a step up in your career by asking for a raise or looking for a new position with a higher salary in your field. Can you see how these are rather simple goals but have an abundant and positive undertone to them? That's what you are after!

The second part of this exercise is to set your long-term abundance goals. Like I said before, this is an exciting part of your journey to wholeness! In the long term, what do you desire, financially, for you and your family? There are no wrong answers here. For me, I wanted to own my own business and grow it because I knew that would bring me the joy and challenge I was craving in my life. I had no idea that I would own a barre studio before or during my divorce. I never got specific about my goal of owning an actual business. What I did get specific about was how it would feel to run my own business. I visualized myself in the role of an owner! I knew that I didn't need to have an exact plan, and I didn't focus on my current situation when I set my long-term abundance goals. As you set abundance goals, do so without focusing on your current situation. You might be in the midst of a chaotic divorce, and if you hold a mindset of, "How on earth will I ever accomplish this??" you will paralyze yourself and eventually quit on your goal. Instead, get excited and intentional about your long-term goals. You can set abundance goals around your salary, how you make your money, how much you have in savings, and/or what you want to plan or save for. Again, there are no rules with abundance goals.

Follow what your gut and intuition tell you here. Write down what comes up and evaluate it later. The first few ideas that come to your head can be expanded on and built up. Avoid judging your abundance goals as too unrealistic or seemingly impossible. You do not need to know "how" you will achieve them. You only need to set the intention by telling yourself, right now, that you will achieve them.

Once you have done the inventory and planning you're ready to step into the actual understanding of personal budget and how it's going to help you feel at ease with your money. Take as much time as you need and make sure you are recording your abundance goals somewhere that allows you to revisit them often and easily.

How to Make Your Plan Come Alive

I want you to think of the difference between using money with and without a plan for a moment. Imagine that you are at one end of a swimming pool and need to get to the other side. You've probably done this in your life at least once before, I promise! You have two options to get from one side to the other. The first is to swim underwater with your eyes closed and hope you don't swim right into the other wall. The second option is swim above the water using breast strokes and cruise all the way down, seeing every obstacle coming at you.

Spending money at times can be an emotional band-aid to a bigger problem, such as ingrained childhood memories, beliefs, or traumas. For example, maybe you grew up with very little money, or you could have grown up where status was determined with the kind of cars your parents drove or the clothes you wore, etc. I want you to do a personal check-in before you step into making your plan. Remember your abundance goals and the work you did in planning because if you let your emotions drive your spending, it will be an unhealthy coping mechanism that drives you to debt and further emotional trauma.

If this resonates with where you are or how you're feeling, please go back to the self-love lessons in chapter five and nurture yourself a bit more. Also remember the importance of your tribe, a vital lesson from chapter five. Your tribe will be a valuable part of your healing journey with money–not to make you spend more money, but help to support you and keep you accountable. I want you to become more aware of the misuse of money as emotional therapy, so you're able to prosper and thrive. I am here with you every step of the way as well. You are not alone, no matter what and when you feel a strong pull of doubt, or you want to spend money on something that doesn't align with your personal goals, become aware that it's an emotional purchase. You can always resort to your inner voice and intuition for a check-in.

GROUNDING MONEY MEDIATION PRACTICE

First, let's get clear:

What is your fear story around money?
What is your money story you keep telling yourself?
What are your limiting beliefs around money?

Be honest with yourself. Once you are clear on what story is holding you back, I want you to sit and pray in a guided meditation with me.

Meditation grounds us and allows us to not only spiritually connect with ourselves most genuinely but it also allows us to ask for help from the Universe. We must release the urge to control our fears and do this all on our own to find our way to freedom and love. This mediation can be done anywhere.

You may find yourself panicked about money at unusual times. You can use this mediation anytime: driving in a car, sitting at your desk at work.

Your fears are only released when you believe in the real power of the Universe and the Laws of Attraction. The truth is both have great power in our journey if you choose to accept them. You must let go of control and fear and believe that there is a power out there working to alleviate your burdens at all times. It doesn't matter if any of it is true! What matters is if you believe it is because that gives it power.

GUIDED MEDITATION:

Close your eyes and sit comfortably.
Imagine a waterfall, a healing waterfall of light, pouring down your body offering you the cleansing of all negative

thoughts around money. You are releasing all fears that you have around money and releasing all negative fear-based thoughts. The waterfall is healing you and cleansing you from your fear-based story. As you breathe, feel the water cleansing you and clearing all negative thoughts. Continue to breathe as you feel this cleanse begin at the crown of your head and be released down to your toes.

Visualize this and feel the recycled energy coming out of your feet and back into the crown of your head. Your new story around the abundance of money is created. Money is abundant, money is free-flowing, money is available to me all the time.

Now feel the same waterfall move through your body filling every cell with light and love surrounding your new story around money.

What is your Personal Budget Plan?

Your personal budget plan is the system you create based on what is important in your life right now, and where you would like to head going forward. It is the part of your wholeness roadmap that aligns with your beliefs and values and tells money what you want it to do for you.

Basically, your personal budget plan gives you the empowering tools to hold yourself accountable and stay on track with what is important to you, regardless of what anyone else thinks or says.

One important thing before we move forward with the actual plan, ALWAYS respect your current financial position. You are working on a journey that is taking you where you want to go. For instance, you would not criticize a house's design and look by just seeing the foundation. It takes time to build a house, and similarly, it takes time to get to your desired financial destination.

When developing your personal budget plan, there are few things to keep in mind.

1. We know that life happens. We know that emergencies happen, which can cost money. Therefore, consider setting aside between $500 to $1,000 that you can have easy access to in the event of an emergency.

2. Develop a plan to pay all of your unsecured debt first. Make this your mission. Remove all of the old debt from your life. Follow a plan that you are comfortable with, and stick to it.

3. Once all of your debt has been paid for (excluding your mortgage and student loans), set aside 3 to 6 months of income for a greater emergency. Do not make this money easily accessible. Make it as inconvenient as possible to access it. That will ensure you do not spend this money unnecessarily.

4. Plan for retirement based on what is important to you, where you would like to be, and how you envision yourself at retirement.

5. Plan on paying off your mortgage as early as possible. One extra payment a year can save seven years of interest.

6. Lastly, plan on building wealth for you, your children (if you have children), and pay it forward to those that helped you along the way in your journey. Consider hiring an expert like a fiduciary advisor that can assist you with wealth management.

The Plan

Step 1: Allocate your Money

For your plan to be effective and successful, you need to know all sources of income on a monthly basis. Then, money has to be told what to do, where to go, and when to go. 100 percent of the income has to be allocated on the plan, where you will tell money what to do on a monthly basis.

Here are some examples of categories and subcategories where you can tell money what to do:

1. Charity
2. Savings
   a. Emergency
   b. Retirement
3. Housing = $1,250
   a. Rent = $1,200
   b. Mortgage
   c. Property Taxes
   d. Homeowner Insurance
   e. Homeowners (HOA)
   f. Home Repairs
   g. Home Supplies = $50
4. Utilities
   a. Electricity
   b. Gas
   c. Phone
   d. Cable
   e. Water
   f. Trash
5. Food
   a. Groceries
   b. Eating Out
6. Transportation
   a. Car Payment
   b. Car Insurance
   c. Gas
   d. Maintenance and Repairs
   e. Car Taxes
   f. Car Replacement
7. Clothing
   a. Self
   b. Children
   c. Dry Cleaning
8. Medical and Health
   a. Health Insurance
   b. Doctors
   c. Prescriptions/ Supplements
9. Personal
   a. Child Care
   b. Hygiene
   c. Haircut/Hair Style
   d. School Tuition/Supplies
   e. Adult Tuition/Books/ Supplies
   f. Gifts (holidays, special events)
   g. Miscellaneous
10. Recreation
   a. Entertainment
   b. Vacation

11. Debt (Working toward

eliminating all debts)

a. Credit Card 1

b. Credit Card 2

c. Credit Card 3

d. Student Loan

e. Personal Loan

f. Other _____

Step 2: Start Creating your Budget

Once you have identified the categories and subcategories that best apply to you based on your plan moving forward:

1. Place the projected expenses (dollar value) of each of the subcategories. For example, Rent (subcategory under Housing) $1,200

2. Add the subcategories under each category. For example, Grocery $600 + Eating Out $200 = Food $800

3. Add the total plan for all of your categories. For example, the total value of all 11 categories might total $2,450 a month (total projected expenses).

4. Let's assume that your total take-home income a month is $2,600 (full-time job at $20/hour and a total of 25% tax liability). Subtract your income from projected expenses (all categories).

5. If the results from subtracting your income from projected expenses is greater than zero, then allocate more money towards creating your easy access quick emergency money, or paying down debt, setting aside 3 to 6 months of income, maximizing your annual contribution towards retirement, paying off your mortgage early, or building wealth.

6. However, if the results from subtracting your income from projected expenses is less than zero, then identify the below zero difference and put it into perspective. For example, your total take-home income is $2,600, and your projected expenses are $3,000. The difference is -$400. Ask yourself the following questions:

    a. What is $400 a month divided into four weeks? (Hint: $100 a week)

    b. What is $400 a month divided into 20 days? (Hint: $20 a day)

    c. If you were to take an additional part-time job, where could you work that you could earn an additional $100 a week? (Hint: $10/hour, 3 hours/day, 4 days/week will give you an extra $104 weekly after 20% tax liability)

    d. OR, identify areas in your plan that could be reduced by an alternative way of doing things (i.e., shopping at a value store) or suspending subcategories temporarily (i.e., premium cable TV).

Even if the results from subtracting your income from projected expenses is greater than zero, consider the following as tips to save money, and place the savings towards some of your planned priorities.

EXAMPLE OF A BUDGET

Category	Planned	Actual	Balance	%
Income	$2,450	$2,450	$0	100%
Housing	$1,250	$1,247	$3	50.9%
Rent	$1,200	$1,200	$0	49.0%
Mortgage				
Home supplies	$50	$47	$3	1.9%
Food	$800	$765	$35	31.2%
Groceries	$600	$575	$25	23.5%
Eating Out	$200	$190	$10	7.8%

Step 3: Consider Ways to Save Money

Once you've developed your budget, if there are areas that you can go back and tighten up even more to save some money, let's go back and do that now. Assess what is absolutely 100 percent necessary and then what is "nice" to have versus what is "needed."

Here are a few creative ways that you can save regularly:

- Go out with your friends in a different way, rather than having lunch, dinner, drinks, or something that costs money. Remind your friends there are different ways to get together that doesn't involve money. Be creative—it could be running in the park together, watching the sunset, going on a bike ride, inviting your friends over and having a potluck dinner, etc.

- Go out during happy hour because food and drinks are cheaper.

- Gain points or extra cash by using credit cards that have points and rewards.

- Shop at other grocery stores that are cheaper. For example, in most cases, Trader Joe's is less expensive than Whole Foods.

- Look for coupons and discounts online and in your local paper.

- Buy in bulk–it can reduce your spending in the long run.

- Get a CSA membership with a local farm for your produce.

- Purchase items that you can get at Costco or other bulk stores.

- Use Amazon Pantry.

- Buy gas cards for a discount at the pump, rather than using your credit card.

Don't make convenience get you into debt and/or overspending. Be consciously aware of where and how you are spending your money. Go the "extra mile" for savings, literally. The "extra mile" could save you a lot of money!

Step 4: Hold Yourself Accountable

This is the fun part–now it's time to hold yourself accountable. I've emphasized the importance of your tribe in chapter five. Reach out to your tribe to help keep you accountable. Having an accountability friend or partner is great, but first and foremost it's important that you are able to hold yourself accountable. I want you to take your budget, no matter how detailed or pretty, and put it somewhere that you can see it every day.

I always like to put things on my bathroom mirror, refrigerator, phone, or in my journal because I love writing and I connect with my journal daily. Think of a place that you will visually see your budget daily and be able to connect with it for at least a minute, send it love, and allow the love and abundance to be received from it.

Then say quietly to yourself the financial abundance prayer.

Quick Financial Check-In Exercise:

I invite you to check-in with yourself every night (at least for a few moments) and look at what you are spending on your credit card (if you use a credit card) or track the cash that you spent.

While reviewing, reflect on whether you spent money on something necessary, or was it convenient, emotional, not so necessary (i.e., Starbucks, which most likely will be considered a luxury for you right now), and a place where you could have saved money.

Creative Ways to Make Money

I can't tell you how many people come to me, both men and women, who don't end up leaving their marriage sooner because they don't know how they are going to make money to support themselves. Now we already covered the mindset part of money and how to shift your thoughts around money, so this part is going to focus on creative ways to help make money and/or supplement your income with more.

I've developed an A-Z list of ways to make money and the important thing I want you to remember is to push yourself beyond your comfort zone. It's important to try and seek a job in your field of study or passion, but sometimes that is just not enough. So be open-minded when reading this list.

If you find yourself in a situation where you haven't been in the workforce for several years or maybe your certification you used to have is no longer valid, whatever the reason is, this list will help you. I've developed this list with the mindset that time is limited and you desire as much flexibility in scheduling because you may or may not have children and let's face it, the more flexible the job, the more time you can take to soak into self-love to get your footing back.

If you have children, this is a time to also talk about the financial freedoms that you were able to experience in your old life that may no longer be accessible. Share with your children that there are sacrifices that you might have to make in your new life in order to have more financial abundance. Children like to know that there is stability, and the same kind of rituals and routines are present like before the divorce. So I invite you to sit down with them and tell them what jobs you are exploring to have the same level of financial abundance as before. Allow them to help you in the process and brainstorm (if children are old enough to understand the job market), make it a fun activity and use this list as help. I have included my children each time I rehab or sell my homes. They learned to enjoy picking out hardwood floor colors, paint colors, or contribute opinions on both big and small improvements. It taught them how to value buying and selling our homes as a tremendous source of income. As my children have grown into teens and young adults, they have embraced moving with great excitement.

The first year after your divorce is going to be the most difficult financially. I won't beat around the bush about it, but I can promise you this, no year after the first will ever be as difficult.

I know not everyone reading this book will be an entrepreneur, maybe you are, perhaps you aren't, but you probably know someone or admire someone who is an entrepreneur. The first year of every entrepreneur's journey is always the hardest because they have to work late nights, early mornings, all hours, be so many things to so many people, wear 17 different hats a day sometimes, and hustle like there is no tomorrow, because literally there might not be, if there isn't money coming in the door. This is what the first year looks like for post-divorce as well when you are finding your financial footing. There will be some wobbly bumps on your journey and combined with your money mindset, there might be times where you have to hustle.

Embrace it and know there is light at the end of the tunnel. Follow your inner voice and inner driver to get you through this and into your abundant success.

A-Z LIST OF CREATIVE WAYS TO MAKE MONEY:

a. Real estate broker

b. Yoga or fitness instructor or manager of a yoga studio

c. MLM programs (beauty, health, and wellness, cleaning products, essential oils, etc.)

d. Substitute teacher

e. Reach out to nonprofits

f. Consider an entry-level position

g. Work at a hospital in the admin department

h. Stay-at-home nanny (moms bring in other kids to take care of)

i. Request monetary gifts on holidays

j. Sell old jewelry, clothes, etc.

k. Be a tutor, teach ESL

l. Learn to web develop (code)

m. Sell goods on places like Etsy and eBay

n. Virtual assistant or personal assistant

o. Translator

p. Freelancer

q. Rent a room or space in your house/have a roommate(s)

r. Personal shopper

s. Sell your skill online: writing, design, etc.

t. Uber, Lyft driver

u. Task and errand services

v. Dog walker

w. Join a virtual call center

x. Be a transcriber and/or have a transcribing service

Remember to have patience and diversify yourself and your gifts, talents, and passions. I used my real estate background and love for homes to sell the homes I live in after I rehab or improve them, looking for new homes that I could make improvements on. I have strategically bought and sold homes at opportunistic times when I saw the real estate market at its prime. At the same time, I bought a barre business and had 20 instructors working for me. Three years later, I sold my house again and bought another home that I could add improvements to and flip. I sold the barre business after five years and went back to school for nutrition and health. And then functional medicine. I wrote a book and embarked on restaurant ownership. Reinventing myself along the way was and still is important to me, it keeps my passion and spirit alive in all that I'm doing.

Show Up and Be Present for Your New Situation and Life

I know the transitional period of stepping out of your marriage and into your new life is that, a transitional period. Where you are today is not going to be where you are a year from now. The transitional period is going to be a period of time where you need to give yourself grace and gratitude. It's a time to create your happiness around you and create the opportunities you desire. If you surround yourself with happiness, then you become happy. If you surround yourself with positivity, then you will have continuous positivity in your life.

As I mentioned earlier, I always had fresh flowers in my kitchen, which made me happy. They were a small piece of life that I could put the intention of happiness in. During my transitional period, I wasn't happy and living in a place of fear, so I knew I needed to bring some small ounce of "light" back into my home and life. The flowers were a representation of hope. Hope that I was creating a happy environment and a bright new beginning. I showed up to my life and was determined to create happiness, abundance *(mind, body, and spirit)*, togetherness, and a homey feel in my house. I stepped into my life and saw it for

what it was, a new life in which I was able to create my own decisions.
This was my new beginning, it was scary but as time went on, it started
to evolve into something lovely and real.

GIVE GRATITUDE FOR WHERE YOU ARE

Be proud of your plan and where you are today. It's not a time to
compare yourself to others or become bitter and vain. There are always
going to be people that have more, have less, and are better than you.
This is a time to always, always, always give yourself gratitude for
taking a step that takes courage and tremendous strength. It's not a
time to compare because then you are focused on what you don't have,
rather than appreciating and embracing what you do have. When
you celebrate positive things and the steps you have made since the
beginning, then you're able to stay focused into the positive light.
Remember when you remain in the light, it opens you up to attract
more positive energy and light into your life.

Gratitude Practice:

This practice is going to be super-simple for you, but in
times of high stress and your new life, you can sometimes
lose sight of what you are grateful for each day. What I'd
like you to do is take out your cell phone because I know
it's the one thing that you will most likely have with you
throughout the day.

Open up your alarm feature on your phone. Now I
want you to program two alarms to go off during the day, it
doesn't matter when, maybe one is in the morning, and one
is in the evening. Whatever times you resonate with and feel
called to set.

Then for the "alert" that is shown when the alarm is
going off, I want you to type in *"what am I grateful for?"* This
is your dose of mindfulness and spontaneous gratitude for
the day.

I want you to program that alarm to go off every day and if you really want to make it fun, program the alarm different times every day, so you are always surprised when it goes off.

Most of the time you will forget about the alarm, so when it goes off, take 30 seconds and just *pause and breathe*, and think about what you are grateful for at that moment. Reflect on your day thus far and just take a moment of gratitude.

Express your gratitude daily!

RESPECT YOUR FINANCIAL POSITION

Of everything that you will take away from this chapter, I want you to remember this: always respect your financial position. One of my favorite spiritual teachers, Gabby Bernstein, shares a practice that will help you spiritually respect your money. I invite you to use this approach, as well as the other physical lessons and tools that I've shared with you in the chapter.

Gabby tells us that to keep your financial energy open, you have to keep the places where you actually keep your money organized and in positive energy. Remember everything is energy. If you look at your wallet for a minute, is it old, ripped, torn, filled with disorganized receipts, or maybe you don't have a wallet and just throw everything in a bag? If everything is energy, then it means we have to respect where we are putting money. If you've had your wallet for 20 years or even five and it's looking like it has seen its best days, it's time to clean things up, clear the clutter, and literally make the physical and energetic space for abundance to fill your wallet.

When you clear clutter out of your life in any area, especially money, more abundance is going to come flowing in. When you respect money, you will be more careful with it. Allow yourself to get a new wallet if that's the case or clean up what you have because your wallet is a physical reflection of how you feel about money. Nobody else is going to come to save you or take care of this for you–it's your job to take back the power and respect where you're at. Love it, cherish it, share the gratitude, praise yourself, and love yourself because you are changing your life for the better now.

The Wholeness Journey

If you are constantly depending on other people's opinions for guidance in decisions and money advice, relying on somebody else to navigate your life, then you are not trusting your gut and your financial position. Embrace your self-love if you need to revisit chapter five. Now is the time, more than ever, to trust your gut, your intuition, and create the stability you need in your life. Apply the lessons and principles in this chapter, and I can promise you that your sense of stress, worry, and fear around money will reduce. Surround yourself with an incredible support system and ask a friend to help keep you accountable. Trust yourself!

I recall my dad wanting to rush into a virtual burning building *(my life)*, during my transitional period, to rescue me from any pain or hardship because he loved me so much. He didn't want to see me hurt and he thought he could lighten my load by making decisions for me. But he couldn't. My heart had to go through the pain, but even more importantly I could not hand over my decisions to him or anybody at that point. Nor did I want to. Keep your loved ones close to you because they offer us a backbone of support; however, do not hand them over your decisions.

I started making decisions that felt right, and they were not always the easiest decisions. I applied the lessons in this chapter that helped make the tough decisions, like selling my homes to put some money back into investments, and the need to pull one child from a school where all of his siblings and cousins attended, to be sent to a new school that could meet some of his processing challenges with reading. That hard decision paid off for him academically because now he thrives. When you make the hard decisions, not only do you grow as a person but your children grow as well. They learn how to take on adversity like you.

Financial decisions and changes are necessary and often even more so with divorce. Don't be afraid to make them and once you make them don't be wishy-washy. Honor your financial position, and it will honor and respect you!

CHAPTER SEVEN

Stress on the Body

One of my favorite spiritual teachers is Eckhart Tolle, author of *The Power of Now*. Tolle teaches us that if we choose to be present in "the now," there can be no stress. Stress is simply erratic thoughts either reliving an experience from the past or worrying about a certain experience occurring in the future. I know personally I would become worried and fixated about having the same negative experience with my ex in the past, and I was inviting this experience into my future by the Law of Attraction. Now, I remind myself every day that stress isn't real. It is our mind creating erratic thought patterns based on our fears. However, all of that stress becomes real disease in our bodies.

Stress had a major impact on my health long after my divorce was finalized. Based on the experiences I had to overcome, I knew that handling stress needed to be a major aspect of this book. The result of being overstressed for extended and consistent periods of time in my life did have one positive impact on me. It pushed me to immerse myself in understanding what stress really is, how it impacts the body, and what needs to be done to minimize stress. My goal for you is to walk away, after reading this book, with a tool box full of tools on how to handle the stress you will inevitably face during and after your divorce.

First off, I was truly amazed by what I learned in the last decade of my life with regard to what causes stress! Your thoughts impact the cells in your body on a biological level, which means you really are what you think! You can compare stress and diet to get a clear picture of what this means. If you eat the world's best diet, completely customized to your body, full of green veggies and organic produce, you will feel great on the inside. That's not new information for most people, and mostly obvious, right? Of course, the opposite side of that is if you eat fast food every single day it's probably going to have a long-term effect on your health. Your thoughts have the same effect! The more positive thoughts you embody, the more positive energy your cells will absorb.

Stress impacts the body both today and in the foreseeable long-term. Long-lasting wellness is key to maintaining a stable stress level, mind, body, spirit. Understanding that both your emotional health and your physical health play a part in your body's wellness gives you a huge advantage. Emotional intelligence is a vital part of lifelong, long-lasting wellness. There have been studies done that show one's emotional understanding (defined as one's awareness of and connection to their emotions), correlates to increased happiness and satisfaction, along with improved stress management. On the other hand, those studies show that a lack of emotional balance and awareness are linked to poor physical health and imbalances in the body which cause disease. This research is eye-opening because here you are, in one of the most stressful times of your life, and totally vulnerable.

The stress-related health consequences I had to deal with years after my divorce led me to learning how important my mindset and self-love practices are. I yearned for a holistic approach to not only healing disease, but also for daily stress management. As time went on, I built this approach through: radically changing my diet away from processed food, diligently focusing on positive thinking, following my intuition, using herbs and supplements, releasing suppressed emotions, embracing social support, and deepening my spiritual practices through meditation and mindful exercise.

Up to this point, I've shared many ways to calm your mind, express your emotions and start to reprogram your thoughts. However, in reality, the stress you are feeling or have felt during your divorce and post-divorce have been building upon each other. The main stress hormone–which you've probably heard of–is cortisol. Cortisol is basically nature's built-in alarm system for your body. It's produced in the adrenal gland and controls mood, motivation, and...FEAR!

The buildup of excess cortisol in your body is at an all-time high when you go through a stressful experience. When your body goes through a divorce, it takes on what is called "fight or flight." It's when your body is in an erratic state and trying to survive as if you were being chased by a mountain lion. And again, stress can be real or simply perceived. Fight or flight is when your body is reactive and in overdrive. We've all been there, it's part of being human! Be confident, right now, that this book will put you in control of how you understand and deal with stress.

We don't always have all the time in the world to unwind and decompress. Especially in difficult times like divorce, finding space for a little rest and relaxation seems like a pipe dream.

BUT...if you are aware, honest and, most importantly, intentional about the nature of thoughts you feed your mind, then you will create this necessary R & R space in your life.

Another way I can say this, more bluntly perhaps, is if you don't slow down to reset your emotions, your stressors will build up and your body will experience symptoms. If you get to this point, it can take years to get yourself back to "normal" again. I don't want this for you, so that's why I am sharing with you the knowledge, steps, and tools you need to keep yourself healthy and as balanced as possible with your body and health.

UNDERSTANDING THE STRESS CONNECTION TO THE BODY

While this is not a medical book, it is essential to be knowledgeable and educated about the benefits and harmful effects of stress on the body. Without actually knowing and understanding the harmful effects, people tend to continue to brush off the reality they are in and face the "problem" when there is a crisis. As you know from reading this far, I want to help you live in an educated, knowledgeable, healing, and preventative state (in the future) as much as possible. So let's begin to talk a bit more on the formality of stress.

When it comes to stress, one body system stands out on how negatively it is impacted–the nervous system. There are several parts to the nervous system, which include the central nervous system (CNS) and the Autonomic Nervous System (ANS). The ANS has two branches: the sympathetic nervous system, which drives the "fight or flight" response, and the parasympathetic nervous system (PNS), which promotes the "rest and digest" state. When you are going through a divorce, your body is in "fight or flight" mode, there is no denying it. Have an awareness of the "fight or flight" mode that you are experiencing, as it will have repercussions on your body. It's important to manage your ANS, to reduce the harm on your tissues and endocrine system. All the tools you've learned up to this point are good resources and things to practice and teach your body how to come down from heightened "fight or flight." There are also deeper-level, specific stress-related tools, and resources later in this chapter, so stick with me!

Okay, let's talk specifically about the central nervous system and a little more in-depth about your autonomic nervous system. The CNS is controlled by your conscious mind, and you control your conscious mind with your thoughts. If you'd visualize with me for a moment, you'll see what I mean by this…if you want to brush your teeth, you pick up your toothbrush; when you are driving your car, the car decides which way you want to go, right? Your ANS, on the other hand, is controlled by your subconscious mind. Meaning you are not immediately able to access the subconscious with your thoughts. For example, your ANS controls how your heart beats, how your liver and kidneys are working, and how fast your hair grows. It is the ANS that is also affected by your level of stress, specifically the sympathetic nervous system, which drives the "fight or flight" response.

Other systems in the body that are negatively impacted with stress are the endocrine system, which includes the adrenal glands (where we make our stress hormones), thyroid, sex hormones, and pituitary glands (the master switch housed inside the brain), and the digestive system. The digestive system only works when the parasympathetic nervous system is active, which is the "rest and digest" mode I mentioned above. Every time you ignite your "fight or flight" response, you are releasing stress hormones such as cortisol and adrenaline into the body. The stress hormones, adrenaline, and cortisol are made in the adrenal glands. Ironically you might be thinking that sounds really bad, but actually, those stress hormones serve a purpose in the body. For example, they would kick in if you were being chased by a tiger.

Adrenaline communicates to every cell in your body and creates a chemical reaction each time, which produces a stress response. Adrenaline tells your body that your life is being threatened even though, for example, all you may be doing is arguing with your ex-spouse, stressing out about bills, rushing to pick your kids up from school, and/or dealing with an energy vampire in your life. Every time you become internally rattled, your stress hormone, cortisol, communicates to every cell in your body as well. The role of cortisol is to warn every cell in your body that food consumption is low and starvation is near - so as a result, it begins to break down muscle in your body and store fat. Can you see now that stress can make you fat? I can imagine you are not starving yourself, so you're thinking, "how does starvation apply to me?" Even though food is plentiful for you and you're not going into starvation mode, your cortisol production is likely being driven from areas of your life that bring you uncertainty, like relationships. Especially in divorce, it brings so many changes and stress with not only your ex-spouse but with kids, families, friends, finances, career, and just overall uncertainty as to where and what the future holds for you. All of these things will drive up your cortisol levels to warn the body.

Overall, the nervous system's response to stress can lead to and be responsible for almost 90 percent of disease in the body. You may not see the impact of stress today or tomorrow, but it's important to have a stress response plan (aka, understand and educate yourself about stress and have exercises, practices, and support in place) now, so you can have the quality of life you imagine in the future.

Bio-Individuality

How do you know what's good for you? Bio-individuality is the answer. Bio-individuality was described by the Institute for Integrative Nutrition® specifically in relationship to food, as "one man's medicine is another man's poison." I'm going to take this one step further and apply this principle to LIFE. This simply means, what works and is suitable for one person, is not always best and what works for another, regarding their overall wellness and well-being. Think about it, you can probably name a person in your life that differs from another in their eating, physical, and exercise habits, and spiritual practices, am I right?

That's why all the content, research, nutrition tips, and spiritual practices in this book are here to support you and be a resource for you on your own individual journey. Every person who reads this book will feel something different from the other, take away something that someone else didn't, and implement into their wholeness journey what works for them. You, my friend, are your own person. You are finding "wholeness" in your life and will be empowered on your journey because you have the education, knowledge, resources, and support around you, to bring you back to balance and happiness. Honoring your bio-individuality is all about restoring your life and finding a diet and finding a peaceful place from your stress.

MY PERSONAL STRESS STORY

I share with you my own bio-individuality; my own personal story of how I was a textbook scenario of how stress creates illness in our bodies and impedes the individual journey to healing. Stress creates disease in our bodies, you already know that. Stress was the precursor of my illnesses. Yes, I said illnesses. The body and all of our organs are interconnected and communicate with one another constantly. Looking back, I was forced to take a pause in life. I think the signs were there for quite some time that I needed a dramatic change in my life and a change in how I was reacting to events in my life. But I never listened to those signs. The signs were loud and clear. Signs like fatigue, achy joints, arthritis in a few joints, swollen joints, thinning hair, weight gain (even though I was working out daily), bloating, stomach distress, food allergies, sugar sensitivities... and these are just to name a few.

At the time, I didn't understand that every one of these symptoms was a piece of a puzzle–just like there is interconnectedness in every system in our bodies. I knew I needed a good doctor to help me and one that was open-minded; I found my way to a doctor who practices Western medicine and functional medicine. This doctor diagnosed me with Lyme disease, Epstein-Barr virus, mineral deficiencies, hypothyroid, low progesterone (hormone imbalances), food allergies (gluten, dairy, eggs, soy, and wheat), vitamin deficiencies, and severe adrenal fatigue. All of these stemmed from the overdrive of stress that I was living in for several years. My gut microbiome consisted of parasites, yeast overgrowth, bad bacteria overgrowth (SIBO), and a fungus overgrowth–my gut lining had been compromised. I was suffering from a leaky gut, which affected my brain by causing inflammation in my brain. Inflammation in the brain can look like brain fog, fatigue, slow responses, lack of energy, anxiety depression, etc. When the gut is not healthy, the brain is not going to function at a healthy capacity either, because our gut and brain are connected and communicate all day long via the vagus nerve. Again, the driving factor that caused these illnesses stemmed from stress.

At this point in my healing journey, a critical event that allowed me to accelerate my healing was going back to school. I was inspired to learn and take my health into my own hands, so I studied for and received my health and nutrition coaching license, and began to dive into the study of functional medicine. Overall, I wanted to feel good again. Although, I didn't want to just "feel good," I wanted to feel amazing. It was in my studies that I learned the entire body is connected and when one system isn't functioning correctly, it is going to compromise the other system(s).

I spent three years treating all of these health issues to get my health back to a balanced and good place. I came to understand that my body in the reactive state of "fight or flight" and ongoing stress, laid the foundation for disease in my body. My level of stress from my divorce and post-divorce literally made me sick. My elevated cortisol levels (stress hormones) were the underlying causes of all of these diseases that developed in my body. It's important to understand that excess cortisol impairs the immune system, which often leads the body to getting sick.

Taking care of your health is so important. We only have one body, and I learned that I am never going to take that for granted again. I will never pretend to be an expert in medicine, but with all of the knowledge I consumed in an effort to heal myself, I did become an expert in reading my own body (bio-individuality). I now understand the components of nutrition, mindfulness, stress management, and how they all play a critical role in maintaining wellness. I am happy to say that today I am healthier than I have ever been in my life. I made the changes that I needed to make. I had to address the gut issues, eliminate the bad stuff in my gut, and nourish my gut with amazing probiotics that change your microbiome in your gut (more on the microbiome, later). I took many supplements that were diminished in my body due to stress: minerals and vitamins like magnesium, zinc, vitamin D, fish oil, vitamin B12, B1, B2, B5, and B6. I embraced herbs to get rid of unhealthy bacteria in my gut and refueled the gut with the most amazing probiotics. I used herbs to reduce my cortisol levels and allowed my body to have healthier responses to stress.

I re-programmed my brain to learn new activities that were stress-reducing like yoga, meditation, and breathing exercises to slow the nervous system down. I had to learn that running and cardio were not good for me any longer because they increased my cortisol levels. I paid attention to everything I put into my body and made sure it was healthily fueling my cells.

I completely transformed the way I had to approach stress, life, food, and I made *me* my number one priority. I knew I could and would bring myself back to a beautiful place of light and health again. And I did just that. That was the greatest love I could have ever given myself. I needed to learn how to treat my body like a beautiful temple. My body was my beautiful temple, and I was determined to make every cell in my body perfect again.

Brain-Gut Connection and Stress

What happens when you are stressed? Do you know all the effects on your body? When we get stressed, we feel symptoms in the body like a racing heart, headache, fatigue, dizziness, muscle twitching, stomach pains or acid reflux, sweating, irritable bowel, and muscle tension or stiffness. These are the symptoms that we can actually *feel* in our body. However, what we don't feel in the body, is what stress is doing to our gut, specifically. Almost 85 percent of our immune system, or a substantial percentage of our immune system, resides in our gut. That's right!

Our gut is sig*nificantly impacted by what we eat and how we live.* The gut is home to an array of trillions of microbes, also known as the microbiome (the gut flora). These microbes are made up of mostly bacteria (good bacteria, when you are healthy), but also archaea, yeast, helminth parasites, viruses, and protozoa (bad bacteria, when you are not healthy). Would you believe this if I told you, the total weight of the gut microbes is equal to the weight of the human brain!

RESTFUL NIGHT SLEEP AND GOOD BACTERIA
The bacteria in our gut doesn't just contribute to disease in the body but also contributes to mood disorders. Can you see how vulnerable you become when you are going through a traumatic life event, such as divorce? The good bacteria can also contribute to a restful night

sleep. Sleep is a natural healing state, so it's of vital importance to have good quality sleep. Although, if your good bacteria are out of balance, anxiety, and depression are just the beginning of the problems that can occur.

The stress hormone cortisol can affect your circadian rhythms and also sleep patterns. When the body functions healthily, cortisol levels will function highest in the morning and lowest at night, to allow you to get a restful sleep. Cortisol levels stay balanced throughout the day to give you the appropriate energy you need.

Gut bacteria play a critical role in producing necessary chemicals called cytokines that work in sync with your cortisol levels. Healthy gut bacteria will keep your cortisol levels functioning like a beautiful orchestra. Bad bacteria on the other hand, or lack of good bacteria, restrict cortisol production or produce cortisol at wrong times of the day, inhibiting the members of the orchestra to be in sync. When gut bacteria are in sync with the chemical cytokines, you are able to produce a healthy and more restorative sleep pattern.

When gut bacteria have been compromised, you have lost the ability to produce the necessary chemicals that allow for healthy circadian rhythms to function and produce the restorative sleep you need. Our bodies can only repair when we receive restorative sleep. If you are experiencing insomnia, the critical step to take is to repair your gut!

STRESS REDUCTION

Our biography becomes our biology—the way we behave, the way we think, our mindset, the people we spend time with, and what we put into our body, dictates our overall wellness and health. Within this book and all the practices that I'm sharing with you, the main focus is on reprogramming the brain and having a positive mindset. The brain-gut connection is directly impacted by how you choose to fuel your mind, body, and spirit. Our thoughts, our beliefs, the food we put into our bodies, are all making changes to our biology at the cellular level. So, if we are in a constant state of stress, not eating proper foods, not getting enough sleep, thinking negative thoughts, etc. we are doing internal damage to the bacteria and cells in the gut, which directly affects our mind and body. A helpful tool for quickly reducing stress is to learn breathing techniques.

BREATHING TECHNIQUES TO REDUCE STRESS:

Clear your mind from all of the financial demands, family matters, career stresses, and divorce stress by using breathing techniques. When you spend just a few minutes on these easy-to-learn breathing techniques, you are not only changing your experience in this world but those around you as well.

1. **Nostril Breathing**

   Did you know that we have one nostril that is more dominant than the other? Scientists have been aware of this for years. Having a dominant nostril that we breathe out of is common, and furthermore, we subconsciously use this nostril for smelling certain chemicals. Other chemicals are detected by our slower moving nostril.

   Why is it important to know this, you may ask? Well, this ability is regulated by the same part of the brain that regulates your "fight or flight" response. When we switch up our nostrils back and forth, we are able to reset our system and lower our stress levels. Pretty cool, huh? The idea is to alternate the nostrils that you breathe through. Let's learn and practice together.

   Step 1: Using your index finger and middle finger, close your left nostril with your finger and breathe in through your right nostril.

   Step 2: Close both nostrils and hold for one count.

   Step 3: Close right nostril only and exhale from your left nostril.

Step 4: Inhale from your left nostril.

Step 5: Close both nostrils and hold your breath for one count.

Step 6: Exhale from your right nostril.

Repeat this cycle for a total of three to five minutes. You will see that your breathing is calmer, more relaxed and slower. This can be done anywhere, so allow yourself the space to do this if you are feeling overwhelmed, anxious, and/or experiencing high amounts of stress. You can do this quietly sitting in a chair, or in the midst of chaos. Make a habit of practicing this twice a day, to begin with. Your nervous system will thank you!

2. **Diaphragm Breathing**

I love this breathing technique as well. When we are in a "fight or flight" state, we breathe shallowly and quickly. We tend to breathe through our chest, which contributes to and exacerbates anxiety. Our bodies are meant to breathe deeply from our diaphragm, in a relaxed and thriving state. Luckily, we can reprogram our bodies to learn how to breathe, and as a result, our brains will follow suit. Diaphragm breathing immediately relaxes the nervous system and allows the lymphatic fluid to flow more easily through the body.

Step 1: Place your hand over your belly and close your eyes.

Step 2: Breathe deeply through your nose and feel your hand being pushed outward by your belly. On the exhale you will feel your hand being moved closer to your body.

Step 3: With every inhale, you should feel your hand push away a few inches, and then with the exhale your hand moves closer to your body.

Continue this pattern for three to five minutes. Practicing this type of breathing will help you become consciously aware throughout the day of your breath. Be mindful of whether you are using diaphragm breathing or chest breathing.

3. **Legs Up the Wall**

   Scoot your bottom up towards the wall. Lay down on your back, allowing your legs to rest above your body and on the wall. Your butt is at the crease of where the wall and floor meet, with your legs above you leaning on the wall.

   This position immediately puts your body in a calm and relaxed state. This position, with your legs above your heart, puts your parasympathetic nervous system in a place of calm, repair, and rest, etc.

   I personally work on my diaphragm breathing in this position. Stay in this position for several minutes. Allow yourself to feel renewed and relaxed while practicing nostril breathing or your diaphragm breathing.

Healthy Eating

By now, I hope you understand further, "we are what we put in our body." What works for one person, might not always work for another because we are made up differently with different bacteria. However, what does work for everyone is consuming a diet that is whole. When I say diet, I don't mean a diet that you're on to lose weight, I mean an eating lifestyle. A whole diet consists of proteins, healthy fats, fruits, vegetables, and whole grains. This type of diet is healthy for everyone because we all need a balanced consumption of each food group. While there are many types of diets available on the market today, such as Paleo, Keto, Ayurvedic, vegan, etc., none are absolutely right or entirely wrong to consume. The critical thing to remember is to have a balanced diet that is whole and works for you.

What's also important to be mindful of with your eating lifestyle, is your relationship with others. I say this because having toxic, negative relationships in your life can also bring poor eating habits to the table. Toxic and unhealthy relationships impede our bodies from thriving. Toxic relationships poison our cells. You want to be mindful of all areas of your life to have healthiness: your spiritual practices, your career, social life, movement, and more. They are all relevant for optimal health and consistent wholesome balance.

FOOD HYGIENE

When we are under stress, most often we are cramming our meals in and not being mindful of how we are consuming our food. Think about it for a moment, how did you consume your last lunch? In front of the computer working? On the go, while driving? Walking on your way to the next meeting? Waiting in the car line to pick up your children? Or perhaps you didn't have lunch at all because you were too busy. It most likely wasn't sitting down, in a calm state to consume the entire meal, then moving onto your next task of the day. When it comes to food hygiene, it's so important that we take into consideration the "how" we are consuming our food. I'll say it again, we are what we eat and we are what we think. If we rush through a meal and multi-task while eating, food is not adequately able to digest in our gut and provide the nourishment our body needs.

Eating, regardless, is a time to stop and be still, be in the present moment and allow the food you are consuming to nourish your mind, body, and spirit. Even if you only have 10 minutes, please slow down and take the 10 minutes that you have to eat with intention and mindfulness–it will support and nurture your overall well-being.

THE STANDARD AMERICAN DIET

Surprisingly, many people are not educated on what foods are good for them and not good for them because what is widely available, even what some doctors will recommend, is the standard American diet (SAD). It sounds like it should be good for us, right? Well, unfortunately, it's quite the opposite. The SAD is low in nutrients and high in toxins. The SAD includes sugar, salt, caffeine, additives, pesticides, and antibiotics. The diet is not designed to provide the right nutrition that the body needs. It does not consider the importance of consuming clean and organic foods because of the high levels of pesticides, antibiotics, and herbicides that are in most American foods.

While this book is not all about foods and our country's food education, I want you to understand the basic level of education you need to know to help minimize the risk of having too many toxins build up in your body. When toxins such as those from non-organic, non-clean foods, and an imbalanced diet, such as SAD, build up in the body, they contribute to inflammation and disease. The toxins can also add more stress to the body because the foods you're consuming are not providing nourishment but instead contributing to fatigue, brain fog, poor digestion, emotional imbalances, depression, mood swings, lack of focus, and more.

Creating the best version of you after divorce not only begins with emotional processing but your diet and food lifestyle as well. You have to look at the whole picture, including your health, food, and stress levels when bringing yourself to wholeness.

Our Stressed and Sugary Society

Did you know that our genes can influence why an individual will experience more weight gain than another? However, science now tells us that genes alone are not the contributing factor.

Epigenetics is the science that shows how our genes and environment both contribute to our outcome. What you eat, where you live, who you spend time with, when you sleep, how you exercise, and even how old you age—all of these can eventually cause chemical modifications around the genes that will turn those genes on or off over time. Epigenetics tells us that our environment most definitely contributes to whether or not specific genes that contribute to disease will be turned on. We have become a more obese society and nation than ever before. And if it isn't due to our genes, then what is it you might ask?

In the last few decades, many circumstances and ways of living have changed. The past few decades have become more toxic with the use of pesticides on our crops, antibiotics and hormones in our food; we use more medications; technology has overtaken our world, we spend less time in sunlight, more time multitasking, we sleep less, have more financial strains, and spend less time with friends. Technology has also significantly reduced our physical interactions with people in the workplace. Processed foods and toxins are among the biggest contributing factors to our obesity problem. Our foods have much more sugar and chemicals than ever before.

One thing that all of these have in common is how they affect our adrenal gland. Remember at the beginning of the chapter I shared that when the body is in a constant state of stress, the adrenals can no longer function healthily; therefore, we store fat. At a time when you are trying to look and feel your best, the excess cortisol makes you gain weight. Excess cortisol that is produced in the adrenal gland is turned to sugar and stored as fat, primarily around the organs, which is called visceral fat. Our adrenal gland cannot distinguish whether you are being chased by a tiger, angry at your ex-spouse, stressed at work, running late for your appointment, or just mad at life. It is our body's way of working to survive in times of stress. And the way it survives in times of stress is it produces more adrenaline and cortisol–cortisol turns to sugar, sugar is stored as fat, fat is stored around your organs, stomach, and thighs, and now your body craves more sugar. Ugh! Can you see how this is a dreaded cycle?

My purpose is to show you in this section how stress, sugar, and weight gain all go together. You may not even be eating very much but if you are in a state of chronic stress, it will have an everlasting negative impact on your body.

Why Functional Medicine?

Functional medicine is a form of medicine that addresses the root cause of disease. Functional medicine teaches us that the gastrointestinal tract (GI) governs how the rest of our body functions. If the digestive system is imbalanced and angry, then nothing else in the body is functioning properly–this includes your brain, immune system, hormones, nerves, muscles, etc. The one-cell-layer-thick lining of your gastrointestinal tract has the hefty responsibility of deciding which of the foods you eat get incorporated into your body and which get eliminated through stool. This is a vital task, which is why it is even more critical to understand why we must replenish and nurture our gut.

In addition to the gut-brain axis being affected by stress, your hormones are significantly impacted by stress as well. There is direct communication occurring between all your sex hormones. Our sex hormones include estrogen, progesterone, and testosterone. The thyroid hormones as well, are impacted by the bacteria that live in our GI tracts. If your hormones are out of balance, then our microbiome in our gut will also be imbalanced and vice versa. You can see how this is a vicious cycle and why it's imperative to feed the body with proper nutrition.

The Wholeness Map Stress Recommendations

While at the beginning I prefaced that this is a chapter to empower you and give you the knowledge to control your stress and eating habits, I also want to provide you with several recommendations from my health coaching and personal background, to add to your "stress response team."

TOP FIVE WHOLENESS RECOMMENDATIONS FOR THE BRAIN

We know that the brain and gut work together. Healthy mind, healthy gut! Here are five recommendations that you can implement to heal and boost your brain and gut health.

1. Eat foods rich in probiotics and prebiotics. Replenish gut with high-quality probiotics.

2. Drink filtered water.

3. Determine what minerals and vitamins you are deficient in and consume in foods and supplements.

4. Eat an organic diet of vegetables (fruits in moderation), proteins, healthy fats, whole grains (carbohydrates).

5. Implement a spiritual practice (daily) that reduces your stress levels.

CLEAN FOODS VS. DIRTY FOODS

I'm encouraging you to eat clean foods (organic or local farm foods) because as mentioned earlier, pesticides and herbicides are used to treat our crops, and antibiotics are used to expedite the growth process of animals (which are also consuming the treated crops). To keep this explanation simple, these pesticides and herbicides destroy bugs and pests by blowing up their stomachs. So imagine what it does to human's stomach linings when we consume these foods. This is one leading contributor to "leaky gut." Leaky gut is known as increased intestinal permeability, it is a digestive condition in which bacteria and "toxins" are able to leak through the intestinal wall. When the gut is "leaky" and bacteria and toxins enter the bloodstream, it can cause widespread inflammation and possibly trigger a reaction from the immune system. Symptoms of leaky gut syndrome include bloating, food sensitivities, fatigue, digestive problems, and skin problems. And as we already know, if your gut is not healthy, your brain is not healthy either. I believe wholeheartedly that your gut health is the highway to your overall well-being.

DIRTY DOZEN LIST:

This list is ranked by the use of higher amounts of pesticides being shown at the top of the list. These are the foods you absolutely want to consume organic because organic foods contain no amounts of pesticides or other residues.

- Strawberries
- Spinach
- Nectarines
- Apples
- Grapes
- Peaches
- Cherries
- Pears
- Tomatoes
- Celery
- Potatoes
- Sweet bell peppers
- Hot peppers*

CLEAN FIFTEEN LIST:

The clean fifteen are produce items known to have fewer pesticides and residues if not consumed organic; however, I still recommend always to choose organic, if possible.

- Avocados
- Sweet corn
- Pineapples

- Cabbage

- Onions

- Sweet frozen peas

- Papayas

- Asparagus

- Mangos

- Eggplant

- Honeydew melon

- Kiwi

- Cantaloupe

- Cauliflower

- Broccoli

THE WHOLENESS MAP (STRESS LESS) RECIPES

I know we all are super-busy and especially reading this chapter, you might be thinking it will be hard to incorporate something new and healthier into your eating routine. Well, I've taken the guesswork out of things for you here, as I'm providing you the key things to include in each meal. My own family and other clients enjoy these same key elements within their wholeness journey. I always keep in mind easy-to-make recipes and foods that store well if prepared ahead of time.

To help you stay in a healthy state throughout the week, I also encourage that you meal prep as much as you can on the weekend or whenever your "weekend" falls (sometimes based on people's work schedules, the weekend might be a Wednesday). Take some time on your day off and establish a routine to prep as much food as you can, so you can have quick "grab and go" food during the week to keep you on a healthy track. Another positive of doing this is to keep your stress level out of "fight or flight" mode, thinking about "what am I going to eat today?" Knowing ahead of time and having a meal plan for the week will keep your body in a state of calm and the tiny but mighty adrenal gland happy. When the adrenal gland is off, it throws everything else off in the body, so keep your stress level neutral, and the body can function at optimal capacity. I shop up to three times a week, buying fresh organic foods.

- Smoothie: Green smoothie (include protein powder, greens, seeds, and fats)

- Breakfast: Eggs, kale, avocado (protein "slam dunk" in the morning)

- Lunch: Vegetables, Fat, Carbs (about 2 golf ball-size carbs)

- Dinner: Vegetable, Protein (palm of a hand-lowest amount of protein), Carbs (about 3 golf ball size carbs)

- Snacks: Carrots, celery, peppers, and hummus; apple and a few almonds (about 5-10)

Keys to Healing Stress and Living Healthy

It's entirely possible for you to experience better health, lower levels of stress, higher levels of happiness and joy, and even lose weight if you desire. Again, while this book is not a medical book or official functional medicine advice, I can assure you that if you seek out the right guidance and support, you will be able to have a higher quality of life. You can begin to lay the foundation by making the smallest adjustments with simply replacing the food you buy at the grocery store and drinking enough water throughout the day. Trust your intuition to guide you and learn to listen to your body as well.

These keys are a combination of everything you've read in this chapter and also things you've read up to this chapter. You will learn even more throughout the transformation part of this book, so be mindful to implement the keys on an even deeper level once you've reached the end of *The Wholeness Map*. Let your journey to healing stress and living healthy begin!

Key One: Detox

Detoxing the body helps not only your body but your lifestyle. When you detox your lifestyle, it becomes part of your way of life. Practices that you've learned earlier in this book are all part of "detoxing" your lifestyle. Reprogramming your brain, invoking positive thoughts, etc. are all detoxing because they are encouraging and inspiring you to eliminate what is no longer serving you. The same goes for the body. Detoxing the body can be done in many ways, but to keep things simple you can begin by replacing processed foods with more vegetables.

Detoxing doesn't have to feel like a burden or "something else to add to the list." It's about looking at what's working and not working and what you need to change. It doesn't have to be hard, as you can start slowly. This could even be as simple as incorporating more water into your day. For me, I take detoxing to a higher level by sitting in an infrared sauna for thirty to sixty minutes a few times a week. Infrared rays are the healthiest rays; they penetrate into your skin deeply, and they dissolve harmful substances accumulated in your body. I purchased one for my home, so if this is something that appeals to you, you can take your detoxing to a whole other level. It not only detoxes the body but it calms the nervous system as well.

Take inventory of what you'd like to change and improve in your diet and lifestyle, then create your own "detox roadmap." Slowly but surely you will begin to see positive changes and improvements in your mind, body, and overall well-being.

Key Two: You are What You Eat and Think

This is simple, as mentioned earlier in the chapter. You are what you eat and think—the body is an interconnected web, so what you eat will affect how you think, and what you think can also change and support how you eat, and even digest, foods.

What you directly put into your body is going to support (or not support) your health. Same for what you think, which we talked about in chapter four. What you think and the actions you take are a direct reflection of what happens in your reality. If you genuinely desire to fill your holes with wholeness, it's imperative to always remember this small nugget of wisdom.

If you find yourself questioning whether something is good for you, be it food, a friendship, relationship, job, travel adventure, etc., think about whether it would enhance or harm your immediate or long-term well-being. If you can answer your question without a shadow of a doubt that it will support your well-being, then you're on the right track. If you hesitate, believing that you may experience high levels of stress, then I guide you to ask for help from your tribe and also from the Universe. Be the best version of you and only consume thoughts, friendships, relationships, food, etc. that support the growth of your well-being.

Key Three: Be Aware

Awareness, as mentioned earlier in the book, is a strong key on your wholeness journey. When you are able to be in tune with your body and hear what it's telling you, you're able to be more aware of the moments when your body is highly stressed and needs support. Awareness is the beginning for your "stress response team." When you are able to quickly identify you are in a state of "fight or flight," stress, or anxiety, then you'll be able to begin to slow down, pause, and reset your nervous system.

Key Four: The Body Always Follows the Mind

Your body will always follow your mind, per the gut-brain connection that we talked about earlier in the chapter. The healthiness of your gut will drive the way your brain processes. Think of it this way–everything begins in the gut. So if you are able to have a clean and healthy gut, it only further supports the overall clarity and health of your mind, body, and spirit.

Key Five: Have Support

As you read in chapter five, having your tribe of like-minded warriors around you supports your growth in life, as well as the growth of your tribe. Overcoming and managing stress isn't always easy, so when there are those moments when you want to "pull your hair out" (literally or figuratively), seek the support of your tribe.

Also having a health/life coach or therapist in your corner can be a tremendous asset because they are able to help, support, and hold you accountable to your goals, desires, and vision. This is what I personally do in my divorce coaching because we all know by now, you have to work through many layers to maintain your lifestyle and stress is one of them. Regulating your stress can be a juggling act, so allow yourself the grace, patience, and gift to work with someone who can support you through your divorce and your personal wholeness journey.

Reflection Exercise:

I'd like you to stop and reflect for a moment, with few distractions around you. You can reflect in your mind, or if you'd like to journal your thoughts, I encourage you to do so.

1. I want you to reflect on what your diet and lifestyle is like today. Do you see that your diet is supporting you in your lifestyle or do you see that your diet can be improved?

2. Does your diet include higher amounts of sugar and processed foods, rather than greens, vegetables, and healthy fats?

3. Knowing what you know now from the chapter, how often would you say you experience depression, bloating, sadness, brain fog, etc.?

4. Do you find the symptoms of stress drive you to eat poorly or contribute to emotional and imbalanced eating?

5. How long have you experienced high levels of stress? Can you reflect back and link stress symptoms to a change in your lifestyle?

6. Do you have a balance of work, life, career, family, etc.? Or are you always on the go and not taking the time to experience "the moment," including eating (remember the lunch example in this chapter)?

7. Do your relationships feed your soul in a positive or negative way?

Allow yourself to be honest here so you can start to incorporate healthier habits into your lifestyle. You need to nourish yourself so you can continue to show up to all the responsibilities that you have. I know after divorce, it is hard to feel a balance because so much is going on and shifting. But I can promise you this, the sooner you are able to get control of your stress levels and nourish your body with fuel and clean foods, the longevity of your happiness, peace, and wholeness will sustain for a lifetime.

The Wholeness Journey

Your body is your vessel for LIFE. You are here on Earth to take care of yourself, the best way that you know how and obviously what you put in your body contributes to this a lot. This is your opportunity to be mindful of what you are putting in your body, the thoughts that you think, and the actions you take, to bring your mind, body, and spirit to spiritual enlightenment, and wholeness. I know everyone indulges and enjoys certain things in life, but creating goals and intentions that allow you to create the best physical body for yourself is of utmost importance. Without a healthy body, inside and out, the wholeness journey would never be "whole." Remember we are working on filling your holes, figuratively speaking, with wholeness.

Have an awareness of what you are feeding your mind and body because it will directly affect your mind, mood, stress level, happiness, and more. Use food as your primary source of medicine for life. Wholeness is a lifetime journey. So take the time you need, as the body always follows the mind. And the mind follows the gut!

LIVE IN THE NOW!

Allow yourself to feel the natural ups and downs of emotions that you are going to feel during the healing phase. Healing can take years, not weeks or months. The important point is that each month and year that goes by, you are more introspective of who you are, and love who it is you are becoming.

I shared with you the practice of mindfulness in the previous section. Mindfulness is a practice that should be sharpened and improved over time. It is like building a muscle in the brain. When you are mindful, it will also allow you to observe the emotions that keep coming up. When you sharpen your awareness of mindfulness, it will enable you to "live in the now."

All of your stresses, fears, worries, and negative feelings occur when you are either living in your past and fixated on something that has already happened, or you are living in the future and worrying or fixating on events that haven't yet happened. Every time you go back into the past, you re-experience those same negative events over and over again, creating the same biochemical reactions that negatively impact your body at the cellular level. Imagine when you relive those events, again and again, your cells absorb the positive or negative emotions as well.

Living in the present is the healthiest mindset and space for you to heal your body, mind, and spirit.

PART THREE

Stepping Into the Transformation of Self

FEEL AND KNOW YOUR WORTH!

To be grounded means you are connected to the earth and your feet are on solid ground. You feel focused and present in the moment. Your soul feels connected to your physical body, and you are able to "be" in the moment.

It is imperative to take everything that you have learned in the healing process and carry it with you into transformation. This will allow you to dive deeper into your practice of self-love, explore your inner depths of your god/goddess, and know your worth before stepping into dating.

When we create a practice of "giving back" we get back what we give. The Universe gives back to us an expansive and abundant amount of love. To give and be of service allows us to expand our self-worth and feel good about who we have become.

CHAPTER EIGHT

Be the Leader of Your Life & Your Inner Voice

Welcome to the transformation of you! I genuinely believe that deep inner connection, peace, love, and wholeness, only become awakened and alive through big life changes. Divorce is one of those big life changes. What I want you to embody, and what I've discovered for myself, is that divorce, although painful, will transform you into a stronger person with limitless control over your thoughts and actions.

In order to facilitate this transformation you'll need to understand two key traits that already exist inside you. The first is your intuition, which we all know about but many people seldom listen to or trust. In this chapter, we will navigate the path to developing an intimate relationship with your inner voice. That inner voice that lives inside all things, works on your behalf. Your inner voice plays on your team by feeding off the energy flowing through your body.

The second trait is your innate ability to lead your life in the direction you want it to go. This trait, like intuition, is ingrained in all humans but only truly understood by those who accept it into their core beliefs.

Have you ever felt like you're not a "natural leader"?

A lot of people, I think, get led to believe that they aren't good leaders. These beliefs can stem back to their earliest years. In an unhealthy marriage, one person tends to be the leader and the other takes the orders, so to speak. That may work out for a time, but in your post-divorce life you'll find yourself face-to-face with the opportunity to seize your life by the horns. From this book, I want you to charge into your new life with the mindset of a leader. Or, at least, a leader-in-training.

The energy of transformation creates and redefines your internal belief system. Beliefs that are with us as adults have been taught to us and ingrained since childhood. You are stepping into a new dimension of shaping your own beliefs, loving yourself, and leading your life with the courage of your internal compass and desires.

The Leader Within

When you take control over your thoughts, like we talked about in chapter five, you are a leader. When you take control of your reactions to high-conflict or narcissistic persons, you are a leader. When you align your actions with your intentions, you are a leader. All the things we've talked about in the book up to this point are traits of a leader. The type of leaders I'm talking about are leaders of their lives. If you can see this in yourself, because it is there, you will navigate the potentially treacherous waters of divorce with grace, ease, and abundance. You can step into this role as a leader right now, and that's what you will do. You need to be a leader, because as a leader you will set an example for your kids. As the leader of your life, you will set an example for other people going through challenging life events, like divorce. Words don't hold much value during divorce, and it's likely that a lot of words will be thrown back and forth in yours. A leader doesn't play into this game because it only slows down progress. If you choose to get a divorce, you are choosing to become a leader!

Your children are going to be subconsciously observing both parents during your divorce. Those observations may not be understood in the moment, but over time their observations will have an impact on how they develop. Children need leadership and we see this every day. Poor leadership from adults can lead to children repeating the same behavior as adults. You must be a leader for your children and for yourself. I knew that I couldn't control what my ex-spouse did while he was with my kids when they were younger, nor could I have any impact on the quality of life that he would go on to create. This can be a scary idea when you don't think your ex-spouse is being a positive leader. I always made sure that I led by example because words don't hold much value.

When it comes to raising my children, they learn best from what I do and not what I say. I am far from perfect (my children would agree), however I make a point to live every day with purpose. I practice everything that I have shared in this book not only for my own growth, but for my children's growth. I eat a clean diet of organic vegetables and fruits, green smoothies with collagen, pea protein, flax and chia. My kids have observed my eating habits and have adjusted their own diets with the intent to eat a fresh and nutritional diet. I practice holistic and functional medicine, consuming probiotics and supplements that fuel my immune system. My kids have observed and watched these habits and have made choices to do the same. When I ever feel a cold coming on, I reach for oregano oil (natural antibiotic and many other benefits) and high doses of vitamin C, which eliminates my symptoms in a day. As my children have matured into young adults and teens, they are taking care of their bodies in a healthy and holistic way as well. I have bought, fixed up, and sold multiple homes in the last 12 years as a single mother. I wanted my children to learn valuable lessons in home ownership, recognize financial gains and opportunities, accept change gracefully, and live an adventurous life. My kids have adapted a similar mindset, in regard to our home improvement projects, seeing them as a creative and fun business opportunity. The gift you can share with your children as a leader are invaluable. When you own your own leader within, that behavior trickles down to them as well.

Your Inner Voice

The job of a leader is one that often comes with criticism and waves of self-doubt. These self-doubts usually stem from the uncertainty and fear associated with not knowing what the future holds. Outside influences, such as friends and family, can add to or take away from your ability to hear and trust your inner voice. I've mentioned in earlier chapters that other people may struggle to cope with how your life is changing during and after divorce. They will tell you what they think you should do, even if they don't know all the facts of the situation. It's what you should expect from the closest people in your life, but that doesn't mean you need to follow their guidance, nor should you if you know it's not what you need. This is where listening to your inner voice will be of the utmost importance.

Your inner voice, or intuition, is the most trustworthy source of guidance you have at your disposal. The people you trust most have valuable opinions and suggestions for you, many of which will be in line with what your inner voice is telling you. Your job is to relinquish any need for validation by accepting that the things you do must feel right to you and to you alone. Validation is kryptonite to your inner voice. The more validation you seek from sources outside your mind and body, the more your inner voice will be stifled and quiet. This is a time when you need to turn up the volume of your intuition, and not stifle it in the face of big decisions. The way to turn up the volume is by doing the self-reflection exercises and implementing mindfulness practices in your life. The art of hearing and following your intuition is a practice itself. The more practice you put in, the better results you will get.

In business, a CEO is expected to lead their company to be more successful as an organization. A CEO will face the same type of outside influence that you will face during divorce. A CEO is a leader of the business just as you are the leader of your life, and a successful CEO will tell you that following your inner voice is the key to making the best decisions given the situation. Embody the idea that your life is like a business and in order for you to create the best life for you and your children, you need to trust your inner voice. That's why being the leader of your life and listening to your intuition go hand in hand!

The first action step to harness the power of your inner voice is accepting the fear and "shakiness" that will come up during your divorce. As I talked about early in the book, sitting with your shakiness, in your alone time, instead of running from it, allows you to look your fear in the face. When you practice this consistently, the fears you have will get smaller. You inner voice will see you face those fears and chime in with hints and guidance. That guidance is what people refer to as "following your heart". You know this feeling because you've heard it before. The issue with divorce is that you have emotions running high, fear, and self-doubt based on all the unknowns that come with a new life. Learn to sit with the shakiness as a means to unlocking more power in your inner voice. If you make decisions without acknowledging the fear you have around all the potential outcomes, you are increasing the chances that you make the best decision for others, not for yourself. Your inner voice is the best teammate you have in life!

The second action step is to remove all the need for external validation in your choices. Validation seeking, as I call it, is the fastest way to backtracking on your inner voice's guidance and changing your mind. Your gut instinct, your intuition, your inner voice, or whatever you prefer to call it, all operate on a higher level than your conscious mind. Your conscious mind can be swayed relatively easily, but your unconscious mind knows the best path for you. In the initial stages of my divorce, and during the two years of separation from my husband, I was often plagued with second-guessing my inner voice because of outsiders telling me what they thought I should do. Even though I knew that they wanted what was best for me, their advice didn't encompass all the facts of our marriage. I went through a lot of unnecessary stress and self-doubt during this time. The moment I finally accepted that I simply cannot follow anyone's but my own inner voice, I saw immediate relief from these stressors.

HOW TO STRENGTHEN YOUR INTUITION

When I tell people to practice strengthening their intuition, they always ask me, *how?* In the beginning, it might be difficult to understand what is your intuition speaking versus your logical mind. What usually works for me is tapping into my strong gut-brain connection, energy will feel great in my gut then I'll experience that same positive message in my brain. It leaves me with a sense of whole-body inner peace.

The most important thing to remember is that tapping into your intuition can be strengthened through any form of self-care. Self-care is all about slowing down and being in the moment. That is exactly what your intuition lives and thrives on–calm moments. Here are a few tools you can use.

TECHNIQUES AND TOOLS TO TAP INTO YOUR INNER VOICE

- Emotional Freedom Technique (EFT) - a psychological acupressure technique that supports your emotional health

- Meditation - the art of practicing mindfulness

- Yoga - spiritual practice including breath work, meditation, and body movement to improve health and wellness

- Acupuncture - complementary medicine that alleviates pain and treats physical, mental, and emotional conditions

- Reiki - a healing technique that channels energy with touch and restores physical and emotional well-being

- Physical Exercise (strength training, circuit training, cardio, CrossFit, etc.) - any type of movement that increases the heart rate

- Breathing Techniques - mindfully breathing and practicing different methods of breathing for stress reduction, wellness, and even restorative sleep

- Infrared Sauna - used for detoxing the body

- Massages - releasing tension in muscles and joints to ease pain

- Mani/Pedi - (I think you get this one!)
- Spiritual Retreats - sacred spaces around the world that focus on Zen and connected oneness
- Visualization - a mental image or picture of something
- Nature walk - walking in nature, without technology to take in all that is around you

If you're always on the go, and never take time for yourself, your intuition is going to be quiet and faint. This book is all about finding your way back to self-love and your center before, during, or after your divorce is finalized. If you're not able to practice some of the examples to strengthen your intuition, simply just be, be still.

And by no means is this a comprehensive list, if there is something else that resonates with you, that allows you to slow down and connect deeper with your higher self, I encourage you to use that practice or exercise. You will be amazed at what you begin to feel and hear if you start to move slower.

THE POWER OF LIVING IN THE NOW

Your ability to harness your natural ability to lead your life and listen to your inner voice will be directly tied to how consciously aware you can become of the present moment. Divorce is a life-changing event that brings with it intense levels of stress, self-doubt, and fear as we've discussed in length up to this point. The present moment is the moment that I want you to live in as much as possible. The present moment is where your leadership will shine and when your inner voice will be heard with the most clarity. In the present moment, stress doesn't exist. Stress exists when you look at the past and the future. The past cannot be changed, and the future hasn't happened yet. Living in the now is all you have to operate from, and with that fact comes a weightless feeling free of fear and scarcity.

The question that gets asked the most before a divorce is, "how am I going to do all this??" This is the question that I let bounce around in my head for years before I embraced the unknown of what my life would look like after my divorce. I see this question in every single person I have ever worked with because it's at the root of all the fear that holds people back from leaving an unhealthy marriage and unhappy life behind. I relate this question to the saying that "it's darkest just before dawn!" As soon as you can find the trust in yourself that everything will work out, you will feel a massive shift in forward momentum towards a more joyful life. All the things that create fear of divorce, such as income, alimony, child support, custody, and more responsibility, will fall apart when you give in to the power of the present moment. In the present moment you cannot experience fear or stress unless you are faced with one of two things. The first is a life-threatening scenario like being chased by a bull through the streets of Spain. There is fear in the present moment if that is happening to you and I won't argue that!

The second way to experience stress and fear in the present moment is through procrastination. The power of procrastination, and the beauty of overcoming it, is a big part of stress in divorce. In my life, I essentially procrastinated on my divorce for two whole years because of fear and stress. I didn't embody the natural leader inside me, I ignored my inner voice that told me it's time to move on from my marriage. I let my focus on image and what my family looked like from the outside take priority over how it was feeling from the inside. I knew the marriage was not working and I didn't feel safe or healthy in my marriage. Students procrastinate homework until the night before the deadline and then try to throw something together quickly without any preparation. In divorce and in school, procrastination breeds a lack of preparedness for the inevitable and unnecessary stress during the time leading up to the moment of truth! Absolve yourself of procrastination by taking charge in the present moment. When your inner voice is yelling at you with the truth of the situation, and you know it's the truth, act on it as a leader straightaway.

The power of living in the moment is indescribable, other than it's so powerful and healing in itself because it's bringing you back to being whole at the moment. When you are going through a divorce and post-divorce you don't know what to expect because most likely you've never been through a divorce before. You have no idea what to expect, and you're afraid of the future because there are so many new things and you're looking down a highway that sees nothing but darkness.

Don't worry about what's happening in the future, when the next argument is going to be with your ex, when and how you're going to get your kids to their team practices, how you're going to pay the bills, and so on and so on. There is nothing you can do at this moment, except overstimulate your nervous system and cause more stress and anxiety.

If you're always living in the future and/or the past, your energy will be depleted and begin crippling you from moving forward. When you're able to practice and apply the mindfulness of "being in the moment," experiencing, feeling and seeing everything that is happening right now, you're able to let go of worry and calm your nervous system. Think of this practice as a muscle in your body. The more you work on living in the moment by making decisions based on your gut instinct, and executing the necessary action steps quickly, the more graceful your life will feel during your divorce. It will show on the inside through a healthy energy that everyone around can feel, and it will show on the outside by being a leader to friends, family, your ex-spouse, and your children.

Creating Your New Story

I remember reading about the power of living in the present years after my divorce thinking, *Wow, this would have really helped me going through my divorce and post-divorce.* The same is true for your story. I had to learn and trust that my inner voice and my story were steering me in the right direction all the time and listening to others' stories, advice, and drama was not the right path. Steve Jobs quoted, "Your time is limited, so don't waste it living someone else's life. Don't be trapped by dogma–which is living with the results of other people's thinking. Don't let the noise of other's opinions drown out your own inner voice. And most importantly, have the courage to follow your heart and intuition. They somehow already know what you truly want to become."

When you look at your divorce and post-divorce as an opportunity, you've just declared to the Universe that you're ready to be the author of your own story–to write a beautiful story that is all yours. Right now, it's time to say goodbye to any old story that is no longer serving you. As a leader, and with the help of your inner voice, it's time to create a new story for your new life.

We create old stories and patterns about ourselves based out of fears, illusions from our past experiences and beliefs that were put onto us by our ex-partners or from our childhood. This is your opportunity to truly recreate who you are and who you are becoming. You are not a victim and that's not the energy you want to carry forward, no matter what your ex-spouse has put you through. The new story that you are creating can be filled with anything you desire, and for that reason it's important to create your life from love and gratitude, not from a victim state of mind.

If you aren't able to shift or change the story that you've been playing over and over, it will merely be that, the same story that you were living in your marriage but the label has just been changed (to post-divorce). If you continue to argue, fight, do the same routines with your kids, continue to surround yourself with energy vampires, and don't develop a tribe of like-minded friends, you'll carry the same energy from your marriage into your new life. Come to terms with your old story, acknowledge your limiting beliefs by bringing them to light. Become aware of these things so that you can replace them with a more authentic life and inspiring goals for yourself.

Have you told yourself that you're not good enough, fearful of the future, will never find love again, can never have a tribe of good friends, or a well-paying career? These limiting beliefs and stories are holding you back from what's possible for you. The Law of Attraction does not work for you here if you are not in a positive mindset. Your old stories could have been ingrained into your subconscious since childhood, or at some point before or during your marriage. I want you to love your scars from living through an unhealthy, potentially unsafe marriage. Every time an old story comes up, immediately recognize and release the story because it no longer serves you. The simple act of reading this book and implementing small but consistent changes, will reprogram your brain and inner voice to come back to a place of self-love and acceptance of your new story.

I was living under tremendous amounts of stress for two years after my divorce. I felt symptoms of health-related issues from the everyday stress in my body. I was living in a story that was killing my body internally and I knew something had to give. One of the best decisions I ever made for myself was to stop listening to traditional doctors that were not solving any of these issues and, mostly, wanted to prescribe medication that I didn't believe in. My inner voice was screaming at me to make a change. I could feel it in the energy flowing through my body! I had to change my story because what I was doing wasn't helping to create a better life for my children or myself. I was putting my health in so many different doctors' hands without getting the results I needed. Then I went back to school to study functional medicine. This was the first step in taking control of my health, and adding to my new life story. My new story, that I was creating and telling the Universe, was that I can heal my stress-related health issues by changing what I eat, how I exercise, and most importantly, the nature of the thoughts in my head. When I took action to change my story in this aspect, it had a ripple effect to other areas of my life. The simple act of ignoring the fear-based thought patterns of, "how can I go back to school while raising five kids?" allowed me the space to actually get it done.

Change Your Story Exercise:

In this exercise, you will begin to test your inner voice, and hone in on what areas of your life need the most attention. This is an exciting way to feel the present moment, and what you need to do to make the right moves going forward.

You will start with five categories and for each category you will answer the same set of questions. These questions are going to set the stage for creating your new story by first identifying what your current story is. The five categories are Lifestyle, Career, Your Tribe, Spirituality, and Self-Care. Grab your journal or a piece of paper and divide it into five sections. For each category answer the following four questions:

1. What is your gut telling you right now about this area of your life? How does this area of your life look and feel to you right now? Are you the leader of this area of your life? Why or why not?

2. How much energy do you feel in this area of your life? Is there excitement around this area of your life?

3. If your answer to #2 is low energy, what are you not happy with? What is one thing that you want to change? Start with just one, maybe two changes that you want to see.

4. What are the obstacles in your way right now with this area of your life?

Here is an example from my life for this exercise. I'm going to answer these four questions under the category of *Lifestyle*, and elaborate on the functional medicine example from the last section. These are notes from when I did this exercise years ago.

1. I feel like I have no control over my ability to overcome stress-related disease in my body. I'm suffering from symptoms caused by living in a "fight or flight" state. I definitely do not feel like I'm leading my life in this area because I am getting different answers from numerous traditional medicine doctors. I've been offered prescriptions that I do not want as the only real solution to dealing with my symptoms.

2. I feel excited because I know from reading a book recently that I am not the only person who has turned away from traditional medicine as the only way to overcome disease in the body. On the other hand, I feel like I'm living with low energy because I don't know what the outcome will be. I have a lot of uncertainty and I know my body is suffering from too much stress. The lack of control I have over how I can beat these symptoms and issues I'm suffering from is causing a low-energy feeling.

3. I'm not happy with the fact that I'm being told that drugs are the only way to fix my overstressed state. I fully believe there must be other ways, but it's really hard to know what those other ways are without having more knowledge on non-traditional medicine.

4. The roadblocks stopping me are basically just the commitments I have to my children. I'm not sure if I can create the time needed to learn more about functional medicine. The other roadblock I'm facing is not having any prior experience studying medicine of any kind!

I remember that soon after I did this exercise, I found a local institute that offered certifications in health and wellness coaching using functional medicine. This was at a point in my life when my overall health was not great and I knew that it was due to stress from my divorce, from my ex-spouse, and from having more responsibilities. I found out that there were programs that worked within my budget, and that I could make time for in my busy life to help myself learn about functional medicine. This reinforced the importance of looking at what was going on in my life, where I needed help, and telling the Universe what I wanted in order for my intentions to be heard! Identifying my roadblocks highlighted the obstacles that I needed to overcome. It's a simple way to get real about what where you're at.

You might find that in some categories you feel a lot of excitement and high energy towards the story you are already creating. That's beautiful. You don't need to only find things to "fix" because that isn't the point of the exercise. This exercise is to identify what parts of your story need more attention than others.

Deservability

What do you feel you deserve out of this life? Sometimes we neglect to put any effort into creating a good life for ourselves. This can stem from feeling like you don't deserve abundance in certain areas or any areas of your life. The theme of my life today is that I deserve everything I want because there's no reason I cannot achieve the dreams I have. If I didn't deserve something, why would I dream about it? The concept of deservability is quite interesting when you break it down, which I will do right now. I want to highlight why I believe that you do deserve what you want out of life, and to do so, I need to simplify the concept.

Imagine two different people, living two completely different lives, with totally different upbringings. The first person was born into a wealthy family, who has always had the latest gadgets, was given a brand new car on their 16th birthday, and has connections to great career choices. You get the idea! I'm talking about someone who has had a lot of things work out in their life for them. They are no better or worse than anyone else, and they have had ups and downs in their life like everyone else. Next, imagine a person that came from a working class family whose parents mostly lived paycheck to paycheck. This person went to normal public schools, wasn't given a clear path to college, didn't always have new clothes for the school year and so on. This person doesn't have a lot of successful connections in life to help them advance forward. Picture this type of person and the other, wealthier, type of person in your mind right now.

When we talk about a beautiful life, full of abundance and happiness, most people would say that the wealthy person is more inclined to have that. That may be true! I mean, how great would it be to get a brand new car on your 16th birthday? Sounds like a good deal to me.

This is a key point to bring up because I want to show you that having a great life and deserving a great life are two very different things. The biggest roadblock for people who don't currently live lives full of happiness and abundance is their inability to embrace the fact they deserve that life. Deservability comes just before obtainability. In order to obtain the life that you really want for yourself and your children, you must first embrace the fact that you deserve it.

If we look at our two imaginary people, one who has wealth and the other who was raised without wealth, the former is far more likely to embrace the fact that they deserve an abundant life. If you've never experienced abundance, it is much more difficult to create abundance. That difficulty starts with believing that you actually deserve abundance. People that have lived more privileged lives naturally feel like they deserve that life. This has nothing to do with who deserves an abundant life and who does not deserve an abundant life. For the most part, everyone deserves a life of abundance from the day they are brought into this world.

If you were raised by parents who struggled financially or never had extra money for vacations and new cars, it will be harder to cultivate the feeling that you do, without a doubt, deserve whatever life you want for yourself. This is extremely important because in order for you to be the leader of your life, you must first believe, with every cell in your body, that you deserve the life you want.

Let's begin by balancing your life experiences with your life dreams by saying "I AM" statements. The first part of awakening the leader within you is to believe and acknowledge that you are free and open to deserve whatever you want. We will use "I AM" statements that are short, powerful affirmations that awaken and invoke what you desire, crave, and want to manifest.

You can say these quietly in your head, anytime. On the other hand say them out loud in the comfort of your own home for an even more impactful result on your body and mind. You want the Universe to hear you, and what better way than standing in front of a mirror and saying these out loud! If you see a word that is capitalized, you should emphasize that word.

I am deserving.
I DESERVE abundance.
Not a little, not some, but PURE abundance.
I am FREE of limit self-beliefs.
I release and let go of the limitations of others. I love them,
    and they deserve abundance.
I am in control of what I want.
I am deserving of EVERYTHING I want.
I am creating abundance RIGHT NOW.
I am SURROUNDED by abundance.
I am only positive thoughts about myself, about others, and
    about life.
I am free of ALL stress.
I am working in harmony with the Universe.
I am living a life FULL of possibilities.
I deserve everything I desire.
I deserve love in all forms.
I deserve good health.
I deserve to prosper.
I deserve joy and happiness.
I deserve freedom.
I deserve abundance.

To awaken deeper levels of your spiritual being, you must be willing to let go of any limiting beliefs that hold you back from believing you deserve an abundant life.

KEY VALUES AND BELIEFS REFLECTIONS

In this section, I'm going to guide you along the path to recognizing your beliefs using your inner voice as a tool. This will require you to be real with yourself, and work from a place of getting more open and honest with yourself. No one will see this work, or know what you write so don't hold back from what comes up. Everything that you have gone through in your life has played a role in your beliefs, especially in what limiting beliefs you have. Your ex-spouse, your parents, all the events you've gone through have shaped the way that you see the world. These questions are designed to spark thoughts inside your head so that you can write them down. That's the key! You must write them down and bring them into the open so you can explore whether you should keep those beliefs or not. Expand on the points with all that comes to mind. Journal and reflect when you hear something pop into your head

Life Purpose & Lifestyle:
(career, money, home, your passions, travel)

- *Do you feel you know your purpose in your life?*
- *How do you view money?*
- *Are there any limiting beliefs around how much money you can acquire?*
- *Do you see money as a consistent stress in your life?*
- *Has money been abundant for you?*
- *What are your beliefs about traveling?*
- *Is traveling something you want more of in your life?*
- *Is traveling, regardless of where you go, important to you?*
- *What are your beliefs on how a home should look and feel?*
- *Is home ownership challenging to you?*

- *Is a home attainable or important for you?*
- *How do you view saving money?*

Body & Wellness:
(healing, fitness, food, rest and relaxation, mental health, sensuality, sex)

- *What does health and wellness mean to you?*
- *What are your beliefs on what healthy eating looks like?*
- *How much do you value physical fitness in your life?*
- *How do you prioritize physical fitness compared to other areas of your life (career, relationships, diet etc.)?*
- *What does rest and relaxation look like in your mind?*
- *How much importance do you place on getting proper sleep? What does good sleep look like? How do you value a good night's sleep (8 hours)?*
- *What is your belief on always being busy or having things to do?*
- *Do you believe it's important to live a busy life?*
- *What do you believe is a healthy sex life for adults?*

Creativity & Learning:
(self-expression, higher education, ongoing learning, hobbies, interests)

- *List three things that you enjoy doing alone? Think of any hobby, activity, or interest.*
- *How difficult or easy is self-expression in your daily life?*
- *How important is higher education and ongoing learning?*
- *How do you define creativity? Where does it come from?*
- *How is creativity channeled in your life right now?*
- *Are you a creative person?*

Relationships, Love, & Society:
(romance, intimacy, friends, family, community, self-love)

- *What are important qualities in your intimate relationships and friendships?*
- *How do you define self-love?*
- *Do you believe self-love plays a role in who we attract in our life?*
- *What are your beliefs about "finding the one" and soulmates? Why?*
- *What does a healthy family look like to you? How does it feel?*
- *How do you value having healthy boundaries in your family?*
- *What is quality family time?*
- *What is a healthy community? What is your role in it?*
- *What does giving to your community look and feel like?*

Parenting:
(this may or may not apply right now, but I encourage you to explore this area)

- *How do you feel about being a parent?*
- *What do you perceive the role of a parent being?*
- *What does having rules, strictness, and structure look like when raising children?*
- *What do you desire for your children to remember about you, your legacy?*

Essence & Spirituality:
(your soul, higher power, intuition, rituals/practices)

- *Do you believe in a higher power? What does it look like?*
- *What is spirituality to you? How is it different from a higher power?*
- *Do you have a daily practice that connects you with your intuition or higher self?*

- *Do you believe there is a right or wrong way to practice spirituality?*
- *Do you feel connected to your intuition? What does it feel like?*
- *Does your intuition navigate your decision-making? And how?*

Your life is beautiful and now is the time to expand on what is possible in life, quiet your ego, and listen to your intuition. You can get as specific and imaginative as you want! Some people prefer to keep things broad, you might prefer to niche down to specifics. Remember, this exercise is for YOU and nobody else, so do this exercise and reflection as it resonates with you. The overall goal is simply to look at your belief system and understand if you have any areas out of balance. An area that is out of balance is one that has beliefs that are holding you back. In doing this exercise, and being completely honest with yourself throughout, you can identify which areas of your life to focus attention on. This is a step on the path to advancing yourself towards the version that you see in your mind in your post-divorce life.

Abundance

Abundance is a word that gets thrown around a lot in this day and age, and often it makes people think about "stuff" instead of passion. Passion is what makes abundance feel real in your life. Abundance isn't clearing your mind so that you can get more stuff in your life. It's not about making your mind focus on having unlimited resources at your disposal. The last thing you want to focus on when you think about abundance is that everything will be going great in your life all the time.

Abundance is an internal mindset that you cultivate from feeling good inside your own body. The best part about abundance is that you can find abundance even when things are not going well. In your divorce, you are going to find things usually don't go great, or at least, not the way you had hoped. When I was going through my divorce, I didn't yet have a strong mindset of abundance. If I had, I would have been able to process the idea of loss (or losing things I was used to having) with less pain and anguish. That's the value of having an abundance mindset before, during and after your divorce. If you can see abundance in your life, even during a painful divorce, you will have an easier time creating more abundance in your life after it's over.

When I look at my divorce, I see tremendous abundance that came from that incredibly difficult time. Over the years walking in nature became a key part of my ability to recognize abundance in my life. Nature walks gave me a chance to disconnect from everything inside my home and issues I was working through in my life. I use my time walking as a way to adamantly reinforce the things I have in life instead of the things I don't have. Abundance is what gave me the momentum to create the life I wanted after my divorce. If I had continued focusing on what I no longer had after my divorce was finalized, I would have reinforced to the Universe that I don't have enough in my life. That's the message you never want to send, and cultivating your abundance mindset today will ensure that you continue to see abundance going forward.

Abundance Practice:

Steps to feeling abundantly whole begin with looking at the areas of your life that you don't feel you have abundance in. Let's go back to our thorough goal categories: love & relationships, finances, health & wellness, spirituality, parenting, work & career, and life purpose. You can certainly add more things to this list but use this list to get you started and let your creativity expand and open up to ideas.

Start with your journal or paper. Answer each question with whatever comes up in your mind first. Avoid second-guessing yourself or getting caught up in a right or wrong answer.

1. Think about your life right now. What are three areas of your life that you have abundance? Name them and

write them down. This could include your social circle, money, time with your children, food, travel etc. There is no wrong answer but there are only true answers!

2. What about these areas is abundant for you? List anything that comes up as you think about the first question.

3. Write down one hardship you've gone through in your life, that is at least one year old. This could be a family death, your divorce, bad break-up, or anything else. Make sure it was something that happened over one year ago so that some time has passed.

4. Write down at least 2-3 things that are positives from that experience. For example, if you had a close friend die, a positive could be that you were able to celebrate the person they were. Or that you see them still in your life even though they are gone.

5. Now, write down the areas of your life where you feel you are lacking in abundance. What do you want to change? What would the changes feel like if you had more abundance? For example, I am lacking abundance in my time with my children. Or, I am lacking abundance in my alone time. A common one is I am lacking abundance in my finances!

Now that you have identified areas in your life that you feel are lacking abundance, you can begin the positive reinforcement that you have abundance in those areas. I want you to take the work you just did and internalize the areas you stated you do not have abundance. In doing so, you can use your positive thinking and set your intention on noticing when you do see abundance in these areas. This might feel like it's not going anywhere at first, but when you consistently open your mind up to noticing abundance, you will also open your life up to receiving abundance. It's the power of the Law of Attraction at work, for you!

I used walking as a way to help me focus on what I wanted more abundance in, and you need to find your own method. I suggest something that allows you to be alone, moving, and without distraction. Other ideas are driving, biking, or running. Find a way to get yourself in motion physically while you pay attention to the abundance you already have or are currently receiving.

Step Into the Lightmaster That You Are

Lightmasters are human beings that are aligned and connected to attracting their desires and focusing on the energy that they radiate to the world around them. Have you ever walked into a room and felt like some people were radiating so bright, their energy felt full, and it just took over the room, and it was truly genuine, not of ego? These people are lightmasters. Lightmasters are leaders and teachers here on Earth– their essence lights up not only a room but the world around them. Even choosing to read this book and moving through your journey of divorce with intention means you are becoming a lightmaster. You are setting the vibration for yourself and others, you are brave, you are courageous, and you are finding strength in every action you take during this difficult time.

Going through the healing process of divorce isn't easy. When you tap into the energy of being a lightmaster you choose to focus on your spiritual nature, your reactions, and your leadership ability. That makes your post-divorce journey graceful and less difficult. That's what this book is here for! I want you to be able to go through something as difficult as a divorce with relative ease compared to most. All the things that we've talked about in this book are part of being a lightmaster.

Things still won't be easy, but I can promise you, you won't feel defeated and depressed every day. In the spirit of transformation, you're going to see the vibration of your energy increase. You're able to see the gifts and opportunities in every wound that you are healing. My post-divorce days were full of highs and lows, they were messy, then they were neat, they were up, and then they were down. I needed consistency in my life. I always knew to find my center before I could grow the life of my dreams. I wish I'd had a clearer understanding of these tools when I was going through my divorce. I didn't have much guidance, but I'm eternally grateful for the experience because of all that it taught me. In the end, my journey has brought me to a point in my life that I am writing a book! I cannot wait to see what you do with your power as a lightmaster.

The Law of Attraction is one of the fundamental mindsets that a lightmaster holds sacred and important. All lightmasters are creating their lives by attracting the energy they put out, and bring it back into their lives. Take your energy seriously, and get excited about the infinite amount of positivity that you will attract back into your life. The Law of Attraction is always at work, you don't need to perform any special ritual or mantra to make it work for you. What a lightmaster does is harness the LOA by choosing to radiate positivity from the moment they wake up. Avoid waiting to choose to be positive each day. Instead, make the choice of positivity from the moment you wake up and that choice will become ingrained inside you!

I suggest this being the best time because once you start moving your body, your mind will begin its daily race. It's my first tip to you if you don't know where to start because your nervous system is still in a state of calm. Utilize this calm energy and start your day by making a list in your head of 2-3 things you're grateful for. The list can be specific or if you're having trouble getting started, start with being grateful for the night's rest you just had, the air you're breathing, the warmth of the sheets, the pillow your head is resting on, etc. Then make a list in your head of all the things that are going to work in your favor that day. You may be struggling to find greatness in the midst of your divorce, but this is an opportunity to see a gift in every difficult or hard situation.

This simple exercise only takes five minutes before you begin the day. Cherish those five minutes because you are setting yourself up for the day with a positive mindset, positive, high-vibrating energy, and overall not allowing your energy to go into a reactive state.

From the time I was a little girl, my dad was showing me that we should all begin the day in greatness. My dad was always encouraging me to have a good day with pure gratitude, and before I got out of the car, he would tell me, *Do a good day.* You read that correctly, *do a good day,* not "have a good day." It's claiming the power and creating the day that you desire with your positive mindset. If we make or create the goodness in our day, then we should never expect a "good" day to be handed to us.

As a lightmaster, it's the most important thing to set your day up for success by not being an energy vampire. A lightmaster is essentially the exact opposite of an energy vampire. You're not going to be the person who brings a low-quality energy into any situation. If you do find yourself sulking with low energy, you'll be able to pick up and correct that behavior quickly. A lightmaster is not a perfect person, rather they are emotionally intelligent and a highly aware person who can spot what their energy is telling the Universe.

When you're able to light up the room, your house, and others around you, you're also being a fantastic example for your children. As a lightmaster, or a lightmaster-in-training, you are leading by example to everyone around you. Even though the people you interact with every day may not understand what a lightmaster is, they will understand that you have something special going on inside of you. It's an energy that you give to people, like a gift, and they use it to improve their lives without even knowing it! You are a leader and motivator to people you come in contact with. As a lightmaster, you know that is the energy you must hold in order to tell the Universe what you want more of in your own life.

How to Teach Your Children to be Lightmasters

Being a lightmaster means you are a leader and teacher for the people in your life, especially children. If you have children, work with children, or are in any way connected with the next generation, then you are their teacher because they are always subconsciously observing you.

In today's society, many children are raised where parents feel they need to have control over every situation, even if there is nothing for them to actually control. Naturally, children who are watching their parents handle conflicts and tense moments will pick up on that behavior and are likely to implement it in their lives.

When you respond with disdain, judgment, or an abrasive reaction to maintain control, you are influencing your child or teen to react the same way. Your reaction is laying the foundation for how your children are going to react in an argument with you as a parent and/or teach them how to need control with their peers. I'm not saying that discipline is not appropriate, but you need to take a step back from the "yelling match" to set the stage for healthy communication with your children. It's not about winning the argument. It's about being the one that leads and steps away to give the argument some space so you can return in a productive, nonreactive state. I have struggled with this at times, especially in a home of five teens and trying to maintain order. Like I said, a lightmaster is not a perfect person who does everything the right way all the time. A lightmaster is someone who is aware and intelligent and can recognize when they are out of touch with their emotions. Be the lightmaster in order to let your child or children see what patience looks like, what non-reactiveness looks like, and what can come of remaining mindful, calm, and reflective in tense situations.

It's not that you have to take control of your kids and have your beliefs and values control their actions. It's about understanding that they are right where they need to be and that's how they're learning.

If you react immediately and start yelling, defining boundaries, and claiming control, they are going to mirror the same energy and reaction back to you. A lightmaster who is a parent always chooses to lead by example. Things aren't always perfect, or easy to handle just because you "are a lightmaster!" It's being mindful of maintaining self-control as a way to train yourself so that one day, with practice, your children will act in the same manner.

I've personally watched how my own kids do not learn from what I tell them, but more by what they observe. They seem to hear very little, are often overstimulated, and not paying full attention. Kids are like that. Given all of those common traits in children, they are still going to be very observant of you, your behaviors, your reactions, your communication, how you carry yourself, how you take care of your health...literally everything. Encourage your children to have their own beliefs as well, even while they are watching and observing yours. Let your kids know it's okay for them to develop into their own lightmaster at a young age, their own being, with their own values and willingness to be vulnerable, share emotions, and be a leader and example for their friends.

Cherish your Vulnerability

Vulnerability is what connects us, on a real level, to the people around us whose relationships are important. Vulnerability allows you to tell your story, share your more painful experiences and open your heart to another person. Your ability to be vulnerable creates a shared experience with that person that invites them to lean in and support us. When you open yourself up to this depth with someone, it feels like your hearts have a magnetic pull towards one another. Vulnerability is healthy for you no matter if it's romantically, in friendship, or any type of relationship. Humans long for connection, and this is how we connect two heart centers together.

We'll talk more about the vulnerability in a romantic relationship in the next chapter but for now, it's important to know before we open ourselves up to another being, we first have to become open and vulnerable with ourselves. You're honoring yourself as a lightmaster by being vulnerable, in control of your emotions, and the leader of your story.

Maybe you're coming out of a marriage where your ex-spouse "threw you under the bus" or felt powerful when he or she exposed your vulnerabilities, leaving you feeling damaged, fragile, and fearful of sharing your vulnerabilities again with others. In addition to a spouse, maybe you've even had friends in post-divorce that abandoned you, exposing your vulnerabilities, making them feel more powerful than you. In divorce, it's not uncommon for people who you thought were friends to expose your vulnerabilities because they want to see you fail.

In all honesty, whatever reason anyone has for turning your vulnerability against you is only affecting their state and the energy they put out to the Universe. As difficult as it can be to let these things slide, it's even worse to let these things impede your ability to open up to others who will not harm you. During your divorce, you will need to reinforce that your ability to be vulnerable is a gift you are giving to yourself, not something you are doing for others. That's the fundamental concept that I want you to walk away from this section with. The power for you to be vulnerable, even if it means you might open yourself up to an energy vampire, is highly valuable to your post-divorce life and growth. These are the times after divorce that positive change takes place within your being because you are making the choice to put yourself in the driver's seat of your life.

Feminine and Masculine Roles After Divorce

When I got divorced, I quickly learned that I had to take on roles in the home that used to be done by my spouse (particularly if you have kids). There are some things you're going to be amazing at and others that will make you want to pull your hair out. When you have one home there are mutual responsibilities that get shared between both parents. Household responsibilities like bills, cars, yard and home maintenance, taking the trash out, money, financial planning, work schedules, doing homework with children, grocery shopping, cleaning, laundry, doctors' appointments, preparing lunches, taking care of sick kids…the list goes on and on and on! I wanted to make this a long list so I can emphasize all the "stuff" that still needs to get done when the houses are divided. Just as the chores around the house need to get done, you're taking on both the masculine and feminine roles as a single parent. This is true even when your ex-spouse lives close by and sees the children regularly. You will still need to own both roles when your children are with you!

The roles of both masculine and feminine energies are within every single person; they are embedded in our biology and our emotional DNA. We have access to it all. Nobody says that you have to be in masculine or feminine energy, exclusively. People are complex and capable of expressing anything, at any given moment, including both the masculine and feminine traits and energies. Society, especially after going through a divorce, encourages you to stay on the move and there is very little encouragement to stop and slow down and get in touch with your soul again. I want to squash that belief and that's one of the purposes of this book. We are reinventing the "normal" rules or unspoken suggestions that are around us. I want you to honor the masculine and feminine energies with equal importance. That's why I shared at the beginning that WE ALL have this energy. It's not about what gender you are because the energy is greater than that. A man does not only have masculine energy, and a woman does not just have feminine energy. There is an equal divide and balance of masculine and feminine energies in every human being.

When you accept that you will be both mom and dad in your post-divorce life, you are being aware and inviting this mutual energy into your life. Embrace this energy and use your intuition to guide you in becoming more aware of the leader your children need at this time. If you are a man or woman and only feel that your dominant trait is that of masculine or feminine energy, then this is showing an imbalance, and you will have a difficult time leading your household and supporting your children. As you get in touch with your spiritual being, life becomes easier and smoother.

The Wholeness Journey

Each of us has a spiritual being within, a divine oneness and inner voice. All of the qualities that I've talked about in this chapter are how you can unleash and strengthen your inner voice further and lead a life by example for your own self-love, as well as the next generation. Creating sacred practices and rituals as part of your daily routine will help you develop and transform your life as you know it.

I became fascinated with spiritual teachers such as Eckhart Tolle, Wayne Dyer, Gabby Bernstein, Oprah, Louise Hay, Buddha, Deepak Chopra, Danielle Laporte, and Tony Robbins. They all have a daily ritual and practices to allow them to connect to their TRUTH, wisdom and inner voice. Seeing how all of these spiritual leaders had rituals, I knew that in order to connect with who I am, it was absolutely necessary to create my own daily practices.

I embarked on a journey of getting deeper into my practice of yoga, I meditated, I practiced reiki to unblock my energies, I journaled, I downward dogged, I cleansed, I took healing probiotics and supplements to nourish what my body was lacking, I dry brushed, I ate fresh whole foods, I prayed, I sat in my infrared sauna every day, I took meditative walks, I did breath work, I found stillness in nature, I took relaxing salt baths. I committed to my barre practice and dove deeper into yoga. I got massages. I loved and took care of myself and found ways back to who I was, at the depth of my soul.

We all have busy schedules, but we need to carve out time in our day to make our way back to our inner goddess, and spiritual being. As long as something feels good and allows you time to connect to your higher self and awaken and ignite your heart and soul, then you are on the right track. Find your sacred practice and commit to it every day. It's your divine birthright to experience deep self-love.

CHAPTER NINE

Soulful Relationships
& Dating

Relationships, and I mean relationships in general, are the strongest energy that humans feel for in life. I'm not just talking about romantic relationships. If you were trapped on a deserted island, full of tropical fruits and fresh fish that's easy to catch, you'd still go crazy because you have no one to talk to and connect with. In general, relationships are what we all long to have present in our lives. The funny thing about it though is that there is no manual or relationships 101 class to take! There are parenting classes, cooking classes, and health classes but when we talk about being the best version of ourselves in a romantic relationship or friendship, you can't find those type of classes. How do we know how to show up as our best self in all our relationships without a guide?

I've put this chapter at the end of the book because it's absolutely not possible, no matter who you talk to, to step right back into the dating world after divorce and expect to show up better than the person you were in your marriage. That's just the plain truth of the situation that is born out of a divorce. Divorce doesn't end because you had too much positivity or too much groundedness! Divorce is caused by having lost those things in your life.

Depending on where you are in life, you may be mourning the loss of a partner that you truly loved and the loss of the perfect life you envisioned, and you need healing from that pain. On the other hand you may be so relieved to be out of an unhealthy relationship but you still need to find love for yourself so you don't get caught in another relationship just like that one. No matter what, a divorce is mourning the loss of your old self, as well as healing from the pain of what you went through during your marriage. Healing and transforming to become the best version of yourself takes time and patience. There is no shortcut for time. The thing that will not work, no matter how badly you may want it to, is jumping head-first into a new relationship without rediscovering your relationship with yourself.

We've been building up your personal development tools and focusing on the importance of self-love first because you'll need that experience in your future relationships. The same way that you need to mirror the type of energy you want to receive back in your life, you need to be able to mirror a healthy relationship with your future partner. The type of person you work to become in the first two years after your divorce will be a great indicator of the type of person you can expect to share your life with down the road. It's infinitely more valuable for your future to work on your self-love before working on creating love with someone else.

You may find that you'll want to jump into dating right out of divorce, and while this isn't a bad thing, it certainly isn't a good thing either. It is a tactic to fill the void that you're feeling from your divorce. I want to empower you by helping you work through personal growth and transformation to have healthy relationships, including your friendships.

My intention for you in this chapter is to help you avoid manifesting your past relationships and avoid trying to fix, change or improve your future partner(s). When we are trying to fix, change, or improve a partner, it stems from something we don't like in ourselves. We are going to work on reprogramming your subconscious dating mind to become much more conscious. It's important to recognize that who you were in your previous relationship didn't serve you and to be mindful of that moving forward into your future relationships. Being mindfully aware of what no longer serves you can help you not fall back into old behavior patterns and the same type of relationship again. At some point, you're going to have to take the time to do the inner work you are reading about in this book.

Without doing the internal work, you are continuing to mask the wounds that stunted you from experiencing authentic love and healthy companionship. The most important thing that I want you to be aware of before we begin the fun of soulful relationships is to have no expectations for how fast you process your emotions during this time. Like the saying goes, this is a marathon, not a race.

Relationship Mindset

Aside from me simply telling you that "getting back into dating will take some unknown amount of time" (that's not really what I'm trying to say), I want to give you the real meat of what that means. You will need the right mindset for a healthy relationship with the right person at the perfect time. The first one, and most important one, we've already covered—you must love yourself first before you can love someone else or expect them to love you back. You must love yourself in order to feel deserving of someone to love you back.

Dating from here on out in your life is going to be fun. If it feels like a chore to find a date or go on a date, then you aren't yet ready. The mindset you should go into dating with is that it's an opportunity to meet a new person who may become a love interest, a friend, or simply a new acquaintance in your life. Drop all the need to have the first, second, or third person you meet fill a role in your life. Let each date, and the big picture idea of finding dates, be an adventure with unknown outcomes!

The next important mindset is that all the dating you do after your divorce is similar to collecting data. You are simply collecting data on what type of traits, qualities, personalities and so on that you like and which ones you don't like. Just like we talked about not judging your ex-spouse during your divorce, this does not mean you should be judging your dates to make sure they check all your boxes. Instead, this mindset is all about letting the experience that comes from each date and each person you meet add to the energy of your perfect partner. It's less of an "I don't want this type of person" vibe and more of a "This person had a great _____ (insert quality you noticed about them) and that's what I would love to have in a partner!" When you can approach your relationship mindset without a set of criteria that must be filled in order for you to be happy with your partner, you open yourself up to new qualities that you can embody yourself. It's completely against the natural order of things to expect someone to have a quality without you also projecting a similar quality in yourself.

To give you a more concrete set of guidelines to consider, here are the timelines that I believe work best based on all the people I've worked with in the last decade. In the first two years of your post-divorce, your only goal should be is to have fun on dates without any need for sex, companionship, or a label (like boyfriend/girlfriend). This is the exploratory period when you still have a lot of inner work to do. Often times, in this period that lack of confidence caused by your divorce will show up on dates. If you don't date with confidence, you can surely expect any relationship that happens during this time won't be in your best interest. If you are playing tennis without confidence and then ask someone to partner up with you for a tournament, it's likely that your team will struggle and feelings will get hurt. It's not fair to yourself or to your partner to commit to anything that you can't deliver. In the first two years of post-divorce life, it will be highly difficult for you to deliver a confident and meaningful relationship.

The second phase is years two through five, when you have spent time working on your energy, your mindset, and your actions. You will know yourself so much more after two years of post-divorce mindset work that it's going to make dating a beautiful experience. This is not going to be true if you are not doing any work in those two years of post-divorce. If you sulk around, stay in a victim state, look for ways to "get back" at people who wronged you during your divorce, it will show in your dating behavior. If you do the work that is required, than usually within two years you will be in a great place to start seriously putting your energy out into the Universe for someone else to discover! And some of us are in a really good place to attract a very healthy relationship during this period.

The last real phase worth mentioning is five years and beyond from your divorce. This is the time when you can form a long-lasting, healthy, highly compatible relationship with another person. During the two-to-five year period, many of us date with intention, we are confident with who we have become, and can form deeper relationships than ever before. Imagine after five years or more of learning to love who you are, learning what you value in another person, and projecting a high vibration energy into the world, you will find a relationship unlike anything you've ever experienced. That's the type of relationship we all want, but few of us are willing to really work for it!

Reflective Exercise:

Use the exercise below to begin your reflective period and help you start to shape what you desire in a meaningful, future relationship. I know there are going to be days that you're not overflowing with self-love but make sure that you are in a good, restorative place before you begin the exercise.

Sit comfortably somewhere, like outdoors in nature, a favorite room in your home, or in your favorite coffee shop. Wherever you find yourself when you're doing this exercise, make sure that you're comfortable, have centered and grounded energy, and a mindset ready for reflecting your relationship desires.

- *Begin with asking yourself what type of partner are you in a relationship? Get in touch with how you've been in past relationships and honest about your behavior and actions.*

- *What kind of experiences are you carrying over from your past marriage, including from childhood, or other less-than-ideal relationships? What things stick out in your mind when you think of these relationships? That's likely what you are carrying over.*

- *In what areas of yourself do you see room for improvement or growth?*

- *What do you desire in a partner? Write down how you want to feel in the presence of your partner. Be specific. It could be feeling deeply connected—spiritually, mentally and emotionally; being heard and supported; a best friend connection; and/or other emotions. Get specific.*

- *How do you desire communication to be with your partner?*

- *Write down the core values and beliefs you desire your partner to have. Be specific.*

I want you to write these down because you are reprogramming your emotional intelligence and sending a consistent intention to the Universe. The important thing here is that you are writing and stating what you are aware of in yourself and what you desire in another. Going forward, these are great questions to focus for manifesting your future partner(s).

Phases of Dating

You might recognize already that I emphasize the importance of utilizing personal time and reassessing your new life goals and priorities first, over dating. Dating can be stressful, and many find it hard to muster up the confidence to step back into dating after divorce. Finding love is a great goal to have, so it's essential to get back out there and date again when the time is right. With this, it's important to understand the phases of dating you're going to go through. Before you even step into dating though, as we talked about previously, have a good mindset around dating and also create the space for dating. These are one and the same.

Phase 1: "Me" Time

It takes time to heal the wounds from your divorce and what you went through dealing with your ex-spouse. This is the time that you're going to work through the immediate transition of living on your own again, and potentially as a single parent. Your energy and attention need to be focused on figuring out how to balance the responsibilities that two people once had but now are all yours. No matter what you may be feeling, the truth is you don't have a lot of emotional bandwidth for dating, nor do you have the capacity to understand what you really desire in a new partner. You might feel the urge to jump right into the dating pool, but this simply isn't the right time. It's also not great if you have kids in your life. They need time to process what is likely a massive change in their lives.

As a frame of reference, I personally believe it takes two years to process the emotions from your divorce and deep dive into the self-healing process after divorce. This is your "me time" stage and it's the most important phase for your future relationships.

It takes time and patience to immerse yourself into setting new life dreams and see them take shape in your life. There is a necessary time frame for you to get used to being alone and forging your way back to you. I have watched people try to jump into dating over and over again and have yet to see it work out. It may not take you two years–or it may be five years for you–but your "me time" must happen first and foremost.

It's during this phase that you will experience feelings of emptiness inside. Those feelings are often what leads divorcees to quickly look for the next relationship with another partner to fill the emptiness with someone else. Nine times out of ten, this is what quickly leads to the same disappointing outcome that you experienced in your marriage.

Happiness is an inside job and will never be fulfilled by finding the perfect partner.

In this phase, I am not saying you should not date at all over the two-year time, I simply think you need to get out there and learn and meet new people. Allow yourself to feel this time of emotions and develop yourself personally. Think of dates you may go on as a way to find friends, have experiences, and get out of the house. I suggest not actively looking for dates during this phase, but I'm also a believer in taking opportunities when the Universe presents them. During this phase of dating, reframing what dating means is a great way to stay grounded.

Phase 2: Casual Dating

This phase still consists of fear, a lack of confidence, uneasiness in your emotions, and potential anxiety carried over from your divorce. This is the data collection phase where you get to approach dating with an open mind. That's really the biggest key to this phase! You want to approach phase two with an open but skeptical mind.

To be open-minded is to naturally be without judgment towards the other person. Being open-minded in the casual dating phase is accepting that you still have roadblocks in your life that may come up at any time during this phase. You still have stuff to work out! On the other hand, if you have spent time alone forming a strong mindset, you will begin to feel excitement towards the potential of meeting new people in a romantic setting. Being open-minded is not only a good mindset for dating in general, it's a great way for you to live without expectation. Removing as many expectations as possible from your dating life (and your life in general) is a key aspect of collecting the most data possible. Expectations tend to cloud your mind and mask what is real.

The second, and equally important, trait for phase two is being skeptical. You don't want to fall back into an unhealthy relationship simply because you are out dating again. In order to be true to yourself, skepticism is a key trait to carry into your dating life.

Be skeptical of the things people tell you on dates. They may try to play against your emotions for an ulterior motive.

Be skeptical of the true nature of the date. Someone may want something different than they let on. Usually, that is sex or material items, and both men and women do it.

Be skeptical of the emotions you are feeling, and where they are coming from! You don't want to simply cast a skeptical gaze at the person you are on a date with, but also at yourself. Is your ego trying to influence you? Are the emotions you feel real or is there lust? Watch to see if your emotions spike, and remember to come back to your grounded center. There are no rules to casual dating but the essence of it is causal. When you can learn to approach casual dating as a genuinely fun experience, or an opportunity to just meet new people, you take a lot of pressure off yourself. Practice this style of dating with no expectation and the Universe will see your ready for an honest, more authentic relationship with the right person.

Phase 3: Ready for Intimacy

This I have to say, is the most exciting time as you are beginning to work through the healing process. You are stepping out of the feeling of losing your identity and establishing who you are and who you want to be in this new life. You are diving deep into creating your own beliefs and goals that come from self-reflection of who you are. You're learning to get rid of old beliefs that were embedded into you by your past or ex-spouse. You've had fun on dates, you've met new people without the need to "get" anything from them (love, sex, stuff, marriage) and you've stayed opened-minded yet skeptical. All these traits create a snowball effect within you and, as people say, causes synergy within your world and the Universe. That synergy is what will open you up to being ready for intimacy.

The important thing is that you've come to realize you are not going to allow yourself to get lost in a relationship again and have no sense of self. This time around, when you are ready for real intimacy with someone, you will remain empowered in your self-love and your *own* happiness. You are not superhuman and can't be someone's happiness, nor they yours. This is such an exciting time because all the work you've done in your post-divorce years is coming back full circle!

Time is the greatest healer and the best way to heal the wounds of a divorce is time. Usually around 3-5 years into your post-divorce life is when you'll start seeing the benefits of putting your own self-love first. This is just my number, but from years and years of experience working with people, as well as my own experience, I feel this is what brings you the best results. The results I'm talking about is more self-confidence than you've had in a long time, because an unhealthy marriage robs you of a lot of who you were and the confidence you once had. When you reach new levels of self-confidence, your ability to find the right partner is much higher. Two healthy individuals, and by that I mean people who put self-love first, tend to have a magnetic pull towards one another. This is the synergy I'm talking about! Be patient, and allow time to heal by giving yourself the necessary time to find your confidence and do the hard work necessary to harness your inner lightmaster.

Dating With Children

At the end of the day, no matter how old they are, most children just want their parents to be happy. Dating is going to be overwhelming for *you* in the beginning, let alone your children. The most important thing that kids want to know is that their lives and the structure of their lives will not change. It's the same feeling they are going to feel when you tell them you're getting a divorce. Knowing that you are dating can make them feel jumpy or nervous post-divorce because of all the changes and transitions happening in their lives. It's important to keep things as normal as possible for them. That means keeping your casual dating life private in the beginning. In the beginning stage of post-divorce, children need time to get over what happened between their parents and how their new lives look. It's a massive transition for everyone involved. Utilize the time that your children are with your ex-spouse to date others, and that will actually help take the pressure off you. There is no need to prove anything to anyone when it comes to dating. You should be focused on exploring what it feels like, what emotions come up, and not what your kids think or how they will like so and so. That's just an unnecessary distraction in the beginning that you don't need. Certainly your children don't need it as they adjust to the change.

Be respectful but don't apologize for wanting to date, obviously because you are the leader of your life. As time passes in your post-divorce, you may find yourself in a relationship where you may want to introduce them to your kids or just be more open with your relationship. Be mindful not to introduce your kids to every person that comes into your life. Be very choosy as to who you bring into your children's lives. When you put in the time, and practice what is in this book, you will be led to the right person. At that point, enough time will have passed and your children will be ready to meet the right person. Even better, you will be able to trust your intuition and you'll simply know that this is the person that you should introduce your kids too. It will feel right. This principle will eliminate so much unnecessary stress for you and your children.

When the time comes to introduce your children to that special person, take it slow. At first, let them know you'll be going out on a date. Plug them into your life and what is happening to create good communication with your children. At a certain point, after enough time has passed, they will truly appreciate your honesty. That honesty will eventually lead to curiosity with who mom or dad is going out with!

At this point, you should begin to introduce them to people you've been seeing and know to be special in your life. Plan to have your date (or boyfriend/girlfriend) step inside your home for a quick hello, or a short meet and greet before going out. This creates a relaxed scenario, with minimal pressure, and that doesn't feel forced. After so many years, my kids became curious about my dating life. They would ask me who I was going out with, or even point out potential matches for me while out in public. As I said, you'll know when the time is right with your children. The energy will be there, they will be excited, and that will translate to a natural, fun meeting.

One thing to be aware of is when you are dating someone who is also divorced and has kids. Just as everyone's divorce is different, so are the post-divorce timelines for each family. If you are in a good place with your dating life and your children, that doesn't mean your potential date is in the same spot. I dated someone whose children were not ready to meet me and it could be felt in the room. I didn't take it as a reflection or judgment against me because I had high self-confidence and I could understand where they were coming from. This is a good way to hone your awareness as we talked about in previous chapters, and put it to good work.

The Modern Era of Dating

So we finally have reached the good part. I think it's safe to say that the new wave of dating certainly begins for many in the digital space, in one way or another. When you are ready to step into the dating world again, start slow. I always suggest you start by sharing with a few friends that you are prepared to get back out there. The hope is by starting here, your friends will be there to support you, first of all, and second, they can set you up with someone and begin to get you out there socially. During the beginning stages of dating again, the key to remember is to have realistic expectations. It's rare that you're going to meet somebody where chemistry is great, and you fall in love right away in your post-divorce journey. I highly encourage you to enjoy the dating process. Look at all of your dates as opportunities to learn to know yourself on a deeper level and what you desire and want in a future partner.

MINDFUL DATING IN POST-DIVORCE

I want to share concrete points of focus for you when your dating life begins to gain momentum. As I've said, early on in your post-divorce life, dating may feel awkward, challenging, and potentially unsuccessful. Those things pass with time, and self-love. When it comes to gaining momentum and putting out an energy that attracts other healthy adults as partners, there are some key behaviors to be aware of.

Validation Seeking: Validation seeking is the act of saying or doing something for the purpose of getting a certain, positive response from someone. It's most common in dating but it happens in everyday life as well. When you seek validation from an external source, like another person you are on a date with, you demonstrate a low level of self-confidence, which subconsciously gets picked up on. I'll give you a modern example of how validation seeking might occur (there are many ways).

Let's pretend you meet someone online and agree to go for a coffee date. Before the date, you look at their social media pages and find out that they love to play volleyball! However, you have never played volleyball and have no interest in it. If you were to go on the date and claim to love volleyball, that is seeking the validation of your date. You are essentially starting the relationship with a lie, but even worse, you are being inauthentic to yourself and you know it. There is no reason that you need this other person to think that you both love the same thing. In fact, if they were to find out that you have zero interest in volleyball, it could be a deal breaker down the road. The better course of action would be complete honesty by saying "I found you on Facebook and saw that you love volleyball! I've actually never played. What do you like about volleyball?" The best thing you can do is turn it into a talking point and be completely honest.

Supplicating: Supplicating is the act of agreeing with everything that your date says. It's really as simple as it sounds! It is the same as "brown nosing" your boss at work in order to get noticed or liked. If you are on a date and have nothing to contribute other than to agree with the things someone else says, you are telling that person you don't have much going for you in life. You want to remember that you don't really know this person at all yet! You don't know if they are worth your time or energy, and by agreeing with them, you validate their beliefs. They may believe things that you are completely against or vice versa. Eventually this type of dishonesty catches up to you. When you can be honest and open during conversation on a date, you will feel more connected to that person. Differing opinions are great for conversation and will increase the chance that someone wants to learn more about you. The best way to avoid supplicating is to get real with yourself first, before even starting to date.

Neediness: Of all the low-quality traits in this section, neediness is the most manipulative and toxic. Needy behavior is an unfortunate by-product of what happens when people seek happiness in others. Needy behavior rises completely from fear-based emotions such as jealousy, lust, and lack of abundance. You will encounter needy behavior in people coming out of a divorce who are not yet ready to date. You may even exhibit this type of behavior yourself if you are not mentally prepared or have the confidence in yourself that is required for a meaningful relationship. Neediness often looks like passive-aggression in an attempt to get you to feel a certain way (usually "bad") for not doing or saying what the other needs. In almost every unhealthy relationship, one partner is needier than the other. If you have been on multiple dates with someone and continue to see needy behavior, it's best to move on instead of trying to fix it. They still have work they need to do on themselves, which means it's best for you to find a partner who has overcome the feeling of needing things from another person to be happy or content.

Outcome Dependency: Outcome dependency is usually mostly internal, meaning only you feel the effects of it. This is something that applies to life massively in so many ways, and especially in new relationships. The art of learning to recognize when you are dependent on a certain outcome will allow you to free yourself of that dependency, which adds to your confidence and your self-awareness. An example of outcome dependency in casual dating is as simple as expecting to have sex with someone after a certain period of time. It can even start before you meet someone, like in messaging or emailing with them. If you expect a certain type of response to a message you send, you take all the fun and excitement out of the experience. Outcome dependency kills attraction quickly and doesn't allow much room for banter or playfulness. Those are two important qualities that you want to use in order to appreciate the journey of dating and meet the right person for you.

When you learn, and practice, being independent of any particular outcome your energy will be different on dates. Be willing to accept that most of your dates won't work out the way you want them to. Be excited about the fact that you have no idea where life will lead you and you are just happy to be along for the ride. That mindset will add greatly to your attractiveness on dates because you'll remove all pressure from dating. If, or when, you feel pressure on or before a date, ask yourself why you are feeling that pressure! There is usually some outcome that you are putting higher on your priorities list. The number one priority you should have on dates is to give the other person a great experience by being yourself, making them laugh, and not expecting anything of them.

DIGITAL DATING

For many, the greatest challenge to dating is finding out the ways dating has changed. For someone who hasn't dated in 15 years, the methods have changed and so have societal norms. This can be stressful for you if you are just getting back in the dating scene. We've all heard the term "online dating" at this point. For the sake of simplicity, I have changed the catchphrase of online dating to digital dating, because there are many more ways to date digitally these days. There are so many great social apps and communities online, so I'm encompassing them all with digital dating.

A real connection can appear tough to find if you don't have a lot of experience digitally dating. Love is a marathon, not a sprint, so it's supposed to take a little time to find the right person for you. That means you'll have to go on dates with people who are not ideal for you in order to figure out what you like and don't like. Digital dating is great because there are so many people out there that you'll never be without options! The opposite side of that is that many people dating digitally are not in the right mindset for a real relationship yet. Digital dating allows you to play a numbers game. What is key to remember, and what most people get hung up on, is that it takes practice to get good at weeding through all the potential options out there. Be ready to look at online dating as skill-based, not just plain luck.

QUICK TIPS FOR DIGITAL DATING:

1. **Meet in person as soon as possible:** Avoid back-and-forth messaging with someone that you're ready to meet in person. This is a big waste of time because some people enjoy the attention but don't have any intention of ever meeting you. The initial messaging phase is great for getting to know someone's vibe to make sure you actually want to meet them. As soon as you feel ready, ask them to meet up.

2. **Don't romanticize the person:** If you create a fantasy of what this person is like based on the emails and texts, without even talking on the phone or meeting in person, you may be disappointed when you meet them. You might not feel like you're in their league or are good enough for them. It's not uncommon for people to put their best foot forward in the online persona, and that doesn't always translate to who they really are.

3. **Talk on the phone:** I know it's not the first step most people take, but my advice to you is always to make sure you connect on the phone before meeting in person. I can generally weed somebody out after having a phone conversation, more so than over text message. If you don't like messaging a lot, but are not ready to meet in person, use the phone as a way to gauge if you want to take it to the next level.

4. **Try out multiple different digital dating avenues:** This is simple! There are so many different websites, apps, and social

meet-ups that sticking to just one route will leave you with far fewer options. Make sure you know what is out there because different people hang out in different spots. Pay sites such as Match.com tend to have more serious people because it costs money. Certain apps connect to your social media page to find people you know in common. Some sites have better quality dates on them, and you want to know which ones don't resonate with you.

5. **Meet in a public place:** Always, always meet in a public place for safety reasons and for a better vibe on the first, second, and third date.

Remember that people will "ghost" or disappear even after it seemed like you had a good time or connection via digital technology. Ghosting happens for so many unknown reasons, and usually has nothing to do with you. If you are getting ignored repeatedly, there is likely some behavior you are exhibiting (such as neediness or validation-seeking) that you need to work on. Be willing to accept you're not perfect in order to work past these issues. You're going to feel rejection, you are going to reject. It's part of the dating journey. Don't let your ego take over when the rejection happens because rejection is part of the process. Again, know that there are going to be some people that you connect with who end up ghosting you and vice versa.

In the era of digital dating, you will find many people are dating numerous people at the same time, trying to figure out who they connect with most and want to pursue more. You are likely to meet several bad apples along the way as well. The digital universe is an easy place for people to disguise themselves as having good intentions. This is a time to tune into your intuition to seek out real people. It's a numbers game, and that's a good thing! You never know—the numbers might play in your favor, and you end up meeting a few good apples.

It's going to be harder on your emotions if you take digital dating too seriously. Most of the apps are always with you, on your phone, and on the computer. You're going to want to check them all the time to see if someone likes you back or becomes a match with you. Again, practice self-love lessons here and don't let this pull at your self-esteem. Don't let an unfit partner or someone you just met talk you into a relationship that doesn't make you feel good or get excited about. Take this time to explore and enjoy the digital dating process.

Sex and Intimacy in Relationships

Let's define the word love, shall we? We could look it up in the Webster dictionary, but I think it would be easier for you and I to understand it better with feelings, wouldn't you agree? I would say that love (in terms of feelings) is good vibes. Good vibes are nature's way of telling you that you're in the right place or with the right person. Just being in the same room with a partner who is in harmony with you lifts your energy; together you create ripple effects that produce high-energy waves.

Bruce Lipton, Ph.D. and best-selling author of *The Honeymoon Effect* explains, "so when you 'entangle' with someone else's energy, you want the interference to be constructive (good vibes) not destructive (bad vibes). You want the interaction to increase your energy, not deplete it.

Whether it is a romantic relationship or non-romantic relationship, we want to be around people who lift our spirits and create positive energy when we are together. We also need to establish boundaries or cut relationships with those that drain us. Great intimacy can only come into your life when you are ready to accept love. You must be in a place that you wholeheartedly love yourself, have done the healing and growth work, and understand all your beautiful layers of who you are.

COMMUNICATION WITH YOUR PARTNER

Communication in a relationship is one of, if not the most critical factor for a successful relationship. Looking back, you may have found in the past that arguments were started out of nowhere and might have stemmed from something so small. When you and your partner are able to understand how to communicate with each other, especially when it comes to giving and receiving of love, relationships have a much longer lifespan and true genuine connection.

Gary Chapman, author of *The 5 Love Languages: The Secret to Love that Lasts*, believes that the romantic love in relationships and marriage is deeply rooted in our physiological makeup. He states that "people speak different love languages." It totally makes sense if you think about it because each person is made up differently. Just like there are different languages and cultures in the world, we all have different ways of showing, speaking, and receiving love.

Most of us, as you've read throughout the book, have been witnesses of our parent's relationships and our friends' relationships. Sometimes the relationships we witness are not always the healthiest examples. These examples we've observed have programmed our brains to think that this is what "healthy love" looks like in a relationship. Just because a couple has been together for X amount of years doesn't always mean that there is genuine communication and love still present. The sad truth is that some couples never learn how to communicate together or even know their own love language. They get married, and all of a sudden things aren't all roses and peaches a few years into the marriage. Gary Chapman tells us that there are five distinct love languages for communicating love in relationships—and this applies both to romantic relationships and friendships. The more in touch you become with self-love, the more in tune you will be with understanding what your love language is and be able to express love in your partner's love language.

The 5 Love Languages:

- Words of Affirmation - this language uses words to affirm or validate the other person.
- Quality Time - this language is all about giving the other person your undivided attention.

- Receiving Gifts - for some people, what makes them feel loved is to receive a gift.

- Acts of Service - for others, actions speak louder than words.

- Physical Touch - to this person, nothing speaks more deeply than appropriate touch.

I encourage you to practice your love language(s) and become one with it or them. You may have more than one love language. Being able to flow with your Divine Essence and understand your love language will only deepen your love for self and also aid your relationships. You'll be able to give and healthily receive love. Once you step into a relationship where you feel you want to explore a more serious connection with your partner, I invite you and your partner to take the *5 Love Languages Quiz* and also read the book together, to further understand what each other's love language is.

Ultimately, you both want to expand and grow your love but also know that you're able to communicate, be vulnerable and open in a safe, sacred space. I promise you will experience communication, intimacy, sex, and every part of your relationship in a whole new way.

INTIMACY

The key to being really intimate—not just physically but mentally, emotionally, and spiritually—is growing together and having the sacred space to feel vulnerable. Vulnerability is the pathway to intimacy. Intimacy requires that you get up close and personal with your partner, feel safe in their presence, and feel like you can share 100 percent of who you are with them. If there is any slight hesitation or fear that is coming up for you when you read this, it means there is still room for growth in vulnerability, and maybe you still haven't met "your special one."

Being in a soulful transparent relationship, both intimately and sexually, is the most healing experience after a divorce. I know this is probably a huge desire of yours and a lot of the holes that are probably being filled on your wholeness map. But trust me when I say, to build a soulful intimate and sexual relationship in the bedroom, you have to allow yourself to be open, be vulnerable, and find your truth.

If you need to go back and revisit chapter eight to work on your personal vulnerability, I invite you to go back. Opening yourself up to the playground of a soulful relationship, can only deepen your level of intimacy with your partner. First, you must experience and work through your own depths of vulnerability. If you are in a relationship and you feel you want to work on vulnerability together, I highly encourage you to do that as well. The power of sharing is healing in itself. Vulnerability will allow you both to grow together as lightmasters and experience a relationship, mind, body, and spirit on a whole new level.

SOULFUL SEX

What exactly is soulful sex? I'm not talking about sex that you see in the movies and on YouTube, I'm talking about the sacred, authentic connection that is present between two human beings. Sex is a sacred experience and one that deserves to be cherished. Coming out of post-divorce you're going to feel the desire to feel like "you still got it," but as we talked about in the healing section, especially with sex, it's not something you want to find comfort in and use as a coping mechanism to mask your emotions. Instead, you want to use sex and lovemaking as just that, a way to open up vulnerably to your partner and experience a soulful connection together.

We know that we possess traits of both masculine and feminine energies and we see how living a life of tapping into our spiritual being can make traumatic experiences and relationships begin to feel like they are flowing easier, more openly, with clearer in communication. Before I give you some quick tips for soulful sex, the key to successful relationships is knowing how to flow in and out of both your masculine and feminine energies and practice mindful communication together with your partner. When you tap fully into your spiritual being, and Divine Essence, it allows the body to embrace and invite more softness into your sexual energy, and surrender to flowing with what the Universe has for you.

I can guess that your ego is going to come knocking at the door especially when you read this section. So let me reassure you, this is a time to put your ego away and soak back into the grounded energy of your spiritual being. This depth of sex and intimacy isn't going to happen overnight for you, and honestly, I hope it doesn't because it takes time to build a relationship where you can experience love and sex this deeply.

You are going to date a lot of people coming out of a divorce, and it's not everyone that you'll be able to open yourself up to like this. It's a natural progression of healing and transformation that allows you to slowly stop judging yourself and shaming yourself about carrying the shadows of pain and hurt from your past. When you feel you're at a place in a relationship where you feel comfortable, like you've never felt that comfortable before, you are stepping into connecting with your Divine Essence. Don't rush into this phase of soulful sex because when you've truly found a partner that you can go this deeply with, it will be genuinely mind-blowing and life-changing for you.

The Wholeness Journey

Be able to create the space for somebody in your life and make your life appealing for them. This person can literally and energetically walk into that space. If you give off a vibe that your life is erratic, whether it is with your finances, career, children, spirituality, etc., then your life is in chaos, and you will not attract the partner you desire. Personally, I knew from the early days I needed to create a very appealing life for myself in every authentic way (career, finances, health, spirituality, and raising five kids). My life needed to feel authentic and flow easily to make it appealing for somebody else to step into it that space.

The earlier years were more chaotic, so it was difficult to make space for somebody. I was busy putting my visions to work like renovating my home, learning to sell a home, operating a business, learning about investments, and how I could make money creatively with different income streams. While that helped keep me busy, I was also doing all the self-love work that I've talked about up to this point! Those early years of really hard work made my later years of raising kids easier, and made my overall quality of life and relationships much easier and more laid-back.

Dating and relationships is not a world where you want to draw conclusions about others because we all have our own individual journey to self-love and wholeness. I look at the life that I created with excitement, so that I would also attract that energy in my dating life.

Your life is what you create of it. It takes work and effort, conscious awareness, and rituals to connect and manifest your desires and goals. My focus today is living a life that flows with ease, and that is communicated and received in my romantic relationships. Don't get caught up in what the future needs to look like or create a false reality of what you think is right based on limiting beliefs. Be open to what the Universe has in store for you. You may get caught up in what you are looking for in a partner. If you are one-dimensional or focused on finding someone right away, you might miss out on a lot of growth and positive experiences through dating.

CHAPTER TEN

Giving and Being of Service

Why Service?

Why would a book on divorce encourage me towards acts of service? It's now time to turn your attention to others in need of help with self-love, encouragement with new challenges, and feedback. Your problems lose significance and power when you are focused on helping someone else who is working through a divorce or contemplating divorce. I've always said that this book isn't just a divorce book. I want this book to offer something for anyone, no matter their relationship status. The greatest gifts you can give someone in need are quite simple when you boil them down.

You can give someone your time when they need a friend.

You can give someone your attention by listening with intention.

You can give someone inspiration, by sharing the value of self-care and mindfulness.

I truly believe, if creating the best version of "you" is your goal, like it is mine, then finding ways to be of service to others is an integral part of overall happiness.

Throughout my whole life, I've watched both of my parents give back in generous ways. They have been lightmasters in every way, with each other and others around them. The examples my father set for me during childhood are the same examples I strive to set for my kids. You want to model that power and responsibility for your kids because it makes all the difference!

My father was inspired by my mother and Mother Teresa. Like Mother Teresa, my dad strives to see God in everyone. My father had the rare opportunity to work with Mother Teresa on projects both in the country and outside of the country. She inspired him to work with the poorest of the poor in our very own city of Chicago.

He started a program in Chicago called The CARA Program. CARA is Gaelic for "friend." The CARA Program has helped people in poverty (and often the challenges of recovery, domestic violence, episodic homelessness, and incarceration), to get and keep quality jobs and, more importantly, rebuild hope, self-esteem, and opportunities for themselves and their families in the process. They have produced hundreds of jobs each year with retention rates over 20 points higher than the national norms and with over 70 percent of those retained residing in permanent housing in which their families can thrive. Seeing and interacting with the people of The CARA Program has made me understand the importance of being of service.

It feels good for the person receiving your kindness and service because they need it. However, you'll be surprised by how much your heart opens up to a new depth as you see that giving feels better than receiving. The act of service is a two-way street of sharing and appreciation. When you've reached a point in your life where you feel whole, being able to pay it forward just comes easily and naturally.

A Longer, Richer Life

Being of service doesn't always have to be giving of financial support. Giving your time, money, possessions, and your energy are all ways that you can be of service to others. Being of service could be as simple as spending a little bit of extra time at work to mentor a new coworker when you weren't asked to. It's taking 10 extra minutes in the morning to take your kids or neighborhood kids to school, instead of them walking or riding the bus. It's all based around thinking more about others than just yourself. This is your opportunity to give with an open heart, because you will get that same energy returned back to you in another form. The power of love comes together and expands when you are giving from the heart.

The ripple effect of this kind of service is hugely important for harnessing the leader within you! If you help just one person, and that person goes on to help someone else, and so on, you are creating an energy of abundance. The ripple effect of service is just as much for you as it is for the person or people you are helping. If every single person reading this book helped one person a day, even with a small act of kindness, the ripple effect of love, happiness, and energy would have a noticeable effect on everyone involved.

There was a research study on longevity that was published in the *New York Times* in 2012, that said *the easiest way to live a short, unimportant life is to consume the world around you, rather than contribute to it. Meanwhile, the people who keep on contributing tend to be the ones who keep on living.* You are here reading this book and taking charge of your life because you've suffered from an unhealthy marriage. That initiative brings you more in line with the best version of yourself. For that reason alone, it's a huge benefit for you to share your time and resources with others.

Think about where you were when you were in your transitional period and all the love and support that you received around you. This love and support is like a universal language, understandable and welcome by all. Once you've reached a certain point in your healing and transformation, the goal of *The Wholeness Map* is to give back and share the lessons in this book that made a positive impact for you. People will need your strong energy, they will seek out your advice on getting through their divorce because of the way you handled yours. I've had this happen in my life and it's helped me build new income streams as well as freely offer myself to those going through what I've been through. You are in that same boat! The more internal work you do to heal your pain, the more experience and inspiration you have to offer.

EXAMPLES OF WAYS TO BE OF SERVICE:

1. Take extra time before, during, or after work to help a new coworker.

2. Help in a local homeless shelter.

3. Ask a coworker that you usually wouldn't have lunch with, out to lunch.

4. Shovel someone's driveway when they aren't expecting it.

5. Smile at someone while you are walking to work, commuting, etc.

6. Let someone who has road rage go ahead of you–wave and smile at them and send them love.

7. Spend time reading to children at a local library.

8. Send holiday gifts to children who might not receive gifts.

9. Mentor a friend or local women's group on how to have a positive interview.

10. Donate time and/or money to a cause or charity that resonates with you and supports greater mankind.

11. Give extra time to a friend in need.

12. Buy flowers for a friend or your office, just because.

13. Pay it forward for the next person in line at your local tea/ coffee shop.

14. Ask the person next to you in the grocery line how their day is going.

15. Declutter your home, closet, or things you don't need anymore and donate them to a local charity, a friend in need, or shelter.

16. Start a conversation with a stranger.

17. Give your local mail and package delivery driver a bottle of water or a healthy snack.

18. Send "kindness cards & notes" for no reason at all.

19. Babysit for a friend so they can have self-care time or take care of errands.

20. Spend time and/or read to an elderly person.

21. Teach someone something new.

22. Do a small act of kindness each day–as simple as letting someone out ahead of you while driving.

23. Volunteer to coach a sports team.

24. Mentor or tutor students at your local school.

25. Ask a friend, brother, sister, or partner if there is something you can do for them to lighten the load of their day.

26. Make or bring a healthy food dish to a friend who you know has been busy.

27. Hold the door for someone.

28. Help someone who looks like they are lost by giving them directions.

29. Mow your neighbor's lawn.

30. Be an active listener with your friends and family.

31. Pick up loose garbage (on the side of the road, in your neighborhood, school, etc.).

32. Give an encouraging word or complement to someone, including strangers and coworkers you don't work with or talk to very often.

33. Help promote someone else's ideas, event, workshop, etc.

34. Talk to people at events that might "look out of place" and introduce them to others.

35. Practice appreciation, inspire others, share gratitude.

36. Live authentically, express your passions, be open about your strengths and vulnerabilities.

37. Be an example for others.

38. Give anonymously.

39. Love. Love all. Be love. Express love. Let love drive your life.

These are just a few ways to help others, and you can create them based on your community's needs. There are infinite ways to be of service, from small acts of kindness daily to larger, more global efforts. We have a responsibility to be an example for our next generation, and if you have children, then you have an even higher responsibility to be an example for helping others.

I am involved in several organizations within my local community. Part of a rich, long, and happy life is getting to know your community and give back in any way you can. Around the holiday times such as Thanksgiving and Christmas, my kids and I spend those days helping in local shelters and organizations to help give back to those in need. My kids spend many Sundays devoting their time to service like making meals for the homeless, baking cookies and treats for shelters, going to the shelters, serving the meals, and cleaning the facilities. My kids see that my work, as well as their own in the community, is so vital for the greater good and building community. It is opening their eyes to see that giving feels even greater than receiving.

Bringing people together, experiencing wholeness as a community, continues to live on as a ripple effect of love and kindness. One simple act of kindness raises the vibration of you, the other person(s), and the greater good of the world.

BEING THE EXAMPLE FOR CHILDREN

As parents, we have a responsibility to teach our children how to be of service. As a result of being an example for my own children, they have even taken to being of service with other kids in their school and those who are struggling and in need. When my dad stepped into a leadership role of service after his retirement, my kids had the privilege of being able to get involved easily. It may not be as easy for you to seek out and find the right service to provide to others, and that's normal. The big picture mindset that you need to adopt is that what you do for others will come back to you. If your intention is to help others, the Universe will light a path for you. The same goes for your children! Teaching children to be of service can be as easy as looking for the underdog in school and helping them step into their light and be the example and ripple effect for other students that surround them.

Dr. Joe Vitale quotes, in Rhonda Byrne's *The Secret*, "You are the masterpiece of your own life. You are the Michelangelo of your own life. The David you are sculpting is you." You can be of service by following your passion. Traditional charity work is not the only way to give back. Following your passion and being resilient in the healing and transformational process of your post-divorce journey is where your service begins. Settling and watching life pass you by is not a healthy use of your energy or potential. *The Wholeness Map* is a continual journey of hope not just for you, but for others as well. Showing up to your life, being resilient, and not settling are all ways to begin your service journey.

I challenge you to think about the activities below, look into your heart and incorporate giving and service into your life. So many people need your love and voice in their lives–I can promise you that. By doing so, you will live a long and richer life–reprogram your being to see acts of kindness daily and help others to do the same.

Being of Service Exercise:

1. **Choose Your Avenue of Service:**

   I've shared many ways that you can be of service to others, from small acts of kindness to larger amounts of time and financial donations. I want you to pause and focus in on your heart center, ask yourself "how would I love to be of service to others?" Don't think about your time or financial abilities when you ask yourself that question. Think big and don't limit yourself. How would you like to spread your love and kindness to others?

Once you determine what feels like a good fit for you, I want you to come back to reality and look at how you can be of support and service presently. Use the resources that you've learned in this book, from finances, self-care, self-love, boundaries, gratitude, and more to determine how this service can fit comfortably into your present lifestyle. Maybe you will donate money, maybe your time, perhaps a weekend of support every quarter…

Whatever your chosen avenue of service is, I want you to schedule it in your calendar right now. When we have things planned in our calendar, we tend to show up for them, more so than when they are not scheduled. So regardless if you are giving time, energy, or money, schedule it as a reminder or event in your calendar so you can commit to being of service on a larger scale.

2. **Small Acts of Kindness Daily:**

There is no right or wrong when it comes to giving and being of service. I understand that everyone is busy, time might be limited, as well as financial resources, so if you are not in a position to give on a large scale either monthly, quarterly, or yearly, there are always the small acts of kindness that you can share daily.

I want you to take a moment to pause and write down something simple that you can do *today* to give back to your community, family, and/or friends. Remember, this does not have to be something that breaks the bank or takes a lot of time, it's something that you can easily commit to and share your love.

Small acts of kindness are easily able to continue that ripple effect that we've talked about throughout the book and especially in this chapter. There are many opportunities for small acts of kindness, even if you simply make a conscious effort to smile at a stranger daily. The power of a smile and recognizing someone can completely change and shift not only your energy and mood but the mood of the other person as well. In a society where many things are at "go-go-go" speed, taking a second to look up and smile at someone can be the best part of your day because you never know what one smile can lead to…perhaps a new friend to your tribe of warriors?!

3. **Get Generous Today!**

    This is super simple for you–it's a reminder that you don't have to put off being of service. Don't let roadblocks stand in your way.

Use this being of service challenge to practice mindfulness daily because small acts of kindness can go a long way!

Rebranding You

You were born free. The more you try and earn your freedom and have inner peace, the more attractive your wholeness and whole being will be. You are worthy of love and respect. You deserve all that you desire in life.

For many people, the divorce itself sometimes ends up being the easiest because there is somewhat of a step-by-step path. It's the redefining yourself after divorce that can sometimes be the most challenging because it's an unknown path. However, that is the entire reason you're reading this book–to come back home to you, your being, your soul, and your life. Define what new life opportunities are there for you and open up to all that the Universe has available. The more you show up to this life, surrender to the outcomes, step back and see the big picture, and release control and fear, the more you step into yourself, your self-love, and heart center.

We are all humans, and we are going to fail, we are going to fall backwards, we are going to have bad days. I want you to embrace them with open arms and welcome them. Becoming consciously aware of your holes, seeing them within you and loving them whole, brings you closer to wholeness and self-love. Whether your holes stem from childhood, bad relationships, an abusive or loveless marriage, whatever the case for your holes, love them.

This book has taught you that self-love is the number one key and foundational element to bring you back to wholeness in your new life post-divorce. Through self-love and dating yourself first, you're able to rebuild your foundation with solid love and inner peace. Spiritual teacher Danielle Laporte states, "You can't always choose what happens to you, but you can always choose how to feel about it." Allow yourself this time and season in life to embrace your new self, gratitude, kindness, and the center of it all, love.

The Wholeness Journey

While this chapter wasn't as long as the rest of the chapters in this book, it's packed full of powerful lessons and ideas of how you can be of service and give to others. In a world where things are changing and moving so quickly, it's always important to remember where we can help others and share the love. I want this short chapter to always be that little note in your back pocket, so to speak, and let love and self-love always guide you to helping others.

Your inner wisdom, intuition, quiet voice, and love are all here to support you no matter what. Always allow yourself the flexibility and grace to not be perfect and flow with your wholeness map. I encourage you to come back to this book often, let it be the one book you have on your nightstand because this is a book that you are always going to get something from. You can always come back to it and see, read, feel, or hear something new that you didn't before. *The Wholeness Map* is a journey for a lifetime, so these tools are always going to be here for you.

Trust that God and the Universe will always have your back and that they are right along with you on this journey to acquiring your dreams and desires. You are never alone. While you can't control all life events, you can control your ultimate destination and desired feelings. Your destination in life is *"wholeness,"*–true inner peace and happiness. Your time is NOW!

PART THREE - TRANSFORMATION COACHING TIPS

Transformation is like reinvention. There is an art to reinventing yourself. You must practice day in and day out, who you want to become.

Create the self-love practice that you can do daily to bring out your inner god/goddess. Examples of mine are salt baths with rose petals or candles, dry brushing, sauna, steam, acupuncture, meditation, yoga, nature walks, mani/pedi, grooming services like a haircut, color, and wax. Anything that brings out your outer beauty will bring out your inner beauty as well. Spend time with people that you admire and who live their lives in a vibrant and positive way. When you surround yourself with these people, it rubs off on you. Remember "your vibe creates your tribe."

VISUALIZATION AND GOALS PRACTICE

Step 1: I want you to take different categories of your life like the examples found below and write them down. Feel free to add more categories if they apply to your life.

1. Family (which includes kids and the home in which you live)
2. Career
3. Financials
4. Dating
5. Nutrition/Exercise/Wellness
6. Spirituality

Begin by writing three goals of what you would like to achieve. Examples for *family* could include: (1) I want to sell my home in one year and make money on this home, then buy a new home that will allow me to put 100k into savings for a college fund; (2) I'm going to create a new ritual where we eat dinner as a family every Sunday night, and we play cards. (Weeknights are busy, so looking forward to cooking a family meal where everyone sits down together and says one thing that they are thankful for can provide a great family ritual). (3) I would like to see my kids not experience any more fighting between my ex and myself.

Step 2: Visualization

Now you will create a visualization of each of your goals. Using the same examples from above, here is what your visualizations might look like...

You're seeing yourself in a new home in one year and Sunday night dinners are so enjoyable. You are all giving thanks, and you are teaching your children to recognize abundance in life and the feeling of gratitude. This all creates more abundance. You visualize your ex-spouse and yourself engaging in a positive way. You can see the stress melt away from your children's shoulders. Your heart is so warm knowing that the load of stress your innocent children feel is lifted when you and your ex can put aside any ego-related arguments. (All arguments are inspired by the ego.)

When we are able to consistently engage our goals and visualize them, match our emotions and energy to our beliefs, then we are able to see our visualizations, desires, and dreams come to life. This is the power of the Universe, the Laws of Attraction, and quantum physics all working together.

Life is a Dance

"Optimize: someone who figures that taking a step backward after taking a step forward is not a disaster, it's more like a cha-cha."

–Robert Brault

Conclusion, Love & Gratitude

CONCLUSION

How to Live
The Wholeness Map

Over the past ninety thousand words, I've shared with you many stories, real-life events, and emotions that you most likely have experienced too. I've also given you the practical and spiritual tools, rituals, and resources you need to awaken your spiritual being to wholeness. As mentioned in the introduction and throughout the book, the wholeness journey is a journey for a lifetime. That's why I've written this book the way I have because no matter when you come back to it, you are always going to learn something new, that you didn't connect with the first time.

This book is like your very own personal development journey, all wrapped up into hundreds of pages. Allow yourself to connect deeper to your intuition, your soul, your inner peace, and your purpose in this life—go deep within and explore depths of yourself that you haven't connected with in a while, or even ever before. Go forth, from within, my friend.

Remember the absolute number one thing I want you to always remember from this book is to love yourself first, love yourself whole. Give yourself credit for making it this far in life and for having the courage to read this book. You are being gentle with yourself and empowering your soul to continue to move forward on your extraordinary journey, with love at the forefront. By you leading your life with love, you are being an example for the next generation and those around you. You are being a messenger for wholeness.

If you feel called, share this book with others and/or a friend or family member who is going through a divorce or ending a relationship and invite them to read it. With the divorce rate in the United States at epidemic proportions, it's imperative that we all come together and hold the compassion and energetic space for healing. When we are able to share our light with others, our voice and love with others, we are spreading the message of wholeness far and wide. I encourage you to spread this message because you care about your friends, your family, your children, and the greater good. When we are able to heal our holes and transform into the light, we've followed our soul's journey to happiness and inner peace. Let's share this message together because it's one that needs to be shared.

My mission has always been to support you where you are and give you the resources you need to improve your life. Life isn't always going to be easy–I know you can relate. It doesn't cost anything to be kind, loving, genuine, and whole. Now that you have the tools to further your adventure on your wholeness journey and transform from divorce, you can thrive and go make your dreams a reality. With everything this book is offering you, please come back to it when you feel called and always take what resonates at that moment and leave the rest. Start small and continually take those steps to be whole–this is your very own wholeness journey! And remember my darling, I am here with you every step of the way! xo

"Healing is the return of the memory of wholeness. Healing, health, whole, and holy all mean inclusiveness. Mind, body, spirit, environment, relationships, social interactions are all one wholeness, and you're a part of that one wholeness."

– Deepak Chopra

Love & Gratitude

This book has been a labor of love, and I want to thank some of the special people in my life that provided me with a foundation of love and support so that I could find me again and explore the depths of healing on such a greater level. It is the many special people in my life that I am grateful for that gave me the courage to step into the light and bring forth this book to you.

First of all, I am grateful to you darling, my reader, for picking up this book and wanting a more transformative map to finding (w)holeness. We are all in this together. We have one shot in life to create the best version of ourselves. So I say, "Go big or go home!" I believe in You!! We got this, my friend!

I want to thank my parents for demonstrating each day what a healthy love and marriage is supposed to look like. They have shared 60 years of marriage. They are two of the greatest lightmasters that I know, never shadowing each other and stepping into their own light each and every day. They put their best selves forward, providing us with unconditional love, support, and acceptance. They created their tribe of other lightmasters (couple friends) who became family to them and gave us kids an extended family of friends for the next generations. They taught me how to create the foundation I built for my own family inspired from love, respect, high morals and integrity. I am so grateful to my mom for teaching me how to be a strong woman and that we all have an inner warrior within us. I am eternally grateful to my dad for his love and ability to believe in me and let me fly on my own. They have taught my children and me so much about service and that the power of giving back feels even greater to the ones that are doing the giving.

To my "Fabulous Five" (by birth order): Katelyn, Grace, Owen, Cullen, and Mary–thank you for making me want to be better and more whole each and every day. I am honored to be your mom. I pray that each of you chooses to look at life as a journey. Life will never be perfect. And when we fall down, it is an opportunity to get back up, brush ourselves off, and find our unique gifts. Our gifts are beautifully wrapped with words like strength, forgiveness, persevere, inner warrior, love, awareness and consciously be finding our gifts in every "good" and "bad" situation. It is our job to find the goodness in everything. I pray that you all create your journey seeking wholeness.

I thank my siblings and their spouses Tom and Sue, Julie and Chris, Mike and Mags, Katie and Tim for being massive inspirations to me at different times in my life. As we all know, life is never perfect and never will be perfect but what we have built together as a family is pretty darn perfect. I love and thank all of you!

Thank you to Daniel McIntire, CEO of "Influncrrs," my editor who jumped in on this project. First, you taught me how to capture an audience on social media and then your edits captured my voice in every way. I appreciate your vision and commitment to *The Wholeness Map*. I am grateful to work with you.

To my amazing tribe of girlfriends (and their husbands): you know who you are. Thank you for helping me find my way back home to "me" and who I am in this world. We can really lose ourselves when we are in the wrong relationship and even more so when we are trying to dissolve a marriage with dignity for ourselves and for our children. Thank you for protecting me from the beginning of this journey until now–and my little people too–and thank you for your ongoing love, never-ending support, and being my rocks over these years, always reminding me that I got this. You beauties are my family by choice: I love you all!!

To my beautiful divorcee warrior friends–this book is dedicated to all of you. We have spent hours chatting over coffee, drinking wine together, taking walks and bike rides together, enjoying nights out in the city and burbs; we have cried together, we have talked about our future and desires, we may even have dated and stayed friends. I am grateful to each and every conversation and experience that inspired me to write this book for people like us needing someone to walk through this journey with them. It is all of my own experiences and experiences you have shared with me that inspired my desire to write a book that could not only heal us but could take someone from the dark and let them stand in their light–a light that shines so bright that it's restored by a beautiful rainbow of colored lights–this is where transformation takes place.

I thank every spiritual teacher, mentor, and coach that I have worked with directly or have studied under. I spent countless hours understanding how to put my spirit back together again, get my physical body back to a place of health and wellness and how to step into my light. I thank these great spiritual teachers for being healers to me so that I could go forward and be a healer to others. Healing our mind, body, and spirits is an essential part of this journey called life. And when we are faced with life challenges, it is "our time" to step forward and embrace the challenge. It is "our time" to choose to step away from darkness and fear and step into living in the Now, which is a place of light, love, and freedom. WE can't grow when we stay in the dark and fear, we can only grow when we are living in a place of light, love, and freedom. I especially thank my late friend Tony Tunney who opened my eyes to a whole new way of seeing life. Tony's passion and strong belief that he, I, you, all of us, have the power within us to create a life that is beautiful, peaceful, a life where you are present in the NOW. Tony brought spiritual teachers like Eckhart Tolle to me and taught me that we attract abundance and goodness into our lives by "what you are," not by "what you want." We can only do this by staying connected to God, to our angels, to our Divine. Tony emulated God in every way he approached life, and now I am sure he is our angel.

He kept showing up and sharing his teachings with me and sharing with me his positive experiences over and over again. I would come to realize later that it wasn't that he had forgotten he had already shared that same story with me; it was that I needed to hear the story over and over again in order for me to learn it. Teachers show up in our lives in many different ways. And the best teachers will repeat their message until they know you have learned it. I am grateful that he shared his teachings with me, and now I can share them with all of you.

I thank Daniel McIntire, owner of "Influncrrs" for teaching me how to capture an audience on social media. I am grateful that you jumped into this project and contributed so much valuable information, ideas and your own experiences. You are truly amazing.

The Wholeness Map
Journal

PART ONE - DIVORCE

PART TWO - HEALING

PART THREE - TRANSFORMATION

About the Author

SHARON OWENS is a serial entrepreneur, certified life coach, and author of the premier personal development and wellness book covering the divorce scene. Sharon is a survivor of divorce, finding her wholeness through self-love and the power of the Law of Attraction. Sharon uses her infectious drive and positivity to empower women and men to take control of their lives and find their wholeness after divorce, without fear. Sharon's motivational words and inspiring story is a refreshing approach that is opening doors and changing the conversation of life after divorce. Sharon has had a varied career that includes, real estate broker, The Dailey Method studio owner, founder of Healthy Living Inside Out, organic restaurant managing partner, life coach, educator, mentor, and now author. She lives in Chicago with her five children. For more information, visit www.SharonMOwens.com.